CHEKHOV:

THE ESSENTIAL PLAYS

ANTON CHEKHOV

THE ESSENTIAL
PLAYS

Translated, with an Introduction and Notes,

by Michael Henry Heim

THE MODERN LIBRARY

NEW YORK

2003 Modern Library Paperback Edition

LIBRARY OF CONGRESS CATALOGING-IN-PUBLICATION DATA
Chekhov, Anton Pavlovich, 1860–1904.
[Plays. English. Selections]
Chekhov, the essential plays / Anton Chekhov ; translated, with an introduction
and notes, by Michael Henry Heim.
p.   cm.
Contents: The seagull—Uncle Vanya—Three sisters—The cherry orchard.
ISBN 978-0-375-76134-8
1. Chekhov, Anton Pavlovich, 1860–1904—Translations into English.   I. Title:
Essential plays.   II. Heim, Michael Henry.   III. Title.

PG3456.A19H45 2003
891.72'3—dc21   2003041349

Modern Library website address: www.modernlibrary.com

Printed in the United States of America

ANTON CHEKHOV

Anton Pavlovich Chekhov was born on January 17, 1860, in Taganrog, a small provincial port in southern Russia located on the Sea of Azov. His grandfather had been a serf who for 3,500 rubles had purchased the family's freedom. Chekhov's domineering father was a lower-middle-class bigot, a petty merchant who kept a grocery store, bullied his wife, and beat his six children. Although Anton Pavlovich's early life was monotonous and oppressive ("In my childhood there was no childhood"), he found his own strange way of compensating for the dismal atmosphere: possessing a natural gift for clowning and mimicry, the boy delighted schoolmates with hilarious imitations of virtually everyone in the village.

Chekhov was sixteen when the family business failed and his father escaped debtors' prison by fleeing to Moscow. The young man's mother and siblings soon followed, but Anton Pavlovich remained behind to complete his education at the Taganrog Secondary School. Three years later, in 1879, he joined them in Moscow and entered the medical school of Moscow University. During his university years Chekhov became the family's chief breadwinner: he supported them by writing stories, sketches, and parodies for humor magazines. All his early works were signed with pseudonyms, most frequently "Antosha Chekhonte." He completed his medical studies in 1884 and practiced medicine intermittently for several years while continuing to publish stories. "Medicine is my lawful wife," he wrote to a friend, "and literature is my mistress. When I get fed up with one, I spend the night with the other. Though it is irregular, it is less boring this way, and besides, neither of them loses anything through my infidelity."

All the while, Chekhov's fiction continued to grow in depth and range. He published his first volume of stories, *Motley Tales,* in 1886; a year later he brought out his second collection, *In the Twilight,* for which he was awarded the Pushkin Prize for distinguished literary achievement by the Russian Academy. Vladimir Nabokov perfectly explained Chekhov's appeal: "What really attracted the Russian reader was that in Chekhov's heroes he recognized the Russian idealist, . . . a man who combined the deepest human decency of which man is capable with an almost ridiculous inability to put his ideals and principles into action; a man devoted to moral beauty, the welfare of his people, the welfare of the universe, but unable in his private life to do anything useful; frittering away his provincial existence in a haze of utopian dreams; knowing exactly what is good, what is worthwhile living for, but at the same time sinking lower and lower in the mud of a humdrum existence, unhappy in love, hopelessly inefficient in everything—a good man who cannot make good. This is the character that passes—in the guise of a doctor, a student, a village teacher, many other professional people—all through Chekhov's stories."

Despite the success of his literary career Chekhov felt guilty about neglecting medicine. Moreover, he still had to write a dissertation to obtain a full medical degree. Partly to discharge this debt and partly for the sake of adventure, he undertook an exhausting— and at times dangerous—six-thousand-mile journey across Siberia to Sakhalin Island. There he made a thorough study of the social, economic, and medical conditions of the Russian settlers (mostly convicts) and native population. Upon his return (by sea, via the Suez Canal) from this "descent into hell," he was quickly forced back into medicine and public health by the terrible famine of 1891 and the cholera epidemic that followed. In 1892 he bought a six-hundred-acre country estate near the village of Melihovo, where for the next five years he served as doctor to the local peasants and helped to build schools, while his literary output continued unabated.

The turn of the century witnessed a dramatic new phase in Chekhov's career: between 1896 and 1903 he wrote the plays that established his reputation as one of the great dramatists of modern times: *The Seagull* (1896), *Uncle Vanya* (1897), *Three Sisters* (1901), and *The Cherry Orchard* (1904). But in 1897 a massive pulmonary hemorrhage forced him to acknowledge that he was stricken with tuberculosis, an illness he had long concealed. For the remainder of his life he was virtually a semi-invalid and lived mostly in a villa at Yalta, his "warm Siberia," where he met Tolstoy and Gorky. In 1901 he married Olga Knipper, the Moscow Art Theater actress who had played the role of Arkadina in *The Seagull.*

Chekhov's last public appearance took place at the Moscow premiere of *The Cherry Orchard* on 17 January 1904, his forty-fourth birthday. Shaken with coughing, he was hardly able to stand and acknowledge the thunderous ovation. In June he was rushed to a health resort at Badenweiler in the Black Forest. He died of consumption on 2 July. His body was transported to Moscow in a refrigerating car used for the transportation of oysters—a quirk of fate he would doubtless have been amused to jot down in his notebook.

Contents

INTRODUCTION

Michael Henry Heim

THE PLAYS

Chekhov was known to balk at the prospect of his works in translation. He believed they were too Russian to travel and would not be understood, much less appreciated, by foreign audiences. Although his innate modesty was clearly at work here, that modesty came not only from within; it had its social roots.

Chekhov was the first major Russian writer of "plebian" origin. Pushkin, Turgenev, and Tolstoy belonged to old and prominent aristocratic families, and even Dostoevsky, whose father was a lowly army doctor, claimed noble descent and the right to own land and serfs. Their lineage made a European upbringing and European contacts (tutors and governesses, friends and lovers) de rigueur. Chekhov grew up with none of this veneer: his grandfather had not owned serfs, he *was* a serf, and Chekhov bitterly recalled having had to "squeeze the slave out of himself drop by drop."* Yet the works that make his reputation are every bit as universal as they are Russian.

* From a letter to his publisher, Alexei Suvorin, dated 7 January 1889 (*Anton Chekhov's Life and Thought: Selected Letters and Commentary,* edited and annotated by Simon Karlinsky, translated by Michael Henry Heim in collaboration with Simon Karlinsky [Evanston, Ill.: Northwestern University Press, 1997], p. 85). Chekhov's letters provide unusually illuminating insights into his mind and creativity.

The four major plays in the present collection are a case in point. The combination of Russian and universal elements is seamless and mutually enriching. What I propose to show is how the two levels complement each other.

The Seagull (1896) is not Chekhov's first full-length play. That distinction belongs to the melodrama *Ivanov* (1887), which itself was preceded by an unfinished play (untitled in Russian, but commonly called *Platonov* in English) and followed by *The Wood Demon* (1889), the predecessor to *Uncle Vanya*. But it is in *The Seagull* that he found himself as a playwright. It is also, not incidentally, a play about the theater.

Russian theater at the time, much like European theater as a whole, was dominated by a repertory of overblown melodramas serving as vehicles for the public's favorite actors. Audiences went to the theater to see stars rather than plays. Arkadina in *The Seagull* is a provincial Russian Bernhardt (Chekhov saw Bernhardt perform and disliked her style intensely); her son Kostya is an aspiring writer who aims to restore literature to the theater. Then there is Nina, an aspiring actress with whom Kostya is in love, and Trigorin, Arkadina's lover and a popular author with whom Nina falls in love.

Had Chekhov been a lesser writer, he might have made Kostya surpass Trigorin, but Chekhov was incapable of black-and-white portrayals. Kostya's play, an attempt to bring the European decadent movement to the Russian stage, is honest but in the end inept. Furthermore, Trigorin is no out-and-out hack; he is sincerely obsessed with his writing. He is merely mediocre—and knows it. As for Arkadina, she is limited, possessive, and self-centered, yet in her own way she adores both her son and her lover. Rarely are Chekhov's characters unmitigated villains, but neither are they heroes, not in the traditional sense at least. In *The Seagull* Nina comes closest to heroism: at the play's end she is by no means the great actress a conventional writer would have made her; she is working hard at life, pulling herself up by her bootstraps. What headway she has made she has made at great cost, but headway it is.

Nina thus provides the link between the local, Russian element I have chosen to highlight—the situation in the Russian theater—

and the universal element I now wish to address—namely, what it means to grow into maturity, to move from adolescence to adulthood. Kostya is well into his twenties, yet he has not cut the umbilical cord: his mother is still all to him; Nina, presumably several years younger than Kostya, has broken with her overbearing father and struck off on her own. Moreover, the local and the universal strands are inextricably intertwined: both Kostya and Nina base their bids for maturity on the theater.

The fateful outcome of Kostya's inability to grow up reflects a strain of melodrama left over from Chekhov's earlier plays, but in other ways *The Seagull* itself solved the theatrical problems it posed. Not only did it call the star system into question in the person of Arkadina; it destroyed it by means of its structure: *The Seagull* has no starring role; it has four equally important characters. In addition, even the less important characters have nothing of the supporting-role attributes of the previous period; they serve to deepen and broaden the play, not to show off the box-office draw. After *The Seagull* Chekhov's plays all followed this innovative pattern.

Even the only major play named after a single character does not highlight that character unduly. The very fact that its title is *Uncle Vanya* and not simply *Vanya* implies another, equally important character, his niece Sonya; indeed, *Uncle Vanya* has five equally important roles—the others being Professor Serebryakov, his wife Yelena, and Dr. Astrov—to *The Seagull*'s four. When reworking *The Wood Demon*, the basis for *Uncle Vanya*, Chekhov made consequent use of his new structural principle.

Uncle Vanya deals with issues that recur in the rest of the plays with enough regularity to make of them a trilogy. True, it retains links to *The Seagull:* Vanya's questioning the validity of the professor's work in art recalls Kostya's questioning the validity of Trigorin's fiction, and Vanya's puerile relationship with his mother recalls Kostya's attachment to Arkadina. (Chekhov's preference for the pet name Vanya over the neutral Ivan suggests that Vanya is still a child, and to make matters worse he is significantly older than Kostya.) But new issues crowd these out.

A prime local issue at the time was the ecological one posed by Dr. Astrov: why destroy forests unthinkingly? It is of course an issue with more universal ramifications as well. But the overriding and to my mind most universal issue in the play is the meaning of work, the part work plays in our day-to-day existence. Is one type of work worthier than another (the professor's scholarly activity, the doctor's not always successful operations, Vanya and Sonya's agricultural efforts)? What are the consequences of doing no work at all (Yelena's idle existence)? Like Nina in *The Seagull*, Sonya in *Uncle Vanya* takes the difficult, unheroically heroic stand of hard work, of plowing through.

A more somber variant of that message emerges from the final speeches in *Three Sisters*. Delivered in solidarity by all three—Olga, Masha, and Irina—they have a melancholic if not mournful ring, the result of the old army doctor's contrapuntal commentary—"What difference does it make?"—and Olga's own refrain—"If only we knew."

"If only we knew" is emblematic of both the Russian issue and the universal issue at stake here. The Russian issue, which again has universal overtones, is the function of education: Olga is a teacher, as is Masha's husband; Irina aspires to be one. There is much talk about the use and misuse of learning, especially—and not surprisingly, given the play's title—among women, who in Russia were for the first time receiving serious education in large numbers. The closely related universal issue is whether the future—which in *Three Sisters* designates the potentialities of life "two or three hundred years" hence—will represent an improvement on the present, thus dwarfing the present in its significance. "If only we knew." Vershinin, Masha's lover, has grandiloquent hopes; Tusenbach, Irina's fiancé, is less optimistic: the externals may change, but life will be as hard as ever. The issue soon turned out to be chillingly pertinent in Russia, where millions suffered imprisonment, forced labor, and death in the name of a radiant Communist future.

Three Sisters is the only mature play Chekhov chose to label a drama. It earns that distinction not only from the cheerless ending but from the dire events that lead up to it and from its two uncharacteristically unredeemable characters: Natasha, the sisters' philistine, social-climbing sister-in-law; and the at first merely irritating but later downright pernicious Solyony. Even if *The Cherry Orchard*, which Chekhov labeled a comedy, ends arguably on an even more somber note—with the death knell of an entire way of life—it has only one pernicious character, the self-important servant Yasha. Besides, Yasha is so vacuous that the consequences of his actions, two broken hearts, are not nearly so dire as the consequences of Solyony's in *Three Sisters*.

The Cherry Orchard is a comedy, though it is also—even first and foremost—about death. Chekhov was dying as he wrote it and, having practiced medicine all his life, he was acutely aware of how soon his end would come. Death puts in an almost personal appearance at the play's end in the dying servant Firs, but it is present symbolically throughout.

Now, Chekhov was anything but a Symbolist; he even made sport of the Symbolists in Kostya's decadent play and in the dead seagull he lays before Nina. ("I suppose it's a symbol," Nina says, "but I'm sorry, I don't understand it.") Still, the chopping down of the cherry orchard is so clearly an allegory of the demise of the landowning class in Russia—the play's main Russian issue—that it fairly begs to be extended symbolically to death in general. In Act Two a group of characters hears a string snapping in the distance, a sound that "seems to come from the sky." They wonder what it is. Lopakhin, the practical man among them and the one who proposes that the orchard be cleared for what we would now call land development, has a practical explanation: it comes from a distant mine. But the consternation among the characters remains. It has since shifted to critics and scholars. I propose that Chekhov introduces the snapping string as a memento mori, to signal the presence of death in life.

Life in *The Cherry Orchard* goes on apace: there is singing and dancing; there are magic tricks and pratfalls. That is the comedy. But behind all the brouhaha the sound of the ax in the cherry orchard makes itself heard much like the sound of the snapping string. Is that a tragedy? No, Chekhov maintains implicitly. In fact, Lopakhin may be seen as a coarse self-portrait: he, like Chekhov, comes from peasant stock; he, like Chekhov, is the first generation of his family to "make it." Life two or three hundred years from now will not (as Vershinin argues in *Three Sisters*) be better, but it will (as Tusenbach argues) be different, and Lopakhin is one of those involved in making it different. There is no point crying over spilt milk, the spilt milk here being the cherry orchard or, allegorically, the gentry and the way of life it represents or, symbolically, death. Life goes on apace. First with us, then without us. That is why a play with death just under the surface from start to finish can—in Chekhov's hands, at least—be a comedy.

"But nothing ever happens!" So goes the fabled cry. Occasionally arising even from Chekhov's most admiring audiences, it reflects a sensibility that expects a "well-made play," the kind Arkadina was wont to star in, a work with a beginning, a middle, and an end. Chekhov's plays have a beginning and a middle all right, but they are open-ended. All sorts of things happen in a Chekhov play, and by the end of each the principal characters' lives have changed irrevocably. But what does happen often takes place beneath the surface and derives as much from what is left unsaid as from what is put into words. Even more disconcerting is Chekhov's refusal to predict what will happen after the play ends. But that is what induces us to take it home from the theater, ruminate on it, not merely file it away. The open-endedness of Chekhov's plays—of his work as a whole, for that matter—results from a conviction that the writer's job is not so much to provide the proper answers as to pose the proper questions.

THE TRANSLATION

Chekhov may not have set great store by translations of his work, but true to form he responded to his translators' queries with alacrity and precision—true to form, because he expended an enormous amount of time and energy on the first drafts of even neophyte writers who sought his comments.* As he did not know English, the assistance he provided to his first English translator

---

* See, for example, the letters to Maria Kiselyova (14 January 1887), Yelena Shavrova (16 September 1891), and even, apparently unsolicited, to his editor Suvorin (30 May 1888) and Maxim Gorky (3 January 1899) in *Anton Chekhov's Life and Thought*, pp. 60–64, 205–7, 104–5, 337–39.

amounts to explanations of unusual words and at one point, this time true to his modesty, a confession that the original word was in fact less than felicitous.

The problems Chekhov's plays have had in English, however, pertain not so much to individual words as to the overall tone. True, I have yet to find an English translation that retains all the famous pauses Chekhov so carefully indicated, and I have included every one of them (as well as all the ellipsis points, which imply briefer pauses). But if retranslations of classics are called for periodically, it is less to correct errors than to address broader issues of interpretation and voice. Early translations of the plays gave the impression that Chekhov's characters were vaguely Shavian in diction and therefore nature, whereas in reality, as Russians have told me again and again, their speech differs surprisingly little from that of their intelligent, educated counterparts today. It was to reproduce the corresponding level of speech that I undertook to retranslate the plays.

Since I was translating for the stage, I had the advantage of being able to work closely with theater professionals. I would read the first draft aloud to the director, answering questions and incorporating suggestions as I went. Then I would listen to the actors' early run-throughs, paying special attention to lines they stumbled over or unconsciously altered. I learned a great deal from those sessions.

At the time, twenty-five years ago, there was a dearth of American translations of the plays, and my initial impulse was to Americanize the diction. After observing the results in a production or two, however, I came to temper that impulse: American diction tended naturally enough to elicit American body language and encourage an informality as inappropriate to the time and place in question as the clipped Shavian formality I was reacting against. Not all the characters speak the same, of course, and I have tried to capture their differences through different registers of English and even varieties of English. But what I hope to have achieved after all the years of fine-tuning on both sides of the Atlantic is a "mid-Atlantic" version, one that sounds as natural—even as neutral—as the Russian.*

* "Chekhov's language is as precise as 'Hello!' and as simple as 'Give me a glass of tea,'" Vladimir Mayakovsky once wrote. (Quoted in "Introduction," *Anton Chekhov's Life and Thought*, p. 31.)

I would like to take this opportunity to thank Gordon Davidson and Ben Shaktman, who first commissioned the translations, the directors I worked with most closely—first and foremost Ben Shaktman, but also Jack Going, Nancy Keystone, Michael McLain, and Ed Parone—and the numerous actors who wittingly and unwittingly influenced me. I am also greatly indebted to Simon Karlinsky, who went through the translations word by word with me, and to my wife, Priscilla, who was my first editor through it all.

An Actor's Guide to
Russian Names and Their
Pronunciation

All Russians have three names: a given name, a patronymic, and a surname. The first and last serve more or less the same function as names in our culture, the main difference being that surnames in -*ov*, -*in*, and -*sky* have feminine forms in -*ova*, -*ina*, and -*skaya*: Chekhov/Chekhova, Pushkin/Pushkina, Dostoevsky/Dostoevskaya. The patronymic consists of the father's given name plus the suffix -*ovich* for a man and -*ovna* for a woman: Pavlovich "son of Pavel" and Pavlovna "daughter of Pavel." Thus Chekhov's full name is Anton Pavlovich Chekhov, his sister Maria's—Maria Pavlovna Chekhova. Russians use a combination of the given name and patronymic—Anton Pavlovich, Maria Pavlovna—to denote a level of formality midway between the surname on its own (Mr. Chekhov, Miss Chekhova) and the given name on its own (Anton, Maria). Russian given names also have a variety of familiar or diminutive forms. I have placed the forms occurring in the plays (Vanya for Ivan, Masha for Maria, etc.) in parentheses after the characters' names in the cast list.

Because stress in Russian is unpredictable—it may fall on any syllable—I have also indicated the accented syllable for every name. For names of characters see the cast list; for other names see the first note to each play.

Placing stress on the proper syllable is the most important factor for correct pronunciation, but a few more points need to be taken into account:

1. Consonants are pronounced as in English with the following exceptions: *kh* is pronounced like the *h* in *help* (Chekhov), *zh* like the *s* in *measure* (Zhuchka).
2. Vowels have the following values: *a* as in *father, e* as in *fed, i* as in *feet, o* as in *fought, u* as in *food, y* as in *fit.*
3. A word has as many syllables as vowels. (*Mikhail* therefore has three syllables (Mi-kha-íl), *Malitskoe* four (Ma-lít-sko-e), and *Nikolaevna* five (Ni-ko-lá-ev-na).

The best way to prepare for saying Russian names on stage is to repeat them as often as it takes—fifty or a hundred times, if need be—to make them roll off the tongue as naturally as one's own name. Otherwise there is a tendency to hesitate slightly before the name, which breaks the rhythm and momentum of the line.

THE SEAGULL

A COMEDY IN FOUR ACTS

CHARACTERS[1]

IRÍNA NIKOLÁEVNA ARKÁDINA (TRÉPLEVA by marriage). An actress.

KONSTANTÍN GAVRÍLOVICH TRÉPLEV (KÓSTYA). Her son, a young
man.

PYOTR NIKOLÁEVICH SÓRIN. Her brother.

NÍNA MIKHÁILOVNA ZARÉCHNAYA. A young girl, the daughter of a
rich landowner.

ILYÁ AFANÁSYEVICH SHAMRÁEV. A retired lieutenant, the manager
of Sorin's estate.

POLÍNA ANDRÉEVNA. His wife.

MARÍA ILYÍNICHNA (MÁSHA). His daughter.

BORÍS ALEXÉEVICH TRIGÓRIN. A writer.

YEVGÉNY SERGÉEVICH DORN. A doctor.

SEMYÓN SERGÉEVICH MEDVEDÉNKO. A schoolmaster.

YÁKOV. A workman.

A MALE COOK.

A HOUSEMAID.

The action takes place on SORIN'*s estate. Two years pass between Acts Three
and Four.*

ACT ONE

The grounds of SORIN'S *estate. A broad tree-lined path leading away from the audience to a lake is cut off by a makeshift stage for an amateur performance. The lake is hidden from view. Bushes to the left and right of the stage. Several chairs, a small table.*

The sun has just set. On the stage behind a lowered curtain YAKOV *and other* WORKMEN *are heard coughing and hammering. Enter* MASHA *and* MEDVEDENKO, *left, on their way back from a walk.*

MEDVEDENKO. Why is it you always wear black?

MASHA. I'm in mourning for my life. I'm unhappy.

MEDVEDENKO. But why? (*Thinking hard.*) I can't understand it . . . You're healthy. Your father may not be rich, but he has a comfortable life. My life's much harder than yours—I make only twenty-three rubles a month minus pension-fund deductions—and I don't wear mourning. (*They sit down.*)

MASHA. Money doesn't matter. Even a pauper can be happy.

MEDVEDENKO. In theory perhaps, but not in practice. I've got myself, my mother, my two sisters, and my little brother to support—and all on twenty-three rubles. We need to eat and drink, don't we? We need tea and sugar. We need tobacco. Just try and make ends meet.

MASHA (*looking at the stage*). The play's starting soon.

MEDVEDENKO. Yes. Nina Zarechnaya in a play by Konstantin Gavrilovich. They're in love, and today their souls will merge in the desire to create a unified artistic image. But my soul and yours have no points of contact. I love you. I miss you so much I can't keep away. Every day I walk four miles here and four miles home, and what do I get? Utter indifference. And no wonder. I have no private means and a large family to support . . . Who wants to marry a man with nothing to eat?

MASHA. Ridiculous. (*She takes snuff.*) I'm touched by your love. I can't return it, that's all. (*She holds out the snuffbox to him.*) Snuff?

MEDVEDENKO. No, none for me.

(*Pause.*)

MASHA. What a muggy day. We're in for a storm tonight. All you do is philosophize or talk about money. You think there's nothing worse than poverty. Well, I think it's a thousand times easier to go begging in rags than to . . . But you wouldn't understand . . .

(*Enter* SORIN *and* TREPLEV, *right.*)

SORIN (*leaning on his cane*). I'm just not myself in the country, my boy. Never will be either, you can be sure of that. I went to bed at ten last night, and this morning at nine I woke up feeling my brain was stuck to my skull. From all that sleep and such. (*He laughs.*) I dropped off again this afternoon, and now I'm a complete wreck. It's a living nightmare, if you know what I mean.

TREPLEV. You're right. You ought to be living in town. (*Seeing* MASHA *and* MEDVEDENKO.) Sorry, but you'll be called when it starts. You can't stay here now. Please go.

SORIN (*to* MASHA). Maria Ilyinichna, do you think you could ask your father to let the dog off the chain? It's always howling. My sister was up again all night.

MASHA. Ask him yourself. I refuse. I don't want any part of it, thank you. (*To* MEDVEDENKO.) Come on.

MEDVEDENKO (*to* TREPLEV). You'll let us know in time, won't you? (*They exit.*)

SORIN. So that dog will howl all night again. You see? I never get my way in the country. I used to take a month off and come here to relax and such, but there was always so much fuss and bother I was ready to leave the day I came. (*He laughs.*) I was always glad to get away from here . . . Now that I'm retired, I have nowhere else to go, if you know what I mean. Like it or not, this is home . . .

YAKOV (*to* TREPLEV). We're going down for a swim, Konstantin Gavrilovich.

TREPLEV. All right. Just make sure you're back in ten minutes. (*He glances at his watch.*) We'll be starting soon.

YAKOV. Yes, sir. (*He exits.*)

TREPLEV (*looking over the stage*). How's that for a stage: curtain, one wing, another, then empty space. No set. You look straight out on the lake and the horizon. Curtain's going up at eight-thirty on the dot, just as the moon starts to rise.

SORIN. Splendid.

TREPLEV. Of course the effect will be lost if Nina's late. She should be here by now. Her father and stepmother never let her out of their sight. Getting away from that house is like breaking out of prison. (*He adjusts* SORIN'*s tie.*) Your hair and beard are a mess. Why don't you keep them trimmed? . . .

SORIN (*combing his beard*). The tragedy of my life. I look drunk all the time. Even when I was young, I looked like a drunkard and all. Never had luck with the ladies. (*Sitting down.*) I wonder why my sister's in such a bad mood.

TREPLEV. Why do you think? She's bored. (*Sitting next to him.*) And jealous. She's dead set against me, my play, and the performance, because her novelist might find Nina attractive. She doesn't know the first thing about the play, but she hates it.

SORIN (*laughing*). You're imagining things. Really . . .

TREPLEV. It galls her to think that Nina will get all the applause. Even on that tiny stage. (*Glancing at his watch.*) She's a psychological oddity, my mother: unquestionably talented and intelligent, capable of weeping over a novel, reeling off all Nekrasov by heart, nursing the sick like an angel—but try praising Duse in her presence.[2] No! She's the only one you can praise; she's the only one you can write about, shout about, rave about in *Camille* or *The Fumes of Life.*[3] But here in the country there aren't any opiates, so she's bored and edgy and thinks we're all her enemies, we're the ones to blame. She's superstitious too: afraid of three candles, of the number thirteen. She's a miser: she's got seventy thousand in a bank in Odessa—I know it for a fact—but try and get a loan out of her. She'll burst into tears.

SORIN. You're so convinced she's against the play you can't think straight and all. Calm down. Your mother worships you.

TREPLEV (*pulling the petals off a flower*). She loves me, she loves me not; she loves me, she loves me not; she loves me, she loves me not. (*He laughs.*) See? My mother doesn't love me. Why should she? What she wants is to live, love, wear bright blouses. And here I am, twenty-five—a constant reminder she's not so young as she used to be. When I'm not around, she's thirty-two; when I am, she's forty-three. That's why she hates me. Besides, she knows I don't accept her theater, the theater she loves. She thinks she's serving mankind, a sacred art, but as far as I'm concerned the theater today is all rote and delusion. When the curtain goes up on an artificially lit room with three walls, and those great talents, those priests of sacred art, show how people eat, drink, love, walk, and wear their jackets; when they take stock lines and stock situations and try to squeeze a moral out of them, a smug, homespun, oversimplified sort of moral; when they serve up the same thing in a thousand variations, over and over and over again—then all I can do is run, flee, the way Maupassant fled the Eiffel Tower, afraid its vulgarity would wear down his brain.

SORIN. But we need the theater.

TREPLEV. What we need are new forms. New forms. And if we can't have them, we're better off with nothing. (*Glancing at his watch.*) I love my mother, love her dearly, but the self-indulgent life she leads—running around with that writer, getting her name in the papers—it's all so tiresome. Sometimes the ordinary selfish mortal in me wishes she weren't a well-known actress. I might be happier if she were an ordinary woman. Can you picture a more hopeless, more ridiculous situation? She has some people over—celebrities all: actors, writers; I'm the sole nonentity present. The only reason they tolerate me is that I'm her son. Who am I? What am I? I left the university in my third year "due to circumstances beyond my control." No money, no talent, and papers that say "Kiev tradesman." Well, my father was from a family of tradesmen, even though he himself was a well-known actor. Anyway, whenever the actors and writers in my mother's drawing room deigned to pay me a little attention, I had the feeling they were sizing up my worthlessness. The humiliation I suffered reading their thoughts . . .

SORIN. By the way, what sort of man is her . . . her writer? I can't make him out. He never says a word.

TREPLEV. He's intelligent, unassuming, melancholy even. Perfectly decent. Not even forty and he's got everything his heart desires. He drinks nothing but beer; his loves are all past their prime. As for his work . . . How shall I put it? It's all very charming and polished . . . but . . . after Tolstoy or Zola you don't want Trigorin.

SORIN. Well, I like writers. I once had two great ambitions: finding a wife and being a writer. Never managed either. Yes, it must be nice to be even a minor writer, if you know what I mean.

TREPLEV (*listening attentively*). I hear footsteps . . . (*He hugs* SORIN.) I can't live without her . . . Even the sound of her footsteps is glorious . . . I'm insanely happy! (*He runs up to meet* NINA *as she enters.*) Enchantress! Light of my dreams! . . .

NINA (*excited*). I'm not late, am I? . . . I hope not . . .

TREPLEV (*kissing her hands*). No, no, no . . .

NINA. I've been nervous all day. And frightened. Afraid Father wouldn't let me come . . . But then he went off somewhere with my stepmother. The sky was red, the moon about to rise. I raced my horse as fast as it would go. (*She laughs.*) I'm so happy to be here. (*She gives* SORIN *a warm handshake.*)

SORIN (*laughing*). Those pretty little eyes have been crying, haven't they? Naughty, naughty.

NINA. It's nothing . . . Look how out of breath I am. I've got to leave in half an hour. We'd better hurry. No, no, don't ask me to stay. Father doesn't know I'm here.

TREPLEV. It's time we got started anyway, time to go and call everybody.

SORIN. I'll go. I'm off and all. (*He starts off to the right, singing.*) "To France were returning two grenadiers."[4] (*Then he stops and turns back.*) Once I burst into song like that at the office, and one of the assistant prosecutors said to me, "That's a powerful voice you've got there, Your Excellency." Then he paused a second and added, "Powerful, but repellent." (*He exits laughing.*)

NINA. My father and stepmother keep telling me not to come here. They say it's too bohemian . . . They're afraid I'll want to be an actress ... But I'm drawn to the lake, like a seagull ... My heart is so full of you. (*She looks about.*)

TREPLEV. We're alone.

NINA. Isn't that somebody over there? ...

TREPLEV. No. (*They kiss.*)

NINA. What kind of tree is that?

TREPLEV. An elm.

NINA. Why is it so dark?

TREPLEV. It's late. Everything is dark. Don't go so soon. Please don't.

NINA. I can't stay.

TREPLEV. What if I followed you home and stood the whole night in the garden looking up at your window?

NINA. You can't do that. The watchman would see you. And Trésor would bark. He's not used to you yet.

TREPLEV. I love you.

NINA. Sh!

TREPLEV (*hearing footsteps*). Who's there? Is that you, Yakov?

YAKOV (*from behind the stage*). Yes, sir.

TREPLEV. Is the wood alcohol ready? and the sulfur? We need that sulfur smell when the red eyes come on. (*To* NINA.) Let's go. Everything's ready. Are you nervous?

NINA. Yes, very. I don't mind your mother. I'm not afraid of her. But Trigorin ... It's so scary, so mortifying to act with him here ... A famous writer ... Is he young?

TREPLEV. Yes.

NINA. What marvelous stories he writes!

TREPLEV. I wouldn't know. I never read them.

NINA. Your play is so hard to act. There are no live people in it.

TREPLEV. Live people! Life must be shown not as it is, not as it should be, but as it appears in dreams.

NINA. Your play has so little action. It's all words. And I always thought a play needs a love interest ... (*Both exit behind the stage.*)

(*Enter* POLINA *and* DORN.)

POLINA. It's getting damp. Go back and put your galoshes on.

DORN. I'm hot.

POLINA. You don't take care of yourself. It's that stubborn streak of yours. You know very well how bad this damp air is for you—you're a doctor. But no, you want me to suffer. That's why you spent the whole evening on the terrace yesterday . . .

DORN (*singing to himself*). "Oh, tell me not that your young years were blighted . . ."[5]

POLINA. You got so carried away talking to Irina Nikolaevna you didn't notice the cold. Admit it. You're attracted to her.

DORN. I'm fifty-five.

POLINA. That's nothing. Fifty-five isn't old for a man. You're as handsome as ever, and women are still attracted to you.

DORN. What is it you want, anyway?

POLINA. You're all just waiting to fall at the feet of an actress. All of you.

DORN (*singing to himself*). "Again I stand before you, enthralled as once before . . ."[6] It's only natural for people to admire actors and treat them differently from, say, merchants. It's a kind of idealism.

POLINA. Women are always falling in love with you and hanging on your neck. Is *that* idealism?

DORN (*shrugging his shoulders*). What can I say? There's been a lot of good in the feelings women have for me. More than anything they've loved my skill as a doctor. Ten or fifteen years ago, if you remember, I was the only decent doctor in the district who would deliver babies. And I've always been honest.

POLINA (*clutching his arm*). Darling!

DORN. Quiet! They're coming!

(*Enter* ARKADINA *on* SORIN'*s arm, followed by* TRIGORIN, SHAMRAEV, MEDVEDENKO, *and* MASHA.)

SHAMRAEV. She was magnificent at the Poltava Fair in '73, magnificent. A sheer delight. Perhaps you know what's happened to Chadin, the comic. Pavel Chadin. His Rasplyuev was incomparable—better than Sadovsky's.[7] Believe me, dear lady. Where is he now?

ARKADINA. How should I know? Why bring up ancient history! (*She sits down.*)

SHAMRAEV (*sighing*). Good old Chadin! A dying breed. The theater's not what it used to be. We once had mighty oaks, Irina Nikolaevna; now we're down to stumps.

DORN. True, we've got fewer celebrities, but the average actor has come a long way.

SHAMRAEV. Can't say as I agree, but I suppose it's a matter of taste. *De gustibus aut bene, aut nihil.*[8]

(TREPLEV *comes out from behind the stage.*)

ARKADINA (*to* TREPLEV). When is it starting, dear?

TREPLEV. In a minute. Please be patient.

ARKADINA (*reciting from* Hamlet).[9]

> O Hamlet, speak no more:
> Thou turn'st mine eyes into my very soul:
> And there I see such black and grainèd spots
> As will not leave their tinct.

TREPLEV (*from* Hamlet).

> Nay, but to live
> In the rank sweat of an enseamèd bed,
> Stewed in corruption, honeying and making love
> Over the nasty sty.

(*A horn plays a fanfare behind the stage.*) Ladies and gentlemen! Attention, please! The play is about to begin.

(*Pause.*)

I'm starting now. (*He taps his stick*[10] *and intones in a stentorian voice.*) O ye hallowed shades of yore floating o'er the lake by night, lull us to sleep and waft us dreams of what shall be two hundred thousand years from now.

SORIN. Two hundred thousand years from now there'll be nothing left.

TREPLEV. Then let them show us that nothing.

ARKADINA. Yes, let them. We're asleep.

(*The curtain rises on a view of the lake. The moon, just above the horizon, is reflected in the water.* NINA, *all in white, is sitting on a large rock.*)

NINA. Men, lions, partridges and eagles, antlered deer, geese, spiders, silent denizens of the deep, starfish and creatures invisible to the human eye—in short, all living things, all living things, all living things have come to the end of their mournful rounds . . . For aeons and aeons the earth has borne no living thing, and this poor moon has lit its lamp in vain. No more do cranes wake calling in the meadow. Beetles have ceased buzzing in the lime groves. All is cold, cold, cold. Barren, barren, barren. Fearsome, fearsome, fearsome.

(*Pause.*)

All living things have disappeared in dust. Eternal matter has turned them into stone, water, and cloud. Their souls have merged into one. And I am that universal soul. I unite in me the souls of Alexander the Great, of Caesar, Shakespeare, and Napoleon, and of the basest leech. I fuse in me the consciousness of man and animal instinct. And I remember all, all, all, and live each life anew within myself. (*Will-o'-the-wisps appear.*)

ARKADINA (*softly*). Sounds awfully decadent.[11]

TREPLEV (*beseeching and reproaching her at the same time*). Mother!

NINA. I am lonely. Once every hundred years I open my lips to speak, and my voice rings out through the void, plaintive and unheard . . . Even you, pale fires, do not hear me . . . Bred by the marsh at dawn, you wander until dusk, lacking thought, lacking will, lacking even a quiver of life. Satan, the father of eternal matter, fearing lest life should enter you once more, promotes in you an endless interchange of atoms—in you and stone and water. You are in constant flux. In all the universe the only element unchanging and unchanged remains the spirit.

(*Pause.*)

Like a prisoner cast into a deep and empty well, I know not where I am or what awaits me. One thing alone has been revealed to me: in my fierce, unyielding battle with Satan, the epitome of material power, I am destined to emerge victorious. Then shall matter and spirit merge in wondrous harmony, and a universal will shall reign. But this shall come to pass over aeons and aeons, after the moon and bright Sirius and the earth have turned to dust . . . Until that time—horror, horror . . .

(*Pause. Two red dots appear over the lake.*)

Behold! My mighty enemy draws near: Satan. I spy his fearsome crimson eyes . . .

ARKADINA. I smell sulfur. Is that part of it?

TREPLEV. Yes.

ARKADINA (*laughing*). I see. Quite an effect.

TREPLEV. Mother!

NINA. He longs for human company . . .

POLINA (*to* DORN). You've taken off your hat. Put it back on or you'll catch cold.

ARKADINA. The doctor's taken off his hat to Satan, father of eternal matter.

TREPLEV (*flaring up, loudly*). That's it! The play is over! Curtain!

ARKADINA. What are you so upset about?

TREPLEV. That's it. Curtain. Bring down the curtain! (*Stamping his foot.*) Curtain! (*The curtain comes down.*) I'm sorry. I overlooked the fact that only a select few are allowed to write for the stage and act. I've encroached on a monopoly. I . . . I've . . . (*He tries to say something, but gives up and exits left.*)

ARKADINA. What's the matter with him?

SORIN. You shouldn't wound the boy's pride like that, Irina dear.

ARKADINA. What in the world did I say?

SORIN. You hurt his feelings.

ARKADINA. He said himself the play was a joke. Well, I treated it like a joke.

SORIN. Even so . . .

ARKADINA. All of a sudden he's written a masterpiece. Really now! So it wasn't a joke. He put together this extravaganza and choked us with sulfur to make a point . . . He wanted to teach us how to write and how to act. What a bore! The thrusts at my expense, the gibes—really, they'd try the patience of a saint. He's just a moody, headstrong little boy.

SORIN. He only wanted to please you.

ARKADINA. Is that so? Then why didn't he pick an ordinary play? Why did he make us sit through that decadent delirium? I'm perfectly willing to put up with delirium for the sake of a joke, but why all those claims for new forms and a new era in art? I don't see new forms; I see bad temper.

TRIGORIN. A writer writes as he feels, as he can.

ARKADINA. Well, nobody's stopping him. As long as he leaves me out of it.

DORN. Thou art angry, Jupiter . . .

ARKADINA. I'm not Jupiter; I'm a woman. (*She lights a cigarette.*) And I'm not angry. I'm just sorry to see a young man wasting his time like that. I didn't mean to hurt him.

MEDVEDENKO. There are no grounds for separating spirit from matter. What we call spirit may well be the sum total of material atoms. (*To* TRIGORIN, *animatedly.*) You know what somebody ought to do? Write a play about the life we schoolmasters live. Put *that* on the stage. It's a hard life, a hard life.

ARKADINA. True enough, but let's stop going on about plays and atoms. What a divine evening it is! Listen, everybody. Hear the singing? (*She listens attentively.*) Lovely!

POLINA. It's from the other side of the lake.

(*Pause.*)

ARKADINA (*to* TRIGORIN). Come and sit here next to me. Ten or fifteen years ago we had music and singing on the lake all the time, every night almost. There are six estates bordering on the lake. I still remember the laughter, the noise, the gunfire . . . And the romances, the romances . . . By the way, the idol, the matinée idol of all six houses was none other than (*nodding towards* DORN)—that's right, Dr. Dorn. Oh, he's still fascinating, but back then he was irresistible . . . Dear me, now my conscience is beginning to bother me. Why did I hurt my poor boy's feelings? I'm so upset. (*Loudly.*) Kostya! Kostya, darling!

MASHA. I'll go and look for him.

ARKADINA. Would you, dear?

MASHA (*exiting left*). Konstantin Gavrilovich! Yoo-hoo! Konstantin Gavrilovich!

NINA (*coming out from behind the stage*). We're obviously not going on with it, so I may as well come out now. Hello, everybody.

SORIN. Brava! Brava!

ARKADINA. Brava! Brava! We all loved you. With those looks and that beautiful voice it's a crime for you to stay buried in the country. I'm certain you've got talent. Certain, do you hear? It's your duty to go on the stage.

NINA. Oh, it's the dream of my life! (*Sighing.*) But it will never come true.

ARKADINA. Who can tell? Here now, let me introduce you to my friend, Boris Alexeevich Trigorin.

NINA. Oh, so pleased to meet you . . . (*Flustered.*) I read everything you write . . .

ARKADINA (*giving her a seat next to them*). No need to be flustered, dear. He may be famous, but he's a simple soul. See? Now he's flustered too.

DORN. We can open the curtain now, can't we? It's so eerie closed like that.

SHAMRAEV (*loudly*). Yakov! Pull open the curtain, will you?

(*The curtain opens.*)

NINA (*to* TRIGORIN). Strange play, isn't it.

TRIGORIN. I didn't understand a word. But I enjoyed watching it. Your acting was so sincere. And the scenery was beautiful.

(*Pause.*)

There must be a lot of fish in that lake.

NINA. Yes.

TRIGORIN. I love to fish. There's nothing I like more than sitting on a riverbank in the late afternoon, watching my float bob up and down.

NINA. But I thought that once an artist had experienced the joys of creation he'd be immune to all others.

ARKADINA (*laughing*). Don't talk to him like that. Whenever people say nice things about him, he gets terribly flustered.

SHAMRAEV. Once when I was in Moscow at the Opera, I heard the great Silva go down to a low C. And it so happened there was a bass from our church choir up in the second balcony, and suddenly—imagine our amazement—suddenly we hear "Bravo, Silva!" a whole octave lower . . . Like this. (*In a deep bass.*) Bravo, Silva! . . . You could have heard a pin drop.

(*Pause.*)

DORN. The angel of silence must be overhead.

NINA. Well, I'd better be going. Good-bye.

ARKADINA. Going? Where? It's so early. We won't let you.

NINA. Father is expecting me.

ARKADINA. No, really. He's impossible. (*They kiss.*) Well, that's that, I suppose. We're so sorry to see you go.

NINA. You can't imagine how hard it is for me to leave!

ARKADINA. Somebody ought to see you home, dear.

NINA (*frightened*). Oh, no! No!

SORIN (*to* NINA, *beseechingly*). Please stay!

NINA. I can't, Pyotr Nikolaevich.

SORIN. Just an hour and all. Really now!

NINA (*hesitating, nearly in tears*). No, I can't. (*She shakes hands with him and exits quickly.*)

ARKADINA. The poor girl. Apparently her mother left all her enormous fortune—every last kopeck—to Papa, and now he's gone and signed it over to his second wife. The girl hasn't a thing to her name. It's disgraceful.

DORN. Yes. To give credit where it's due: Papa dear is quite a swine.

SORIN (*rubbing his hands to warm them*). What do you say we move inside, ladies and gentlemen? It's getting damp. My legs are bothering me.

ARKADINA. They're stiff as boards. You can hardly walk. Here, let's go, you poor old thing. (*She takes* SORIN *by the arm.*)

SHAMRAEV (*offering his arm to* POLINA). Madam?

SORIN. There's that dog howling again. (*To* SHAMRAEV.) Please have it unchained.

SHAMRAEV. I can't or we'll have thieves in the barn. I've got my millet in there. (*To* MEDVEDENKO, *who is walking alongside him.*) Yes, a whole octave lower: "Bravo, Silva!" And no opera singer either. An ordinary member of the choir.

MEDVEDENKO. Tell me, how much does a choir member make a month?

(*They all exit except* DORN.)

DORN (*alone*). I don't know. Maybe I don't understand these things, maybe I'm out of my mind, but I liked the play. There's something to it. When that child started talking about loneliness and the devil's eyes appeared, I was so moved my hands started shaking. It was fresh and innocent... Oh, here he comes. I want to say all the nice things I can.

TREPLEV (*entering*). Everybody's gone.

DORN. I'm here.

TREPLEV. That Masha. I can't stand her. She's been hunting all over for me.

DORN. I really liked your play, Konstantin Gavrilovich. Oh, it's a little strange, and I didn't hear the end, but even so it made a deep impression on me. You've got talent. Don't give up. (TREPLEV *grasps his hand warmly and gives him an impulsive hug.*) Oh, you're so high strung. Look—tears in your eyes. Now what was it I wanted to say? You've taken your plot from the realm of the abstract, and rightly so: a work of art needs a great idea behind it. Nothing can be beautiful without being serious. You look so pale.

TREPLEV. So you think I should keep at it?

DORN. Yes . . . But stick to what's important, what's eternal. You know, I've had a decent life, full of variety. I'm satisfied. But if I'd ever had the chance to feel the exaltation an artist must feel in the process of creation, I think I'd have spurned my material self and all that goes with it and taken wing, soared into the heights.

TREPLEV. Excuse me, but where's Nina?

DORN. One more thing. A work of art must have a clear-cut, well-defined purpose. You must always know why you are writing. If all you do is paint pictures with no definite goal in mind, you'll go astray, your talent will be the end of you.

TREPLEV (*impatiently*). Where's Nina?

DORN. She's gone home.

TREPLEV (*in despair*). What can I do? I want to see her ... I need to see her ... I'm going after her ...

(*Enter* MASHA.)

DORN (*to* TREPLEV). Calm down, my boy.

TREPLEV. I'm going no matter what. I've got to.

MASHA. Come inside, Konstantin Gavrilovich. Your mother's waiting for you. She's upset.

TREPLEV. Tell her I've gone. And leave me alone, please, all of you. Leave me alone. Stop following me.

DORN. Now, now, Kostya . . . You mustn't go on like this . . . It's not right.

TREPLEV (*nearly in tears*). Good-bye, Doctor . . . Thank you . . . (*He exits.*)

DORN (*sighing*). Ah youth, youth.

MASHA. Whenever people are at a loss for what to say, they say, "Ah youth, youth." (*She takes snuff.*)

DORN (*taking the snuffbox from her and flinging it into the bushes*). Disgusting!

(*Pause.*)

I think I hear piano playing inside. We'd better go in.

MASHA. Wait a minute.

DORN. What is it?

MASHA. I want to tell you again. I feel like talking . . . (*Troubled.*) I don't love my father . . . But I'm close to you. I don't know why—I've got a strong feeling there's a bond between us. Help me. Help me before I do something foolish, make a mockery of my life, ruin it . . . I can't go on like this . . .

DORN. What do you mean? How can I help?

MASHA. Oh, the pain. Nobody, no one knows the pain I'm in. (*She puts her head on his chest. Softly.*) I'm in love with Konstantin.

DORN. So high strung. They're so high strung. And all that love . . . O magic lake! (*Tenderly.*) But what can I do, my child? What can I do?

CURTAIN

ACT TWO

A croquet lawn. Upstage right is a house with a large terrace, left—the lake with the sun playing on its surface. Flower beds. It is midday and hot. ARKADINA, DORN, *and* MASHA *are sitting on a bench near the lawn in the shade of an old linden tree.* DORN *has a book open on his lap.*

ARKADINA (*to* MASHA). Come, let's stand up. (*They both stand.*) Side by side. You're twenty-two; I'm nearly twice that. And which of us looks younger, Doctor?

DORN. You, of course.

ARKADINA. There you are . . . And why? Because I work, I feel, I'm always on the move. While you, you never budge, you haven't lived . . . I make it a rule never to look into the future. I never think about old age or death. What will be will be.

MASHA. I feel I was born ages ago. I drag my life after me like a gown with an endless train . . . There are times when I've no desire to go on living. It's ridiculous, of course. All I need to do is pull myself together and snap out of it.

DORN (*singing softly*). "Tell her, tell her for me, o flowers, do . . ."[12]

ARKADINA. And then I'm as proper as an Englishman. Yes, dear. I keep myself in hand: always dressed and coiffed *comme il faut*. Would I leave the house—even come into the garden—wearing a dressing gown or with my hair undone? Never! The reason I look so young is that I've never let myself get dowdy, let myself go, like some people . . . (*She parades up and down the lawn, arms akimbo.*) See what I mean? Light as a feather. I could play a girl of fifteen.

DORN. Yes, well, why don't I start again. (*He picks up the book.*) We'd just come to the part about the grain merchant and the rats . . .

ARKADINA. And the rats. Go ahead. (*She sits.*) No, let me have it. I'll read. It's my turn. (*She takes the book and looks for the place.*) And the

rats . . . Here it is . . . (*She reads.*) "Clearly it is every bit as dangerous for society people to dote on novelists and entice them into
their homes as it would be for grain merchants to raise rats in
their granaries. Yet writers are much in demand. Thus, when a
woman sets her sights on a writer, she besieges him with all manner of compliments, attentions, and favors . . ." Well, that may be
true of the French, but we're different. We don't plan things. By
the time a Russian woman sets her sights on a writer, you can be
sure she's fallen head over heels in love with him. No need to go
far. Look at me and Trigorin . . .

> (*Enter* SORIN, *leaning on his cane, with* NINA *at his side.*
> MEDVEDENKO *is pushing an empty wheelchair behind them.*)

SORIN (*fondly, as if to a child*). Really? Good news, eh? We're going to
have a good time today, if you know what I mean. (*To* ARKA-
DINA.) Good news! Father and Stepmother have gone to Tver,
and we're on our own for three whole days.

NINA (*sitting next to* ARKADINA *and hugging her*). I'm so happy. I'm all
yours now.

SORIN (*sitting in his wheelchair*). My, doesn't she look pretty today!

ARKADINA. Attractive, nicely dressed . . . There's a good girl! (*She
kisses* NINA.) We'd better not praise her too much, though: it
might bring bad luck. Where's Trigorin?

NINA. Down at the bathing shed, fishing.

ARKADINA. How he can stand the boredom I don't know. (*Getting
ready to return to the book.*)

NINA. What's that you're reading?

ARKADINA. Maupassant, dear. *On the Water.* (*She reads several lines to
herself.*) Oh well, the next part isn't interesting. Or true either.[13]
(*She closes the book.*) I'm terribly worried. Tell me, what's wrong
with my son? Why is he so gloomy and out of sorts? Spending
day after day on the lake like that. I hardly see him.

MASHA. He's deeply troubled. (*To* NINA, *timidly.*) Would you recite
a passage from his play for us?

NINA (*shrugging her shoulders*). You really want me to? It's so uninteresting.

MASHA (*trying to curb her enthusiasm*). When he recites it himself, his eyes light up and his face turns pale. He has the most beautiful, mournful voice. And the bearing of a poet.

(SORIN *gives a loud snore.*)

DORN. Good night.
ARKADINA. Petrusha.
SORIN. Huh?
ARKADINA. Are you asleep?
SORIN. No, not in the least.

(*Pause.*)

ARKADINA. You need medical attention. It's no good going on like this.
SORIN. I'd be only too glad. It's the doctor here who's against it.
DORN. Medical attention at sixty!
SORIN. Even sixty-year-olds want to live.
DORN (*annoyed*). Oh, all right, then. Take some valerian drops.
ARKADINA. I think a trip to a spa would do him some good.
DORN. Fine. Go ahead ... Or stay at home.
ARKADINA. Now what is that supposed to mean?
DORN. Just what I said. It's perfectly clear.

(*Pause.*)

MEDVEDENKO. Pyotr Nikolaevich should give up smoking.
SORIN. Nonsense.
DORN. No, it's not nonsense. Wine and tobacco rob you of your individuality. After a cigar or a glass of vodka you're not just Sorin anymore; you're Sorin plus somebody. Your image of yourself gets blurred and you start seeing yourself in the third person: him.
SORIN. That's easy for you to say. You've lived a full life. But what about me? I spent twenty-eight years at the Department of Justice, but that's not living. I've had no experiences, if you know what I mean, so of course I want to live. You've had your fill, so you don't care. You can afford to wax philosophical. I want to live. That's why I drink sherry with dinner and smoke cigars and all. Well, that's it.
DORN. Take life seriously, by all means. But going to a spa at sixty?

Complaining you didn't live it up when you were young? I'm sorry, that's just plain silly.

MASHA (*standing*). Must be time for lunch. (*She starts off sluggishly, listlessly.*) My foot's asleep . . . (*She exits.*)

DORN. Off for a couple of quick ones before lunch.

SORIN. She's unhappy, poor thing.

DORN. Ridiculous, Your Excellency.

SORIN. The response of a man who's had his fill.

ARKADINA. Oh, could anything be more boring than this pleasant country boredom? So hot, so still. Nobody doing anything, everybody philosophizing . . . I like it here with you, friends; I enjoy hearing you talk . . . But oh, to be sitting in a hotel room learning lines.

NINA (*ecstatic*). Yes, I know what you mean!

SORIN. Of course. Everything's better in town. You sit in your study, your servant won't let anyone in unannounced, you've got your telephone . . . There are cabs outside and all . . .

DORN (*singing to himself*). "Tell her, tell her for me, o flowers, do . . ."

(*Enter* SHAMRAEV *followed by* POLINA.)

SHAMRAEV. Here they are! Hello, everybody! (*He kisses* ARKADINA's *hand, then* NINA's.) Terribly glad to see you looking well. (*To* ARKADINA.) My wife tells me you're planning to go into town with her today. Is that true?

ARKADINA. Yes, we are going into town.

SHAMRAEV. Hmm! Perfect. And how do you plan to get there, my dear lady? Today's our day to bring in the rye. All the men are busy. And what were you planning to do for horses, if I may ask?

ARKADINA. Horses? How should I know?

SORIN. We do have carriage horses.

SHAMRAEV (*upset*). Carriage horses! Where do you expect me to find collars for them? It's unbelievable! I can't understand it! I'm sorry, dear lady. I have the greatest of admiration for your talents, I'd gladly give ten years of my life for you, but horses—no, I can't let you have any.

ARKADINA. And if I *must* go? This is all very peculiar.

SHAMRAEV. My dear lady, you have no idea what it means to run an estate.

ARKADINA (*losing her temper*). The same old story! Well, if that's the case, I'm leaving for Moscow today. Have somebody hire me some horses in the village or I'll *walk* to the station.

SHAMRAEV (*losing his temper*). Well, if that's the case, I resign. You can find yourself another manager. (*He exits.*)

ARKADINA. Every summer it's the same; every summer they insult me. I'll never set foot in this place again! (*She exits left in the presumed direction of the bathing shed. A moment later she crosses back and goes into the house. She is followed by* TRIGORIN *with fishing tackle and a pail.*)

SORIN (*losing his temper*). The nerve of that man! What's going on here? I'm sick and tired of this. I want every one of those horses here this instant!

NINA (*to* POLINA). Saying no to a famous actress like Irina Niko-laevna! Can't you see? Her slightest wish, her merest whim means so much more than all your farming. It's unbelievable!

POLINA (*in despair*). But what can I do? Put yourself in my place. What can I do?

SORIN (*to* NINA). Let's go and find her . . . We'll all beg her to stay, agreed? (*Looking in the direction* SHAMRAEV *took.*) That man is impossible. Tyrant!

NINA (*stopping him from standing*). No, no. Don't get up . . . We'll push you in . . . (*She and* MEDVEDENKO *start pushing the wheelchair.*) Oh, isn't this terrible!

SORIN. Yes, yes. Terrible . . . But he won't resign. I'll have a talk with him. (*They exit.* DORN *and* POLINA *are left alone.*)

DORN. People are so boring. Your husband deserves to be tossed out on his ear, but before the whole thing's over, that old biddy Sorin and his sister will be apologizing to him. Just wait.

POLINA. He sent the carriage horses into the field. Every day it's something different. You have no idea what it does to me. Even physically. See? I'm trembling . . . I can't stand it when he's coarse like that. (*Begging him.*) Yevgeny, dearest darling. Let me come and live with you . . . Time is slipping by. We're not so young as we used to be. Are we going to keep lying and hiding till the end of our lives? . . .

(*Pause.*)

DORN. I'm fifty-five. It's too late for me to change my ways.

POLINA. I know why you won't have me. There are other women in your life. You can't have all of us living with you. I understand. I apologize. You must be fed up with me.

(NINA *appears near the house picking flowers.*)

DORN. No, it's all right.

POLINA. I'm tormented by jealousy. You're a doctor, of course. You can't avoid women. I understand . . .

DORN (*to* NINA, *who is coming up to him*). How are things going in there?

NINA. Irina Nikolaevna is crying, and Pyotr Nikolaevich is having an asthma attack.

DORN (*standing*). I'd better give them both some valerian drops . . .

NINA (*giving him her flowers*). For you.

DORN. *Merci bien.* (*He walks towards the house.*)

POLINA (*walking with him*). What pretty little flowers! (*Near the house, in a low voice.*) Give me those flowers! Give them to me! (*He hands them to her. She tears them to pieces and flings them aside. They both enter the house.*)

NINA (*alone*). It's so strange to see a famous actress crying—and over such a trifle. And a celebrated author—a public idol who's in all the papers, whose picture is on sale everywhere, whose books come out in foreign languages—spending the whole day fishing, asking for nothing more than a carp or two. I thought celebrities were proud and remote. I thought they had contempt for the crowd and used their fame and brilliant names to get back at people for making so much of money and birth. But here they are—crying, fishing, playing cards, laughing, and losing their tempers just like the rest of us.

TREPLEV (*entering hatless, carrying a gun and a dead seagull*). Are you alone?

NINA. Yes. (TREPLEV *lays the seagull at her feet.*) What is that supposed to mean?

TREPLEV. I did something contemptible today: I killed this seagull. Let me lay it at your feet.

NINA. What's wrong with you? (*She picks up the seagull and looks at it.*)

TREPLEV (*after a pause*). And soon I'll kill myself the same way.

NINA. You've changed.

TREPLEV. Since you started changing. You're different with me. You look at me so coldly. I'm always in your way.

NINA. You're so moody lately, and I don't understand the way you use words anymore: you talk in symbols. This seagull now. I suppose it's a symbol too. But I'm sorry, I don't understand it . . . (*She puts the seagull on the bench.*) I'm too simple to understand you.

TREPLEV. It all started that night my play was such a fiasco. Women can't forgive failure. I've burned the whole thing, every last scrap of it. You can't imagine how unhappy I am. Your coldness is terrifying. I can't believe it. It's like waking up one morning and finding the lake suddenly dry, drained of all its water. You say you're too simple to understand me, but what is there to understand? You didn't like the play, you have contempt for my creativity, and now you think I'm nobody, nothing, part of the crowd . . . (*Stamping his foot.*) Oh, it's clear, so clear. It's like having a nail driven into my brain. Damn that nail and damn the pride that sucks my blood, sucks it like a viper. (*Seeing* TRIGORIN, *who enters reading a book.*) Now here comes a real master, striding along like Hamlet himself, and with a book too. (*Mocking him.*) "Words, words, words . . ." The sun hasn't reached you yet, and you're all smiles, your eyes melting in its rays. I won't stand in your way. (*He exits quickly.*)

TRIGORIN (*making notes in his book*). Takes snuff and drinks vodka . . . Always wears black. Loved by the schoolmaster . . .

NINA. Hello, Boris Alexeevich.

TRIGORIN. Hello. Things have taken an unexpected turn: we seem to be leaving today. We'll probably never meet again. Pity. I don't often have a chance to meet young girls, young and attractive. I've forgotten how it feels to be eighteen or nineteen, I can't picture it, so the young girls in my stories tend to be unconvincing. I wish I could change places with you just for an hour and find out how your mind works, what you're really like.

NINA. And I'd like to change places with you.

TRIGORIN. What for?

NINA. To see how it feels to be a famous gifted writer. What does fame feel like? What does it make *you* feel?

TRIGORIN. Oh, nothing special, really. I've never given it much thought. (*After a moment's reflection.*) There are two possibilities: either you're making too much of my fame, or it has no feeling at all.

NINA. But reading about yourself in the papers . . .

TRIGORIN. I like it when they praise me; when they're hard on me, I'm depressed for a day or two.

NINA. What a marvelous world! You can't imagine how I envy you. People have such different destinies. Some can barely drag themselves through their dull, dreary lives—each one like the next and all of them unhappy; others, like you—though you're one in a million—others live brilliant, meaningful, fascinating lives . . . You are happy . . .

TRIGORIN. Me? (*He shrugs his shoulders.*) Hmm. All the things you say about fame and happiness and a fascinating life, all your fine words—I'm sorry, but they're just so many gumdrops, which I never touch. You are very young and very kind.

NINA. Your life is beautiful!

TRIGORIN. What's so good about it? (*He glances at his watch.*) I'd better go and write now. Sorry. My time is up . . . (*He laughs.*) You've found my weak spot, as they say, and that riles me, makes me a little angry. All right, then. Let's talk about it. Let's talk about my wonderful, beautiful life . . . Well now, where shall we begin? (*After a moment's thought.*) There are times when you can't get something out of your mind. Day and night all you can think of is, say, the moon. Well, I've got my own moon: day and night I'm obsessed with the idea of writing. I've got to keep writing and writing. I've no choice . . . As soon as I finish one story, I feel a compulsion to write another, and a third, and a fourth . . . I can't stop. I'm driven. There's nothing I can do about it. Tell me, what's so beautiful, what's so wonderful about that? Mad is more like it. Here I am with you and all excited, but not for an instant can I forget I have an unfinished story waiting for me. I look up and see that cloud in the shape of a grand piano, and I say to myself, "I'll have to use it somewhere in a story: 'A grand piano of a cloud drifted by.' " I notice the scent of heliotrope in the air and make a mental note: "Cloying fragrance, widowlike; use for describing a summer evening." I can't let a sentence, a word go by—yours or my own—without locking it up in my literary larder: it may just come in handy.[14] Whenever I finish a piece of work, I run off to the theater or a place where I can fish. All I want is to relax and forget. But no. Before I know it, a cannonball starts rumbling around in my brain—a new plot pulling me back to my desk. So off I rush, to write and write. And on it goes. I never give myself a moment's peace, I'm devouring my own life, and for the honey I pass on to an anonymous public I'm robbing my best flowers of their pollen. No, worse: I'm pulling them up and trampling on their roots. I must be out of my mind. How can my friends and relatives treat me as if I were sane? "What are you writing these days? What have you got in store for us?" It's always the same, over and over, and I can't help feeling the concern and praise and enthusiasm are all make-believe: they're only pretending I'm sane. There are times I'm afraid they're going to creep up on me, grab me, and carry me off to a madhouse, like Poprishchin in the Gogol story.[15] Even when I was young, in the best years of my life, writing was pure torture. A minor writer, especially when he's down on his luck, feels awkward, out of place, expendable. He's always tense, on edge. He's irresistibly drawn to people in art and literature, but they don't recognize or even notice him, and he's too scared to look them in the face. He's like a passionate gambler with no money. I can't see my readers, of course, but somehow I picture them as hostile and suspicious. I was afraid of the theater audience, terrified, and whenever a new play of mine was produced I would think the dark-haired men in the audience were antagonistic and the fair-haired men cold and indifferent. Oh, how awful it was! Pure torture!

NINA. Even so, don't you feel moments of ecstasy and bliss, when you're inspired and actually in the process of creation?

TRIGORIN. Yes, I enjoy the writing; I enjoy reading proof. But . . . the moment the thing's published, I can't bear it. I realize it's not what I intended, it's all wrong, I never should have written it in the first place, and I get all depressed and disgusted with myself . . . (*Laughing.*) And then the public reads it and says, "Very nice, shows talent . . . Very nice, but a far cry from Tolstoy." Or "Fine work, but no *Fathers and Sons*."[16] "Very nice, fine work; fine work, very nice" till the day I die. You know what my friends will say as they file past my grave? "Here lies Trigorin. A good writer, but no Turgenev."

NINA. I'm sorry, I refuse to accept that. You're just spoiled by success.

TRIGORIN. Success? I've never liked myself as a person; I don't like myself as a writer. And the worst of it is I live in a kind of daze and often don't even understand what I'm writing . . . What I do love is this water, the trees, the sky. I have a feeling for nature. It arouses a passion in me, an irresistible urge to write. But I'm not just a landscape artist; I'm a member of society as well. I love my country and my people. As an author I feel duty bound to speak out about them, about their sufferings, their future, about science and the rights of man, and so on and so forth. I try to cover them all, I do my best, but there's always somebody after me, angry, and I race back and forth like a fox at bay. I watch science and society forge ahead while I drop farther and farther behind, like a peasant running after a train. And then I start feeling I'm no good at anything but landscapes and when I do anything else I'm an imposter, an imposter to the marrow of my bones.

NINA. You've been working too hard. You're either too busy or too stubborn to see what you mean to others. What if you are dissatisfied with yourself? Other people see you as a great and wonderful man. If I were a writer of your stature, I'd give my life to the crowd, knowing that the only thing that can make them happy is to rise to my level. They would draw my chariot.

TRIGORIN. Chariot, eh? . . . Who do you think I am? Agamemnon? (*Both smile.*)

NINA. If I were lucky enough to be a writer or actress, I'd gladly put up with my family's rejection, with poverty and disappointments. I'd live in a garret and eat nothing but dry bread. I'd be very hard on myself and acknowledge all my shortcomings, but in return I'd demand fame . . . Real fame! Resounding fame! . . . (*She covers her face with her hands.*)

ARKADINA (*from inside the house*). Boris Alexeevich!

TRIGORIN. They're calling me ... To pack, I suppose. But I don't feel like leaving. (*He turns to look at the lake.*) Look at it! Heavenly!

NINA. You see that house with a garden on the other side?

TRIGORIN. Yes.

NINA. It was my mother's when she was alive. I was born there. I've spent my life on this lake. I know every little island in it.

TRIGORIN. It's so beautiful here! (*Noticing the seagull.*) What's that?

NINA. A seagull. Konstantin Gavrilovich shot it.

TRIGORIN. Nice bird. I don't feel like leaving, really. Why don't you try and talk Irina Nikolaevna into staying? (*He jots something down in his notebook.*)

NINA. What's that you're writing?

TRIGORIN. Just making a few notes ... An idea for a story ... (*Putting away the notebook.*) An idea for a story. About a young girl who has lived on a lake since childhood, a young girl like you. She loves the lake like a seagull; she's happy and free like a seagull. Then a man comes along, notices her, and—for want of anything better to do—destroys her. Just like the seagull.

(*Pause.*)

ARKADINA (*appearing in the window*). Boris Alexeevich, where are you?

TRIGORIN. Coming! (*He starts walking, then looks back at* NINA. *At the window, to* ARKADINA.) What is it?

ARKADINA. We're staying.

(TRIGORIN *goes into the house.*)

NINA (*going up to the footlights and thinking for a moment*). I must be dreaming.

CURTAIN

ACT THREE

The dining room in SORIN'*s house. Doors right and left. A sideboard. A medicine cupboard. A table in the middle of the room. A trunk and some hat-boxes. Other signs of impending departure.* TRIGORIN *is having lunch.* MASHA *is standing at the table.*

MASHA. The reason I'm telling you all this is you're a writer and can make use of it. I really mean it: if he'd wounded himself badly, I couldn't have lived another minute. But I'm brave. I've decided to tear the love from my heart, tear it out by the roots.

TRIGORIN. And how do you plan to do that?

MASHA. By getting married. To Medvedenko.

TRIGORIN. The schoolmaster?

MASHA. Yes.

TRIGORIN. I don't see what for.

MASHA. What good is love without hope, with long years of wait-ing? ... There'll be no time for love when I'm married. New wor-ries will bury the old. And if nothing else, it will be a change. How about another round?

TRIGORIN. Don't you think we've had enough?

MASHA. Come now! (*She pours them each a glass.*) Don't look at me like that. Women drink a lot more than you think. The ones who do it openly like me are in the minority; most of them do it on the sly. That's right. Vodka or cognac! (*She clinks glasses with him.*) Your health! You're a good man. I'm sorry to see you go. (*They drink.*)

TRIGORIN. And I don't want to.

MASHA. Then why not ask her to stay?

TRIGORIN. No, she won't stay now. Not with her son behaving so tactlessly. First he tries to shoot himself; then he wants to challenge me to a duel. And what for? He sulks and sneers and preaches forms . . . Well, I say there's room for both old and new. Why push and shove?

MASHA. It's jealousy too. But that's none of my business.

(*Pause.* YAKOV *crosses from left to right with the trunk. Enter* NINA. *She stops at the window.*)

My schoolmaster's not too bright, but he's a kind man and a poor man and he loves me very much. I feel sorry for him. For his old mother too. Well, good-bye. Think of me now and then. (*She shakes his hand warmly.*) And thank you for being so nice. Send me your books, and be sure to inscribe them. Only don't write "Best wishes"; write "To Maria, who knows not whence she comes or why she lives." Good-bye. (*She exits.*)

NINA (*holding out a clenched fist in* TRIGORIN*'s direction*). Odd or even?

TRIGORIN. Even.

NINA (*sighing*). No, odd. Only one pea in my hand. I'm trying to decide whether to go on the stage or not. I wish someone would give me advice.

TRIGORIN. You can't give advice about that sort of thing.

(*Pause.*)

NINA. Once we say good-bye . . . we may never meet again. Take this medallion to remember me by. Please. I've had your initials engraved on it . . . And the title of your book *Days and Nights* on the other side.

TRIGORIN. Exquisite! (*He kisses the medallion.*) A charming gift.

NINA. Think of me now and then.

TRIGORIN. Oh, I will. I'll think of the way you looked that sunny day a week ago, remember? You were wearing a bright dress . . . We talked a while . . . And there was a white seagull lying on the bench.

NINA (*pensively*). Yes, the seagull . . .

(*Pause.*)

We'd better stop. Someone's coming . . . Let me have two minutes with you before you go. Please . . . (*She exits left.*)

(*At the same time* ARKADINA *and* SORIN *enter right.* SORIN *is wearing a frock coat with a star-shaped medal on it. They are followed by* YAKOV *carrying luggage.*)

ARKADINA. No, you stay here, old man. You can't go gallivanting about with that rheumatism of yours. (*To* TRIGORIN.) Who left just now? Nina?

TRIGORIN. Yes.

ARKADINA. Oh, *pardonnez-moi.* We didn't mean to disturb you . . . (*She sits.*) Well, I think I've got everything packed. I'm exhausted.

TRIGORIN (*reading the inscription on the medallion*). *Days and Nights,* page 121, lines 11 and 12.

YAKOV (*clearing the table*). Do you want me to pack the fishing rods too, sir?

TRIGORIN. Yes, I'll be needing them. But you can give away the books.

YAKOV. Yes, sir.

TRIGORIN (*to himself*). Page 121, lines 11 and 12. I wonder what's in them. (*To* ARKADINA.) Do you keep my books anywhere in the house?

ARKADINA. In Pyotr's study, the corner bookshelf.

TRIGORIN. Page 121 . . . (*He exits.*)

ARKADINA. Really, Petrusha, you ought to stay here at home.

SORIN. But you're all leaving. It will be lonely without you.

ARKADINA. And in town?

SORIN. Nothing special, but still . . . (*He laughs.*) I can go to the ground-breaking ceremony for the new County Building and all . . . I just want to shake off this terrible lethargy for an hour or two. I'm as stale as an old cigarette holder. I've ordered the horses for one o'clock. We can all start out together.

ARKADINA (*after a pause*). Well, have a good winter. Don't let yourself get bored or catch cold. And keep an eye on my son. Take care of him. Give him some guidance.

(*Pause.*)

Now that I'm going, I'll never know for sure what made him put a gun to his head. I think the main reason was jealousy, so the sooner I get Trigorin away from here the better.

SORIN. I don't know quite how to put this . . . but there were other reasons as well. After all, an intelligent young man living in the country, the back of beyond, with no money, no job, no future, nothing to do, ashamed and afraid of just sitting around. I love him very much, and he's fond of me, but he doesn't really feel he belongs here, if you know what I mean. He feels he's sponging, living on charity. He's got his pride, after all . . .

ARKADINA. The trouble he gives me! (*Thoughtfully.*) Maybe he should find a job . . .

SORIN (*whistles a little, then speaks hesitantly*). I think it would be best if you . . . well, gave him a little money. He really ought to have some decent clothes and all. I mean, look at him. He's been wearing the same miserable jacket for three years now. He doesn't even own an overcoat . . . (*He laughs.*) And it wouldn't hurt the boy to have a little fun . . . go abroad or something . . . It doesn't cost that much.

ARKADINA. I know, but . . . Well, I might be able to afford a suit, but a trip abroad . . . No, I can't even afford the suit now. (*Firmly.*) I haven't got any money. (SORIN *laughs.*) I haven't!

SORIN (*whistles a little*). I see. I'm sorry, my dear. I believe you. You're a generous, noble woman.

ARKADINA (*nearly in tears*). I haven't got any money!

SORIN. If *I* had, you can be sure I'd give him some myself. But I haven't, not a kopeck. (*He laughs.*) Shamraev takes all my pension and spends it on crops and cows and bees. I never see it again. The bees die, the cows die, I can't get near the horses . . .

ARKADINA. Well, I do have some money, actually, but remember, I'm an actress. My wardrobe alone is enough to ruin me.

SORIN. You're a kind, good-hearted woman . . . I have the greatest respect for you . . . Yes . . . Oh dear, it's starting up again . . . (*He staggers forward.*) I'm dizzy. (*He grabs hold of the table.*) I feel faint and all.

ARKADINA (*frightened*). Petrusha! (*Trying to hold him up.*) Petrusha,

dear . . . (*Shouting.*) Help! Help! (*Enter* TREPLEV *and* MEDVE-
DENKO. TREPLEV's *head is bandaged.*) He feels faint.

SORIN. It's all right, it's all right . . . (*He smiles and drinks some water.*)
It's over . . . and all . . .

TREPLEV (*to* ARKADINA). Don't be frightened, Mother. It's not serious. It's been happening a lot lately. (*To* SORIN.) How about lying
down for a while.

SORIN. All right, but just for a while . . . I'm still going to town . . . I'll
lie down for a while before I go . . . After all . . . (*He moves off, leaning on his cane.*)

MEDVEDENKO (*supporting him on his arm*). Here's a riddle for you.
What walks on four legs in the morning, two legs at noon, three
legs in the evening . . .

SORIN (*laughing*). And spends the night on its back. I know that one . . .
I can manage by myself, thank you.

MEDVEDENKO. Now, now. Don't put on a front for my sake. (*He and*
SORIN *exit.*)

ARKADINA. That was a real scare he gave me.

TREPLEV. Country life is bad for him. Depressing. If you had a sudden fit of generosity, Mother, lent him fifteen hundred or so, he
could spend the whole year in town.

ARKADINA. I haven't got any money. I'm an actress, not a banker.

(*Pause.*)

TREPLEV. Change my bandage for me, will you, Mother? You do it
so well.

ARKADINA (*taking some antiseptic and a box of gauze out of the medicine
cupboard*). The doctor's late.

TREPLEV. He promised to come by ten, and here it is twelve.

ARKADINA. Sit down. (*She takes the bandage off his head.*) It's like a
turban. Yesterday in the kitchen a visitor asked what nation-
ality you are. Oh, it's almost healed, all gone. (*She kisses him
on the head.*) No more bang-bang while I'm away, now, understand?

TREPLEV. Yes, Mother. It was a moment of wild desperation. I lost
control of myself. It will never happen again. (*He kisses her hand.*)

You've got magic hands. I remember once a long time ago when you were still with the state theaters—I was just a boy then— there was a fight in our courtyard, and one of the tenants, a washerwoman, was nearly beaten to death. Remember? She was unconscious when they found her ... And you went to see her all the time, took medicine to her, gave her children baths in the washbasin. You really don't remember?

ARKADINA. No. (*She puts on a fresh bandage.*)

TREPLEV. There were two girls, ballet dancers, living in the house ... They used to come and have coffee with you ...

ARKADINA. That I do remember.

TREPLEV. They were very religious.

(*Pause.*)

Just recently, these past few days, I've loved you in the same tender, selfless way I loved you as a child. You're all I have left. But why, why do you let that man come between us?

ARKADINA. You don't understand him, Konstantin. He has a very noble character.

TREPLEV. But when he heard I was planning to challenge him to a duel, that noble character of his didn't keep him from changing color. And now he's leaving. An ignominious flight.

ARKADINA. Don't be silly. He's leaving because I asked him to.

TREPLEV. A noble character! Here we are, on the verge of squabbling over him, and he's off in the drawing room or garden somewhere having a good laugh at our expense ... Cultivating Nina, trying to convince her he's a genius.

ARKADINA. You take great delight in saying nasty things to me. I respect the man, and I ask you not to speak ill of him in my presence.

TREPLEV. Well, *I* don't respect him. You want me to think he's a genius too, but I'm sorry—I'm not a good liar. His stories make me sick.

ARKADINA. That's envy talking. What can pretentious nonentities do but malign true talent. Not much in the way of consolation, if you ask me.

TREPLEV (*ironically*). True talent! (*Angrily.*) I've got more talent than all of you put together, so there! (*He tears the bandage off his head.*) You're nothing but a bunch of hacks, and just because you've got a stranglehold on the arts you think the only legitimate way of doing things is your own. Everything else you smother and suppress. Well, I don't accept your supremacy! Yours or his!

ARKADINA. You decadent!

TREPLEV. Go back to your precious theater and your trashy, third-rate plays!

ARKADINA. I've never done a trashy play in my life, and you couldn't write a third-rate vaudeville sketch! Out of my sight, you upstart Kiev tradesman, you! You sponger!

TREPLEV. Penny pincher! (TREPLEV *sits and weeps quietly.*)

ARKADINA. Nonentity! (*Pacing up and down in her excitement.*) Don't cry. Stop crying. (*She starts crying.*) Don't . . . (*She kisses his forehead, cheeks, and head.*) Forgive me, my darling. Forgive your wicked mother. Forgive me. I'm so unhappy.

TREPLEV (*embracing her*). If you knew what I'm going through! I've lost everything. She doesn't love me. I can't write . . . All my hopes are gone . . .

ARKADINA. Don't despair . . . Everything will turn out fine. I'm taking him away; she'll love you as before. (*She wipes his tears.*) That's enough now. There, we're friends again, aren't we?

TREPLEV (*kissing her hands*). Yes, Mother.

ARKADINA (*tenderly*). Now make friends with him too. There's no need for a duel, is there now.

TREPLEV. All right . . . As long as I don't need to see him. That would be too hard . . . too much to ask . . . (*Enter* TRIGORIN.) There he is . . . I'm going . . . (*He quickly puts the medicine and bandages back in the cupboard.*) The doctor will take care of the bandage.

TRIGORIN (*looking through the book*). Page 121 . . . lines 11 and 12 . . . Here it is . . . (*He reads.*) "If ever you should need my life, come and take it."

(TREPLEV *picks up the old bandage from the floor and exits.*)

ARKADINA (*glancing at her watch*). The horses will be here soon.

TRIGORIN (*to himself*). If ever you should need my life, come and take it.

ARKADINA. You're all packed, I hope.

TRIGORIN (*impatient*). Yes, yes . . . (*Lost in thought.*) Why do I sense such anguish in the appeal of that innocent girl? Why do I find it so moving? . . . If ever you should need my life, come and take it. (*To* ARKADINA.) Let's stay on another day. (ARKADINA *shakes her head.*) One more day.

ARKADINA. I know what's keeping you here, darling, but try and control yourself. You're a bit intoxicated, that's all. Time to sober up.

TRIGORIN. And time for you to be sober and reasonable and understanding. Please, please try and see it like a true friend . . . (*He presses her hand.*) You're capable of sacrifice . . . Be a friend. Set me free . . .

ARKADINA (*greatly agitated*). Is it as bad as all that?

TRIGORIN. I feel drawn to her. It may be just what I need.

ARKADINA. The love of a provincial girl? Oh, how little you know yourself!

TRIGORIN. You know how people walk in their sleep? Well, while I'm here talking to you, I feel I'm asleep, dreaming of her. Sweet, wonderful dreams . . . Set me free . . .

ARKADINA (*trembling*). No, no . . . I'm just an ordinary woman. You mustn't talk to me like that . . . Stop torturing me, Boris . . . I'm frightened.

TRIGORIN. You could step out of the ordinary if you really wanted to. Young love, the kind that's all poetry and magic and whisks you off into the world of dreams—it's our only chance for happiness on earth. I've never felt it before . . . I was too busy when I was young: I spent all my time on editors' doorsteps struggling with poverty . . . And now here it is, that love; it's come at last, it's calling to me . . .

ARKADINA (*angry*). You must be out of your mind!

TRIGORIN. What if I am?

ARKADINA. You're all conspiring to torture me today. (*She cries.*)

TRIGORIN (*clutching his head*). She doesn't understand! She refuses to understand!

ARKADINA. Am I really so old and ugly that you can talk about other women to my face? (*She hugs and kisses him.*) You must be out of your mind! My wonderful, marvelous man ... The last page of my life! (*She goes down on her knees.*) My pride, my joy, my ecstasy ... (*She hugs his knees.*) If you leave me for a single hour, I won't survive. I'll go out of my mind. My wonderful, magnificent lord and master ...

TRIGORIN. People might see us. (*He helps her up.*)

ARKADINA. Let them. I'm not ashamed of loving you. (*She kisses his hands.*) You want to be wild and reckless, my treasure, but I won't have it, I won't let you. (*She laughs.*) You're mine ... all mine. This forehead mine, these eyes mine, and this beautiful silky hair ... You're mine completely. You're so talented and intelligent. You're the best writer in Russia today, Russia's only hope ... You've got such sincerity, simplicity, freshness, vibrant humor ... With a stroke of the pen you go straight to the heart of a person or landscape. Your characters are so alive. No one can read you without going into raptures. You think I'm just flattering you, playing up to you? Well then, look me in the eye ... Look me in the eye ... Do I look like a liar? There, you see? I'm the only one who really appreciates you, the only one who tells you the truth. My darling, my own ... You *will* come with me now, won't you? You won't abandon me? ...

TRIGORIN. I've no will of my own ... Never had ... How can a woman care for anyone so weak-kneed and spineless, so ready to give in? Take me, carry me off, but don't let me out of your sight for an instant ...

ARKADINA (*to herself*). He's mine now. (*Casually, as if nothing had happened.*) Of course, if you really want to stay, why not? I'll leave today, and you can follow later, in a week. What's the hurry, after all.

TRIGORIN. No, we might as well leave together.

ARKADINA. Whatever you say. We'll leave together then ...

(*Pause.* TRIGORIN *jots something down in his notebook.*)

What's that?

TRIGORIN. I picked up a good expression this morning: "a vestal pine grove..." Might come in handy. (*He stretches.*) So we're going, are we? Another round of trains and stations, railway chops and railway chitchat.

SHAMRAEV (*entering*). It is my honor and sad duty to inform you that the horses are ready. Time to leave for the station, dear lady. The train's due in at 2:05. You *will* do me that favor now, won't you, Irina Nikolaevna, and find out the whereabouts of Suzdaltsev, the actor, and whether he's alive and well. We were once drinking companions ... He was inimitable in *The Mail Robbery* ... Now that I think of it, there was a tragedian named Izmailov in the same company in Yelizavetgrad. Another fine man ... No need to rush, dear lady. We've got five more minutes ... They were playing conspirators in a melodrama once, and when they got caught they were supposed to say, "We've fallen into a trap," but Izmailov said, "We've trallen into a fap." (*He chuckles.*) A fap!

(YAKOV *has been tending to the trunks during* SHAMRAEV's *speech. The* MAID *has brought* ARKADINA *her hat, coat, parasol, and gloves. They all help* ARKADINA *to dress. The* COOK *peeks in through the door left and after a few moments of hesitation enters haltingly. Enter* POLINA, *followed by* SORIN *and* MEDVEDENKO.)

POLINA (*with a small basket*). Here are some plums for the trip ... Nice and sweet. You might feel like a bite ...

ARKADINA. That's very kind of you.

POLINA. Good-bye, my dear. Please forgive us if things haven't been as they might have. (*She cries.*)

ARKADINA (*hugging her*). Everything's been fine, just fine. No need to cry.

POLINA. We're not getting any younger.

ARKADINA. But there's nothing we can do about it.

(*Enter* SORIN *from the door left wearing a hat and overcoat with a shoulder cape and carrying a cane.*)

SORIN (*crossing the room*). Time to go, Irina. We don't want to be late for the train, after all. I'll get in the carriage. (*He exits.*)

MEDVEDENKO. I'm walking to the station ... To see you off. I'll be there in no time ... (*He exits.*)

ARKADINA. Good-bye, everybody ... We'll see you again next summer if all goes well. (*The* MAID, YAKOV, *and the* COOK *kiss her hand.*) Don't forget me. (*She give the* COOK *a ruble.*) Here's a ruble ... for the three of you.

COOK. Much obliged, ma'am. Have a good trip. We're very grateful.

YAKOV. God be with you.

SHAMRAEV. Don't forget to drop us a line. Good-bye, Boris Alexeevich.

ARKADINA. Where's Konstantin? Tell him I'm leaving. We need to say good-bye. Well, think kindly of me. (*To* YAKOV.) I've given cook a ruble. It's for the three of you.

(*They all exit right. The stage is empty. Standard farewell patter offstage. The* MAID *comes back, takes the basket of plums from the table, and exits again.*)

TRIGORIN (*coming back*). Now where is my cane? Must be out there on the terrace. (*Walking towards the door left, he meets* NINA, *who is on her way in.*) Oh, it's you. We're leaving ...

NINA. I had a feeling we'd meet again. (*Excited.*) I've made up my mind once and for all. The die is cast: I'm going on the stage. I'll be away from here tomorrow ... I'm leaving my father, leaving everything, starting a new life ... I'm going to Moscow, just like you. We can meet there.

TRIGORIN (*looking round*). Take a room at the Slav Bazaar ... Let me hear from you immediately ... My address is Grokholsky House, Molchanovka Street ... I've got to go now ...

(*Pause.*)

NINA. Just one more minute.

TRIGORIN (*almost whispering*). You're so beautiful ... Oh, how happy it makes me to think we'll be meeting again soon. (NINA *rests her head on his chest.*) And I'll see those wonderful eyes again, that indescribably beautiful, tender smile ... those gentle features, that look of angelic purity ... Darling ... (*A long kiss.*)

CURTAIN

Two years pass between Acts Three and Four.

ACT FOUR

The drawing room in SORIN's *house.* TREPLEV *has converted it into his study. Doors right and left leading to other rooms. In the center a French window opening onto a terrace. Besides the usual drawing-room furniture there is a desk in the right-hand corner and a low daybed near the door left. A bookcase, books on the windowsills and tables.*

It is evening. A single shaded lamp is burning in the semidarkness. A wind is whistling in the trees and howling in the chimneys. A watchman shakes his rattle in the distance.

Enter MEDVEDENKO *and* MASHA.

MASHA (*calling out*). Konstantin Gavrilovich! Konstantin Gavrilovich! (*Looking round.*) Nobody here. Every minute the old man asks, "Where's Konstantin? Where's Kostya?" He can't live without him . . .

MEDVEDENKO. He's afraid of being alone. (*Listening hard.*) What terrible weather. Two days in a row.

MASHA (*turning up the flame in the lamp*). There are waves on the lake. Giant waves.

MEDVEDENKO. The garden's pitch black. Somebody ought to tell them to take down that stage out there—standing all naked and ugly like a skeleton, curtain flapping in the wind. Last night I thought I heard someone crying there as I walked past . . .

MASHA. What next . . .

(*Pause.*)

MEDVEDENKO. Let's go home, Masha.

MASHA (*shaking her head*). I'm staying the night.

MEDVEDENKO (*pleading*). Please, Masha. The baby will be hungry.

MASHA. Ridiculous. Matryona will feed it.

(*Pause.*)

MEDVEDENKO. Poor thing. Third night in a row he's been without his mother.

MASHA. What a bore you've become. You used to do a little philoso-phizing at least; now it's all home and baby, baby and home.

MEDVEDENKO. Let's go, Masha.

MASHA. You go.

MEDVEDENKO. Your father won't give me a horse.

MASHA. Yes, he will. Go and ask him.

MEDVEDENKO. All right. I'll try. Will you come home tomorrow?

MASHA (*taking snuff*). Oh, I suppose so. Just stop pestering me . . . (*Enter* TREPLEV *and* POLINA. TREPLEV *is carrying pillows and a blanket,* POLINA *sheets. They drop everything on the daybed, and* TRE-PLEV *goes over to his desk and sits down.*) What's all that for, Mother?

POLINA. Pyotr Nikolaevich asked me to make up the bed in Kostya's room for him.

MASHA. Here, I'll do it . . . (*She makes up the bed.*)

POLINA (*sighing*). An old man is twice a child. (*She goes up to the desk and, propping herself on her elbows, looks at a manuscript.*)

(*Pause.*)

MEDVEDENKO. Well, I'll be going. Good-bye, Masha. (*He kisses* MASHA*'s hand.*) Good-bye, Mother. (*He tries to kiss* POLINA*'s hand.*)

POLINA (*irritated*). Oh, go if you're going.

MEDVEDENKO. Good-bye, Konstantin Gavrilovich. (TREPLEV *shakes hands with him silently.* MEDVEDENKO *exits.*)

POLINA (*still looking at the manuscript*). Who'd have thought you'd turn into a real writer, Kostya. The magazines even pay you now. (*She runs her fingers through* TREPLEV*'s hair.*) And you've been looking so handsome lately . . . Dear Kostya, good Kostya, be nice to my Masha.

MASHA (*still working on the bed*). Leave him alone, Mother.

POLINA (*to* TREPLEV). She's a fine girl.

(*Pause.*)

A woman doesn't need much, Kostya. A kind glance now and then. I know. (TREPLEV *gets up from his desk and exits without responding.*)

MASHA. Now you've made him upset. Why hound him?

POLINA. I feel sorry for you, Masha dear.

MASHA. Just what I need.

POLINA. My heart aches for you. I see it all. I understand.

MASHA. Don't be silly. Unrequited love happens only in novels. It's ridiculous. The thing is to keep a firm grip on yourself and stop expecting things, a sudden change ... Once love worms its way into your heart, your only choice is to tear it out. Semyon's been promised a transfer to another district. As soon as we're settled there, I'll forget the whole thing ... tear it out of my heart, roots and all.

(*A melancholy waltz comes from two rooms away.*)

POLINA. That's Kostya playing. It means he's depressed.

MASHA (*taking two or three noiseless turns*). The main thing, Mother, is not to see him. All I need is for the transfer to come through. I'll forget him in a month once we're away from here. It's all so ridiculous.

(*The left door opens.* DORN *and* MEDVEDENKO *wheel in* SORIN.)

MEDVEDENKO. I've got six mouths to feed now, and flour is up to two kopecks a pound.

DORN. Just try making ends meet.

MEDVEDENKO. You can laugh. You're rolling in money.

DORN. Me? It took me thirty years of general practice to scrape together two thousand rubles, thirty years of hard work without a minute of the day or night to call my own. And now I've spent it all on my trip abroad. It's all gone.

MASHA (*to* MEDVEDENKO). Haven't you left yet?

MEDVEDENKO (*apologetically*). No, it's ... They won't let me have a horse.

MASHA (*deeply resentful, under her breath*). I wish I'd never laid eyes on you.

(*They have wheeled* SORIN *to stage left.* POLINA, MASHA, *and* DORN *sit near him.* MEDVEDENKO, *crestfallen, moves off to the side.*)

DORN. I see you've made a lot of changes around here. Turned the drawing room into a study.

MASHA. It's a good place for Konstantin Gavrilovich to work. He can go out into the garden and think whenever he feels like it.

(*The watchman shakes his rattle offstage.*)

SORIN. Where's my sister?

DORN. Gone to the station to meet Trigorin. She'll be right back.

SORIN. I must really be ill if you had to send for my sister. (*After a short silence.*) But I can't understand it. If I'm so ill, why don't you give me any medicine?

DORN. What do you want? Valerian drops? Bicarbonate of soda? Quinine?

SORIN. Here comes the philosophy again. Oh, the torment! (*Turning his head in the direction of the daybed.*) Is that for me?

POLINA. Yes, Pyotr Nikolaevich.

SORIN. Thank you.

DORN (*singing to himself*). "The moon drifts through the skies at night . . ."[17]

SORIN. I've got an idea for a story I want to give Kostya. It will be called "The Man Who Meant To"—"L'homme qui a voulu." When I was young, I meant to be a writer—I never was. I meant to speak well—I speak atrociously. (*Making fun of himself.*) "Um . . . and all . . . um . . . if you know what I mean . . ." Every time I had to sum up in court, I broke into a cold sweat. I meant to get married—I never did. I meant to live in town—and here I am ending my days in the country and all.

DORN. You meant to become a state councilor—and you did.

SORIN (*laughing*). No, I didn't mean to do that. It just happened.

DORN. You must admit, though, it's not very magnanimous all this talk of how badly life has treated you. And at sixty-two.

SORIN. Stubborn, aren't you? Can't you see? I want to live!

DORN. Don't be silly. According to the laws of nature every life must have its end.

SORIN. You talk like a man who's had his fill. You're content, you've lost interest, you don't care anymore. But when your time comes, you'll be frightened too.

DORN. Fear of death is an animal fear, something to be overcome. The only people who consciously fear death are people who believe in Life Eternal and are afraid of retribution for their sins. But you're no believer, and then, what sins can you have committed? Twenty-five years at the Ministry of Justice, that's all.

SORIN (*laughing*). Twenty-eight.

(*Enter* TREPLEV. *He sits on a stool at* SORIN's *feet.* MASHA *never takes her eyes off him.*)

DORN. We're keeping Konstantin Gavrilovich from his work.

TREPLEV. No, that's all right.

(*Pause.*)

MEDVEDENKO. Tell us, Doctor. Which city did you like best?

DORN. Genoa.

TREPLEV. Why Genoa?

DORN. The wonderful street life. You step out of your hotel at night and the street is teeming with people. You move with the crowd—aimlessly, this way and that. You live with the crowd, merging with it spiritually. You start believing there really might be a universal soul like the one in your play, the one Nina performed for us a few years back. By the way, where is she now? How is she?

TREPLEV. All right, I suppose.

DORN. Somebody told me she'd been leading a rather irregular existence. What happened?

TREPLEV. It's a long story, Doctor.

DORN. Well, give us an abridged version.

(*Pause.*)

TREPLEV. She ran away from home and had an affair with Trigorin. You knew that, didn't you?

DORN. Yes, I did.

TREPLEV. She had a child. The child died. Trigorin tired of her and returned to his former attachments, as was to be expected. Or rather, he'd never given them up. No, in his own spineless way he'd managed to keep going back and forth. From what I can piece together, Nina's personal life has been a shambles.

DORN. And her stage career?

TREPLEV. Even worse apparently. She made her debut at a small summer theater near Moscow. From there she went to the provinces. I didn't let her out of my sight. Wherever she went, I followed. She got big parts, but she was vulgar in them, crass—ranting and raving, gesticulating wildly. True, she had her moments— a convincing shriek, a convincing death—but they were only moments.

DORN. Then she does have some talent.

TREPLEV. She may have. It's hard to tell for sure. I saw *her,* but she wouldn't see *me:* they wouldn't let me into her hotel room. I understood how she felt and didn't insist.

(*Pause.*)

What else is there to tell? Later, back at home, I started getting letters from her. Warm, intelligent, thought-provoking letters. She never complained, but I could tell how unhappy she was: every line was a taut, aching nerve. Her mind must have been affected too: she signed all her letters "The Seagull." The miller in Pushkin's *Water Nymph* says he's a raven.[18] Well, she kept calling herself a seagull. She's here now.

DORN. Here? What do you mean?

TREPLEV. She's had a room in town for four or five days. At the inn. I was planning to go and visit her—Masha actually did go—but she won't see anybody. Medvedenko says he saw her in a field yesterday afternoon a mile or two from here.

MEDVEDENKO. That's right. She was going back to town. I bowed and asked why she hadn't been to see us. She said she'd come.

TREPLEV. She won't.

(*Pause.*)

Her father and stepmother will have nothing to do with her. They've posted guards around their estate to make sure she can't get near the place. (*He goes over to the desk with* DORN.) It's one thing to be a philosopher on paper, Doctor, and another thing to be one in life.

SORIN. She was a charming girl.

DORN. How's that?

SORIN. I said, "She was a charming girl." State Councilor Sorin was even in love with her for a time.

DORN. The old rake.

(SHAMRAEV *is heard laughing offstage.*)

POLINA. They must be back from the station . . .

TREPLEV. Yes. I hear Mother.

(*Enter* ARKADINA *and* TRIGORIN, *followed by* SHAMRAEV.)

SHAMRAEV (*entering*). We're all getting older, wearing down under the influence of the elements, but you, dear lady, you're as young as ever . . . Your bright blouse, your vitality . . . your grace . . .

ARKADINA. Trying to bring me bad luck again, you awful man?

TRIGORIN (*to* SORIN). Hello there, Pyotr Nikolaevich. Under the weather as usual? Bad boy! (*Seeing* MASHA. *Happily.*) Maria Ilyinichna!

MASHA. You mean you remember me? (*She shakes his hand.*)

TRIGORIN. Married?

MASHA. For ages.

TRIGORIN. Happy? (*He exchanges bows with* DORN *and* MEDVEDENKO, *then goes up to* TREPLEV *a bit uneasily.*) Your mother tells me you're willing to let bygones be bygones. (TREPLEV *holds out his hand.*)

ARKADINA (*to* TREPLEV). Boris Alexeevich has brought along a magazine with a new story of yours in it.

TREPLEV (*taking it, to* TRIGORIN). Thank you. It's very kind of you.

(*They sit.*)

TRIGORIN. Your admirers send their greetings. All Moscow and Petersburg are intrigued. People never stop asking me about you. They want to know what you're like, how old you are, whether you've got dark hair or light. For some reason they seem to think you're getting on in years. Nobody knows your name, you publish under a pseudonym, you're as mysterious as the Man in the Iron Mask.[19]

TREPLEV. Will you be staying long?

TRIGORIN. No, I'm planning to go back to Moscow tomorrow. I really must. I've got one story due soon and another promised to an anthology. In other words, the same as ever. (*While* TREPLEV *and* TRIGORIN *talk*, ARKADINA *and* POLINA *set up a card table in the middle of the room.* SHAMRAEV *lights the candles and puts the chairs in place. They take a lotto set out of a cupboard.*) Can't say the weather's given me a nice welcome. The wind is fierce. If it lets up by tomorrow morning, though, I'll go down to the lake and get some fishing in. Which reminds me, I wanted to have a look at the garden and the place where you did your play. Remember? I've got an idea for a story. It's all ready. All I need is to refresh my memory about the setting.

MASHA (*to* SHAMRAEV). Let Semyon have a horse, Father. He's got to go home.

SHAMRAEV (*mimicking her, sharply*). A horse . . . To go home. You saw the horses coming back from the station. I can't go chasing them out again.

MASHA. But there are other horses . . . (*Realizing* SHAMRAEV *will not respond, she makes a gesture of resignation.*) Oh, what's the use.

MEDVEDENKO. I can walk, Masha. Really . . .

POLINA (*sighing*). Walk in this weather . . . (*She takes her place at the card table.*) Come and sit down, everybody!

MEDVEDENKO. It's only four miles, after all . . . Good-bye. (*He kisses* MASHA's *hand.*) Good-bye, Mother. (POLINA *reluctantly holds out her hand for him to kiss.*) I wouldn't have troubled anyone if it weren't for the baby . . . (*He bows to everyone.*) Good-bye. (*He exits slowly, apologetically.*)

SHAMRAEV. He's no general. He can walk.

ARKADINA (*to* TRIGORIN). Lotto is very popular around here in the autumn when the evenings start getting long. Look! The same ancient set we used with Mother when we were children. How about a round with us before supper. (*She sits at the table with*

TRIGORIN.) It's a boring game, but not so bad once you're used to it. (*She deals each of them three cards.*)

TREPLEV (*leafing through the magazine*). He's read his own story, but hasn't even cut the pages of mine. (*He lays the magazine down on his desk and moves towards the door left. As he passes* ARKADINA, *he kisses her on the head.*)

ARKADINA. How about you, Kostya?

TREPLEV. Sorry, I'm not in the mood ... I'm going out for a walk. (*He exits.*)

ARKADINA. Everybody put in ten kopecks. You'll take care of mine, won't you, Doctor?

DORN. Of course, madam.

MASHA. All the money in? Here goes ... Twenty-two.

ARKADINA. Here.

MASHA. Three.

DORN. Right.

MASHA. Is your three down? Eight. Eighty-one. Ten.

SHAMRAEV. Slow down.

ARKADINA. They really loved me in Kharkov. Goodness! I still can't get over it!

MASHA. Thirty-four.

(*The melancholy waltz is heard again offstage.*)

ARKADINA. The students cheered and cheered ... They gave me three baskets of flowers, two wreaths, and see ... (*She takes a brooch off her dress and tosses it onto the table.*)

SHAMRAEV. Well, look at that ...

MASHA. Fifty.

DORN. Five-oh?

ARKADINA. I was wearing a fantastic outfit ... One thing you can say for me: I know how to dress.

POLINA. That's Kostya playing. He's depressed, poor thing.

SHAMRAEV. The papers have been very hard on him.

MASHA. Seventy-seven.

ARKADINA. Who cares what the papers say.

TRIGORIN. He's unlucky. He can't seem to find his own voice. His stuff's so bizarre, so vague. It even reads like delirium at times. And not a single living character.

MASHA. Eleven.

ARKADINA (*looking over at* SORIN). Bored, dear?

(*Pause.*)

Asleep.

DORN. The state councilor is asleep.

MASHA. Seven. Ninety.

TRIGORIN. If I lived on an estate like this, near a lake, do you think I'd write another word? No, I'd smother the urge and spend all my time fishing.

MASHA. Twenty-eight.

TRIGORIN. Catching a nice perch or carp is my idea of heaven.

DORN. Well, I have faith in the boy. He's got something, he's onto something. He thinks in images; his stories are intense and vivid. I find them moving. I'm only sorry he doesn't write with a definite purpose in mind. It's all impression. You can't go far on impression alone. Are you glad your son's a writer, Irina Nikolaevna?

ARKADINA. You know, I've been so busy I haven't found time to read him.

MASHA. Twenty-six.

(TREPLEV *enters quietly and goes over to his desk.*)

SHAMRAEV (*to* TRIGORIN). By the way, Boris Alexeevich, we've been keeping something for you.

TRIGORIN. What?

SHAMRAEV. Konstantin Gavrilovich once shot a seagull here, and you asked me to have it stuffed.

TRIGORIN. I don't remember. (*Thinking hard.*) I don't remember.

MASHA. Sixty-one. One.

TREPLEV (*opening the window wide, but keeping an ear on the conversation*). It's pitch black out. I wonder why I feel so restless.

ARKADINA. Close the window, Kostya. There's a draft.

(TREPLEV *closes the window.*)

MASHA. Eighty-eight.

TRIGORIN. I win!

ARKADINA (*happily*). Bravo! Bravo!

SHAMRAEV. Bravo!

ARKADINA. That man has all the luck. (*She stands.*) Let's have a bite to eat, shall we? Our celebrity here hasn't had a thing since breakfast. We'll play another round after supper. (*To* TREPLEV.) Leave your manuscripts and come to supper now, Kostya.

TREPLEV. I don't want any, Mother. I'm not hungry.

ARKADINA. As you please . . . (*She wakes* SORIN.) Time to eat, dear. (*She takes* SHAMRAEV'*s arm.*) Let me tell you how much they loved me in Kharkov . . .

(POLINA *blows out the candles on the table. She and* DORN *wheel out the wheelchair. They all exit through the door left.* TREPLEV *remains alone on stage at his desk.*)

TREPLEV (*preparing to write, going through what he has finished*). After all my talk about new forms in art, I'm slipping into a rut myself. (*Reading.*) "A poster on the fence announced . . ." "A pale face framed by dark hair . . ." Announced . . . Framed . . . How amateurish! (*He crosses it all out.*) I'll start with the protagonist being awakened by the sound of rain, and cut the rest. The description of the moonlit night goes on too long. It's pretentious. Trigorin has his devices all worked out. It's easy . . . He takes the neck of a broken bottle glittering on a dam, adds the shadow of a mill wheel, and before you know it—a moonlit night. And I've got flickering light and the stars' quiet twinkling and the chords of a distant piano dying away in the hushed, fragrant air . . . Oh, the agony!

(*Pause.*)

Yes, I'm more and more convinced it's not forms that count, old or new; it's writing with no thought for form, writing that flows freely from the heart. (*There is a tap at the window nearest the desk.*) What's that? (*He peers through the window.*) Can't see a thing . . . (*He opens the French window and gazes out into the garden.*) Somebody's run down the steps. (*He calls out.*) Who's there? (*He goes outside and is heard walking briskly along the terrace. A moment later he comes back with* NINA.) Nina! Nina! (NINA *rests her head on his chest and sobs quietly. He is deeply moved.*) Nina! Nina! It's you. It's you . . . I had a feeling you'd come. My heart's been aching all day . . . (*He takes off her hat and cape.*) She's here! Dear, kind, precious Nina! Don't cry! Let's not cry.

NINA. We're not alone.

TREPLEV. Yes we are.

NINA. Lock the doors. Somebody may come in.

TREPLEV. Nobody will come in.

NINA. Your mother's here. I know she is. Lock the doors . . .

TREPLEV (*locking the door right and crossing left*). This one hasn't got a lock. I'll put a chair against it. (*He pulls an armchair against it.*) Don't be afraid. No one will come in.

NINA (*staring at his face*). Let me have a look at you. (*Looking round.*) It's nice and warm in here . . . This used to be the drawing room. Have I changed a lot?

TREPLEV. Yes . . . You're thinner, and your eyes look bigger. It's so strange to see you, Nina. Why wouldn't you ever let me in? Why did you wait so long to come? I know you've been here nearly a week . . . I've been trying to see you, several times a day, standing under your window like a beggar.

NINA. I was afraid you hated me. Every night I dream you look at me without seeing who I am. If only you knew. I've been walking and walking since I came . . . Down by the lake. I've been here at the house a lot too, but I couldn't bring myself to come in. Let's sit. (*They sit.*) Let's sit and talk and talk. It's so nice in here and warm and cozy . . . Hear the wind? There's a passage in Turgenev that goes: "Happy is the man who on a night like this has a roof over his head and a warm corner of his own."[20] I'm a seagull . . . No, that's not right. (*She rubs her forehead.*) What was I talking about? Oh, yes . . . Turgenev . . . "And God help all homeless way-farers . . ." Never mind. (*She sobs.*)

TREPLEV. Not again, Nina . . . Nina!

NINA. Never mind. It will do me good . . . I haven't cried for two years. Late last night I came to see whether our stage was still standing in the garden. And there it was. I cried for the first time in two years. It gave me a sense of relief, set my mind at ease. There, you see? I've stopped. (*She takes his hand.*) So you're a writer now ... You're a writer; I'm an actress ... Drawn into the whirlpool, the two of us. Once I lived the happy life of a child. I woke up in the morning with a song. I had my love for you and my dreams of glory. And now? Tomorrow bright and early I'll be on the train to Yelets, surrounded by peasants in a third-class compartment. And when I get there, I'll have the attentions of the "enlightened" merchants to contend with. Not a pretty life.

TREPLEV. But why Yelets?

NINA. I've got a contract for the winter. I must go now.

TREPLEV. There were times I cursed you, Nina, hated you. I tore up your letters and pictures. But every second I knew I belonged to you forever, all of me. I can never stop loving you. Ever since I lost you and started having my stories published, life has been impossible. I'm so miserable ... All of a sudden my youth was gone. I seemed to turn ninety overnight. I call out your name. I kiss the ground you walk on. Everywhere I look I see your face, that gentle smile that lit up the best years of my life ...

NINA (*bewildered*). Why is he saying these things? Why is he saying these things?

TREPLEV. I'm all alone, unwarmed by anyone's affection. I'm cold. It's like a dungeon here. Everything I write is dry, stale, gloomy. Stay with me, Nina, please. Or let me go away with you. (NINA *quickly puts on her hat and cape.*) Why, Nina? Why? Nina, for God's sake ... (*He looks on as she dresses.*)

(*Pause.*)

NINA. My horses are at the gate. Don't bother to see me out. I'll go on my own ... (*Almost crying.*) Give me some water.

TREPLEV (*giving her a glass of water*). Where are you going now?

NINA. Back to town.

(*Pause.*)

Your mother is here, isn't she?

TREPLEV. Yes . . . My uncle's illness took a turn for the worse on Thursday, and we wired for her to come.

NINA. Why do you say you kiss the ground I walk on? I ought to be done away with. (*She leans down over the desk.*) I'm so tired. If only I could rest . . . rest! (*She lifts her head.*) I'm a seagull . . . No, that's not right. I'm an actress. Yes, that's it. (*She hears* ARKADINA *and* TRI-GORIN *laughing, listens closely for a moment, then runs over to the door left and peeks through the keyhole.*) So he's here too . . . (*Going back to* TRE-PLEV.) Yes, that's it . . . Well, it doesn't matter . . . Yes . . . He never believed in the theater—he always laughed at my dreams—and little by little I stopped believing too and lost heart . . . I was afraid he didn't love me, I was jealous, I worried all the time about the baby . . . And I started being mean and petty. My acting made no sense . . . I didn't know what to do with my hands, how to stand, I couldn't control my voice. You can't imagine what it's like to know you're terrible onstage. I'm a seagull. No, that's not right . . . Remember when you shot the seagull? Well, one day a man came along and saw it and—for want of anything better to do—did away with it . . . An idea for a story. No, that's not right . . . (*She rubs her forehead.*) What was I saying? . . . I was talking about the stage. That's not the way I am now . . . I'm a real actress now. I enjoy acting, I adore it. I feel exhilarated onstage, I feel beautiful . . . I've been walking a lot since I've been back, walking and thinking, thinking and feeling myself grow, spiritually, day by day . . . Now I know, Kostya, now I understand that what really counts in our work—acting or writing—is neither fame nor glory, the things I dreamed of; what really counts is endurance. Bearing your cross and having faith. I have faith, and I don't suffer so much anymore. And when I think of my calling, I'm not afraid of life.

TREPLEV (*sadly*). You've found your way, you know where you're headed. I'm still rushing about in a maze of dreams and images with no idea of who or what any of it is for. I have no faith. I don't know what my calling is.

NINA (*listening in on the conversation next door*). Sh! . . . I'm going now. Good-bye. Come and watch me when I'm a great actress. Promise?

And now ... (*She shakes his hand.*) It's late. I can hardly stand ... I'm exhausted, famished ...

TREPLEV. Stay a while. I'll bring you supper ...

NINA. No, no ... Don't bother to see me out. I'll go on my own ... My horses are just outside. So she brought him along. Oh well, it doesn't matter. Don't tell Trigorin anything when you see him. I love him, love him even more than before. An idea for a story ... I love him, love him passionately, desperately. Remember how nice things used to be, Kostya? What a simple, warm, pure, and happy life we had, with feelings like gentle, delicate flowers ... Remember? (*Reciting.*) "Men, lions, partridges and eagles, antlered deer, geese, spiders, silent denizens of the deep, starfish and creatures invisible to the human eye—in short, all living things, all living things, all living things have come to the end of their mournful rounds ... For aeons and aeons the earth has borne no living thing, and this poor moon has lit its lamp in vain. No more do cranes wake calling in the meadow. Beetles have ceased buzzing in the lime groves..." (*She gives* TREPLEV *am impulsive embrace and runs out through the French window.*)

TREPLEV (*after a pause*). I hope nobody sees her in the garden. Mother might be upset if she heard ... (*He spends the next couple of moments silently tearing up his manuscripts and throwing them under the desk. Then he unlocks the door right and exits.*)

DORN (*trying to open the door left*). That's strange. The door seems blocked ... (*He enters and puts the armchair back in its place.*) A regular obstacle course.

(*Enter* ARKADINA *and* POLINA, *then* MASHA *and* YAKOV,
who is carrying some bottles, and finally SHAMRAEV
and TRIGORIN.)

ARKADINA (*to* YAKOV). Put the red wine and the beer for Boris Alexeevich over here, on the table. We'll have our drinks while we play. Everybody take your seats now.

POLINA (*to* YAKOV). And bring the tea in immediately, will you? (*She lights the candles and sits down at the card table.*)

SHAMRAEV (*taking* TRIGORIN *over to the cupboard*). Here's that thing I was telling you about . . . (*He takes a stuffed seagull out of the cupboard.*) Just as you ordered.

TRIGORIN (*looking at the seagull*). I don't remember. (*After a moment's thought.*) I don't remember.

(*The sound of a shot comes from offstage right. Everyone starts.*)

ARKADINA (*frightened*). What was that?

DORN. Don't worry. Probably something going off in my medical bag, that's all. (*He exits through the door right and comes back a short time later.*) Just as I thought. A bottle of ether exploded. (*He sings to himself.*) "Once more enthralled, I stand before you . . ."

ARKADINA (*sitting at the table*). Phew, I was so frightened! It reminded me of the time . . . (*She covers her face with her hands.*) Everything went black for a moment . . .

DORN (*leafing through a magazine, to* TRIGORIN). Two months ago there was an article in this magazine . . . a letter from America, and I've been meaning to ask you . . . (*Putting his arm around* TRIGORIN's *waist and walking him up to the footlights.*) You see, I'm very interested in the matter . . . (*Dropping his voice, in an undertone.*) Try and get Irina Nikolaevna away from here. Konstantin has just killed himself . . .

CURTAIN

Uncle Vanya

SCENES FROM COUNTRY LIFE
IN FOUR ACTS

CHARACTERS[1]

ALEXÁNDER VLADÍMIROVICH SEREBRYAKÓV. A retired professor.

YELÉNA ANDRÉEVNA (LÉNA, HÉLÈNE). His wife, twenty-seven years old.

SÓFYA ALEXÁNDROVNA (SÓNYA). The professor's daughter by his first wife.

MARÍA VASÍLYEVNA VOINÍTSKAYA. The widow of a privy councilor, mother of the professor's first wife.

IVÁN PETRÓVICH VOINÍTSKY (VÁNYA, JEAN). Her son.

MIKHAÍL LVÓVICH ÁSTROV. A doctor.

ILYÁ ILYÍCH TELÉGIN. An impoverished landowner.

MARÍNA. An old nursemaid.

A WORKMAN.

The action takes place on SEREBRYAKOV's *estate.*

ACT ONE

A garden. A terrace and part of the house are visible. There is a table set for tea under an old poplar in a tree-lined walk. Benches, chairs. A guitar is lying on one of the benches. There is a swing near the table. It is shortly after two on an overcast afternoon. MARINA, a sluggish, heavyset old woman, is sitting at the samovar, knitting a stocking. ASTROV is pacing up and down nearby.

MARINA (*pouring him a glass of tea*). How about some tea.

ASTROV (*taking the glass reluctantly*). I don't really feel like it.

MARINA. A little vodka, then.

ASTROV. No. I don't have vodka every day. Anyway, it's too muggy.

(*Pause.*)

Marina, how long have we known each other?

MARINA (*giving it some thought*). How long? Let me see now . . . When was it you came to these parts? . . . Sonya's mother was still alive. You were here all the time her last two winters . . . That makes it eleven years. (*She thinks again.*) Maybe more . . .

ASTROV. Have I changed a lot since then?

MARINA. Certainly have. You were young then, and handsome. You're old now. You've lost your looks. And you like your vodka.

ASTROV. Yes . . . I'm not the man I was ten years ago. And the reason? Overwork, Marina. On my feet, dawn till dusk. Never a moment's rest. At night, when I lie down at last and pull the blanket over me, I'm always afraid they'll come and drag me off to some patient or other. I haven't had a free day the whole time I've known you. How can I help looking old? And then this life is so dull and stupid and foul . . . A life that drags you down. I'm surrounded by crackpots, nothing but crackpots. Spend two or three years with them and little by little, without noticing, you turn into one yourself. There's nothing you can do about it. (*Giving his long mustache a twist.*) Just look at this huge mustache I've grown . . . Stupid mustache. I've turned into a crackpot, Marina. Oh, I've still got a head on my shoulders, thank God; my brains are still intact. But my feelings have gone dull. I don't want anything, I don't need anything, I don't love anybody . . . Except maybe you, only you. (*He kisses her head.*) I had a nursemaid like you when I was a boy.

MARINA. Something to eat?

ASTROV. No. The third week of Lent I went to Malitskoe. There was an epidemic . . . Typhus . . . Huts crammed with people flat on their backs . . . The filth, the stench, the smoke. Calves on the floor, right next to the sick . . . Calves and baby pigs . . . I ran around all day, didn't sit down for a minute, didn't eat a thing. Even after I got home they wouldn't leave me in peace. They drove up with the signalman from the station. I laid him out on a table to operate, and before I knew it he'd died on me under the chloroform. Just when I didn't need them, my feelings came alive again. You'd think I'd gone and murdered the man the way my conscience bothered me . . . I sat down, shut my eyes— like this—and wondered whether people who come a hundred or two hundred years after us—the people we're paving the way for—whether they'll remember us. They won't, Marina, will they.

MARINA. People no, but God will.

ASTROV. Thank you, Marina. That was well put.

(*Enter* VANYA *from the house. He has had a nap after lunch and looks disheveled. He sits on a bench and straightens his stylish tie.*)

VANYA. Yes . . .

(*Pause.*)

Yes . . .

ASTROV. Had a good nap?

VANYA. Yes . . . Very. (*He yawns.*) Things are out of joint since the professor and his spouse got here . . . I sleep odd hours, eat spicy foods for lunch and dinner, drink all kinds of wine . . . It's bad for me. I never used to have a moment to spare. The work we did, Sonya and I—unbelievable. Now Sonya does it all. I just eat, sleep, and drink . . . It's no good.

MARINA (*shaking her head*). Everything's topsy-turvy. The professor's in bed till noon, but the samovar boils all morning for him. Before they came, we ate at twelve, like normal people; now we don't eat until six. The professor stays up all night reading and writing, and suddenly—it's one in the morning—there goes the bell. Dear Lord, what's the matter? Bring me some tea. So I go and wake the servants for him, start the samovar boiling . . . Everything's topsy-turvy.

ASTROV. And have they come for long?

VANYA (*whistles*). A hundred years. The professor's decided to settle here.

MARINA. Look. A perfect example. The samovar's been ready two hours now and they're off walking.

VANYA. Here they come, here they come . . . Calm down.

(*Voices are heard.* SEREBRYAKOV, YELENA, SONYA, *and* TELEGIN, *back from their walk, enter from the far end of the garden.*)

SEREBRYAKOV. Beautiful, beautiful . . . The scenery's marvelous.

TELEGIN. Exquisite, Your Excellency.

SONYA. Tomorrow I'll show you the woods, Father. Would you like that?

VANYA. Tea's ready, ladies and gentlemen!

SEREBRYAKOV. Dear friends, would you be good enough to have my tea sent to the study? I have a few things to finish off today.

SONYA. I'm sure you'll like the woods . . .

(YELENA, SEREBRYAKOV, *and* SONYA *exit into the house.* TELEGIN *goes over to the table and sits down next to* MARINA.)

VANYA. It's hot and it's muggy, and our eminent scholar is wearing an overcoat, galoshes, and gloves and carrying an umbrella.

ASTROV. Just taking care of himself.

VANYA. And isn't she lovely! Isn't she lovely! I've never seen a more beautiful woman in my life.

TELEGIN. You know, Marina, riding through a field or strolling in a shady garden or just standing here looking at this table, I feel indescribable bliss. The weather is delightful, the little birdies sing, we live in peace and harmony—what more could one ask for? (*Taking a glass.*) I thank you from the bottom of my heart.

VANYA (*dreamily*). Those eyes . . . A marvelous woman!

ASTROV. Tell us a story, Ivan Petrovich.

VANYA (*listlessly*). A story?

ASTROV. Isn't there anything new?

VANYA. Nothing. Everything's old. I'm the same as always. Well, maybe a bit worse. I'm lazier than I used to be. All I do is grumble like a grump. As for the old magpie, *maman*, she still babbles on about the emancipation of women. She's got one eye on the grave and the other in those wise little books of hers, searching for the dawn of a new life.

ASTROV. And the professor?

VANYA. The professor, as usual, sits in the study and scribbles from morning till far into the night.

> With brain belabored, furrowed brow,
> We write our odes—some good, some worse—
> But no kind word or reverent bow
> Accrues to us or to our verse.

The poor paper! He'd be better off writing his autobiography. A magnificent subject! A retired professor—know the type?—a dried crust, a dried kipper with an education . . . and with gout, rheumatism, migraines, and a liver swollen by jealousy and spite . . . Now this kipper lives on the estate of his first wife. Not because he wants to but because he can't afford to live in town. He does nothing but complain about his misfortunes, though in fact he's been extraordinarily fortunate. (*Wrought up.*) You can't imagine how fortunate he's been. The son of a common sexton, a seminarian—and he's got advanced degrees, a full professorship plus the right to have people call him Your Excellency. He's the son-in-law of a senator, et cetera, et cetera—but none of that's important. Listen to this. For twenty-five years that man has been lecturing and writing about art without understanding a thing—not a thing—about it. For twenty-five years he's been chewing over other people's ideas about Realism, Naturalism, and who knows what other nonsense. In other words, for twenty-five years he's been pouring one empty glass into another. But oh, how sure of himself he is, how pretentious! Now that he's retired, he's completely forgotten, a complete unknown. In other words, for twenty-five years he kept a better man out of a job. And just look at him. Strutting about like a demigod!

ASTROV. You sound jealous.

VANYA. Well, I am. The success he's had with women! No Don Juan could equal it. His first wife—my sister and a radiant and gentle creature, as pure as that blue sky, noble and generous and sought after by more suitors than he had pupils—his first wife loved him as only angels can love beings as pure and radiant as themselves. My mother, his mother-in-law, adores him to this day; to this day he inspires a feeling of awe in her. His second wife, a beautiful and intelligent woman—you saw her just now—married him when he was an old man. She gave him her youth, her beauty, her freedom, her brilliance, and for what? What for?

ASTROV. Is she faithful to him?

VANYA. Unfortunately.

ASTROV. Why "unfortunately"?

VANYA. Because that kind of fidelity is false from beginning to end. It's all rhetoric, no logic. Deceive an old man you can't stand and you're immoral; stifle your vitality, the little youth you have left, and you're not.

TELEGIN (*with tears in his voice*). I don't like to hear you say those things, Vanya. Really . . . People who betray their wives or husbands are disloyal and might even betray their country!

VANYA (*annoyed*). Oh, dry up, Waffles.

TELEGIN. No, let me speak. The day after our wedding my wife ran off with the man she loved, the reason being my unprepossessing appearance. Since then I have never shirked my duty. To this day I love her and am faithful to her. I do whatever I can to help her. I gave her everything I owned to support the children she had by the man she loved. I have lost all hope of bliss, but retained my pride. As for her, her youth is gone, her beauty—for such is the law of nature—has faded, the man she loved has passed away . . . What is she left with?

(*Enter* SONYA *and* YELENA, *followed shortly by* MARIA VASILYEVNA *with a book.* MARIA VASILYEVNA *sits and continues reading. She drinks the tea she is served without looking up.*)

SONYA (*hurriedly to* MARINA). There are some peasants at the door, Nanny. Go and see what they want. I'll take care of the tea . . . (*She pours tea.*)

(*Exit* MARINA. YELENA *picks up her cup and drinks her tea on the swing.*)

ASTROV (*to* YELENA). Your husband's the reason I'm here, you know. You wrote he was ill—rheumatism and something. He looks fit as a fiddle to me.

YELENA. Last night he was depressed and complained of pains in his legs, but today everything seems fine . . .

ASTROV. And I broke my back galloping twenty miles to get here! Oh well. It's not the first time. At least I can stay the night and catch up on my sleep *quantum satis.*[2]

SONYA. Wonderful. You so rarely spend the night with us. You probably haven't eaten yet.

ASTROV. No, I haven't.

SONYA. Well then, you can eat with us. We don't sit down till after six these days. (*She takes a sip of tea.*) The tea's cold!

TELEGIN. The temperature in the samovar has decreased considerably.

YELENA. That's all right, Ivan Ivanovich. We'll drink it cold.

TELEGIN. Excuse me. My name is Ilya Ilyich, not Ivan Ivanovich.

Ilya Ilyich Telegin or—as some people call me for my pockmarked face—Waffles. I was Sonya's godfather, and His Excellency, your husband, knows me very well. I live here now, on your estate ... You may have noticed me. I dine with you every day.

SONYA. Ilya Ilyich is a great help to us. He's our right-hand man. (*Tenderly.*) Give me your glass, Godfather. Let me pour you some more tea.

MARIA VASILYEVNA. Oh!

SONYA. What's the matter, Grandmother?

MARIA VASILYEVNA. I forgot to tell Alexander something ... Must be losing my memory ... I had a letter today from Pavel Alexeevich in Kharkov ... He sent me his new pamphlet too ...

ASTROV. Is it interesting?

MARIA VASILYEVNA. Very, but there's something odd about it: he's refuting what he defended seven years ago. Isn't that awful?

VANYA. Not in the least. Drink your tea, *maman*.

MARIA VASILYEVNA. But I want to talk!

VANYA. We've been talking for fifty years, talking and reading pamphlets. It's time to stop.

MARIA VASILYEVNA. For some reason you find listening to me distasteful. I hate to say it, Jean, but you've changed so much this past year I hardly know you ... You used to be a man of strong convictions, a light in the darkness.

VANYA. A light in the darkness! A light that's enlightened no one ...

(*Pause.*)

A light in the darkness ... You couldn't have made a crueler joke. Here I am, forty-seven years old. Till last year I tried like you to pull the wool over my eyes, shut out the real world with all that pedantry. I thought I was doing the right thing. But now—oh, if only you knew. I lie awake at night, distressed and bitter over the time I let slip through my fingers so stupidly, the time I could have had everything I'm too old for now.

SONYA. Uncle Vanya. Please.

MARIA VASILYEVNA (*to* VANYA). You seem to be blaming your former convictions ... Well, the convictions aren't to blame; you are.

You're forgetting that convictions in themselves don't mean a thing, they're a dead letter ... It's what you do that counts.

VANYA. What you do? Not everybody has it in him to be a scribbling perpetuum mobile like your Herr Professor.

MARIA VASILYEVNA. And what do you mean by that?

SONYA (*beseechingly*). Grandmother! Uncle Vanya! Please!

VANYA. I won't say another word, not a word. I beg your pardon.

(*Pause.*)

YELENA. Nice weather we're having ... Not too hot ...

(*Pause.*)

VANYA. Nice weather to hang yourself ...

(TELEGIN *starts tuning his guitar. Enter* MARINA *near the house, calling the chickens.*)

MARINA. Here chick, chick, chick ...

SONYA. What did the peasants want, Nanny?

MARINA. Same old thing. That plot of unused land. Here chick, chick, chick ...

SONYA. Which one are you calling?

MARINA. The speckled one. She's gone off with her chicks ... The crows may get them ... (*Exit* MARINA.)

(TELEGIN *plays a polka. Everyone listens in silence. Enter the* WORKMAN.)

WORKMAN. The doctor here? (*To* ASTROV.) Some people to see you, Doctor.

ASTROV. Where are they from?

WORKMAN. The factory.

ASTROV (*irritated*). Much obliged. Well, got to go ... (*He looks around for his cap.*) Damn it. It's so frustrating ...

SONYA. So annoying ... Come back after the factory and eat with us.

ASTROV. No, it'll be too late. No, impossible ... No ... (*To the* WORKMAN.) How about bringing me a glass of vodka, my friend. (*The* WORKMAN *exits.*) No, impossible ... No ... (*He finds his cap.*)

One of Ostrovsky's plays has a man with a generous mustache and meager capabilities . . .³ Well, that's me. And now it's time to say good-bye . . . (*To* YELENA.) If you ever feel like dropping in with Sonya, I'll be delighted to see you. My estate isn't very large, eighty acres or so altogether, but if you're interested, I have a model orchard and nursery the like of which you won't find for miles around. Besides, my property borders on a state-owned forest . . . The forester's old and ailing, so I'm basically in charge.

YELENA. Yes, I've heard you love the woods, and of course what you do may be very useful. But doesn't it interfere with your true calling? You *are* a doctor.

ASTROV. Only God knows what our true calling is.

YELENA. And is it interesting?

ASTROV. Yes, it's interesting work.

VANYA (*with irony*). Oh, very!

YELENA. You're still young. You don't look more than . . . say, thirty-six, thirty-seven . . . It can't be as interesting as you say—trees, trees, and more trees. Sounds rather monotonous to me.

SONYA. Oh, no! It's extremely interesting. Mikhail Lvovich plants new forests every year. He's been awarded a bronze medal and a certificate of achievement. He does everything he can to keep the old forests from being destroyed. Just listen to what he has to say and you'll agree with him. He says that forests make the earth beautiful, that they teach man to appreciate beauty and instill a sense of majesty in him. Forests make a harsh climate milder. In countries with a mild climate people use less energy in their struggle with nature, so man himself is milder, gentler. People are soft and beautiful, yet full of passion. Their speech is elegant, their movements graceful. Art and learning flourish among them. Their philosophy is joyous, their attitude towards women refined and noble . . .

VANYA (*laughing*). Bravo, bravo! . . . That's all very nice, but not very convincing, so (*to* ASTROV) I hope you won't mind, my friend, if I go on burning logs in my stoves and building my barns of wood.

ASTROV. You can burn peat in your stoves and build barns of stone. I can see chopping trees if you *need* to, but why simply exterminate them? Russian forests are groaning under the ax, millions of trees are dying, the homes of animals and birds being ravaged, rivers subsiding and drying up, splendid landscapes vanishing for good. And all because people are too lazy or haven't got the sense to bend down and pick up fuel from the ground. (*To* YELENA.) Don't you agree? Anyone capable of burning this beauty in his stove and destroying what we can't create is nothing but a mindless barbarian. Man is endowed with the reason and creativity to increase what's been given him. So far all he's done is destroy it. There are fewer and fewer forests, rivers are drying up, game animals are all but extinct, the climate is being ruined, and day by day the land gets poorer and uglier. (*To* VANYA.) I can see the irony in your eyes. You think everything I'm saying is trivial, and . . . and maybe I *am* just a crackpot, but when I walk past a peasant's trees I've saved from the ax, when I hear the rustle of young trees I've planted with my own hands, then I know I have at least some control over the climate, and if man is happy a thousand years from now I'll have played my little part. When I plant a birch and watch it turn green and sway in the wind, my heart swells with pride, and I . . . (*He catches sight of the* WORKMAN, *who has brought him a glass of vodka on a tray.*) I think . . . (*He tosses down the vodka.*) I think it's time for me to go. Maybe I *am* just a crackpot after all. Good-bye, everybody. (*He starts off in the direction of the house.*)

SONYA (*taking his arm and walking with him*). When will you come back and see us?

ASTROV. I don't know . . .

SONYA. Not for another month again?

(*Exit* ASTROV *and* SONYA *into the house.* MARIA VASILYEVNA *and* TELEGIN *remain by the table.* YELENA *and* VANYA *go over to the terrace.*)

YELENA. You've been misbehaving again, Ivan Petrovich. What was the point of provoking your mother with that talk about the per-

petuum mobile? And today at lunch—picking a quarrel with
Alexander. It's so petty.

VANYA. But I hate the man.

YELENA. Well, you've no reason to. He's the same as everyone else.
No worse than you.

VANYA. If you could see your face, the way you move . . . You're so
listless. Life seems too much of an effort for you.

YELENA. An effort and a bore! Everyone finds fault with Alexander;
everyone looks at me with compassion: poor thing, her husband's
an old man. The sympathy—how well I understand it. Remember what Astrov said just now about how we were mindlessly destroying the forests and soon there wouldn't be any nature left?
Well, you're mindlessly destroying humanity, and soon, thanks
to you, there won't be any fidelity or purity or capacity for self-
sacrifice. Why can't you look with equanimity at a woman who's
not your own? Because—the doctor's right—you're obsessed by
a demon of destruction, all of you. You have no pity for forests
or birds or women or one another.

VANYA. I don't like this philosophy of yours. .

(*Pause.*)

YELENA. The doctor has a haggard, sensitive face, an interesting
face. Sonya obviously finds him attractive. She's in love with him,
and I can see why. He's been here three times now, but I'm so shy
I haven't once had a good talk with him or been decent to him.
He must think I'm cross. I wonder if the reason you and I are
such good friends, Ivan Petrovich, is that we're both such dull
and dreary people. Dull and dreary. Don't look at me that way—
I don't like it.

VANYA. How else can I look at you? I love you. You're my life, my
youth, my happiness! I know there's little chance, no chance of
your loving me in return. All I ask is that you let me look at you,
hear your voice . . .

YELENA. Sh! They might hear you. (*She walks towards the house.*)

VANYA (*following her*). Let me tell you about my love. Don't chase
me away. That alone will give me the greatest joy.

YELENA. This is agony . . .

(*They exit into the house.* TELEGIN *plays some chords and then his polka.* MARIA VASILYEVNA *makes a few jottings in the margins of her pamphlet.*)

CURTAIN

ACT TWO

The dining room in SEREBRYAKOV'*s house. It is night. A watchman is heard tapping in the garden.* SEREBRYAKOV *is sitting in an armchair in front of an open window, dozing.* YELENA *is sitting next to him, also dozing.*

SEREBRYAKOV (*waking with a start*). Who's there? Is that you, Sonya?
YELENA. No, it's me.
SEREBRYAKOV. Oh you, Lena . . . The pain's unbearable.
YELENA. Your blanket's on the floor. (*She wraps it round his legs.*) Let me close the window.
SEREBRYAKOV. No, don't. I'm suffocating . . . I dozed off just now and dreamt I had someone else's left leg. Then I was awakened by an excruciating pain. It's not the gout; it must be rheumatism. What time is it?
YELENA. Twenty past twelve.

(*Pause.*)

SEREBRYAKOV. Get me Batyushkov from the library in the morning.[4] I think we have a volume.
YELENA. What's that?
SEREBRYAKOV. Bring me Batyushkov in the morning. I recall seeing it on the shelves. Why am I having so much trouble breathing?
YELENA. You're tired. You haven't slept for two nights in a row.
SEREBRYAKOV. They say Turgenev's gout developed into angina pectoris. I'm afraid it's going to happen to me. Damn, old age is a nasty business! Now that I'm old I find myself repulsive. All of you must find it repulsive to look at me.
YELENA. The way you talk about your age you make it seem our fault.

SEREBRYAKOV. And you're the one who finds me most repulsive. (YELENA *moves away and takes a seat at some distance.*) You're right, of course. I'm no fool. I understand. You're young, healthy, and beautiful. You want to live. I'm an old man, practically a corpse. You think I don't notice? It's stupid of me to go on living, of course, but wait—soon I'll set you all free. I can't hang on much longer.

YELENA. Be quiet, for heaven's sake ... I'm exhausted.

SEREBRYAKOV. You'd think everyone was exhausted, bored, and wasting his youth on account of me and I was the only one who enjoyed life and was happy. Yes, yes, of course.

YELENA. Oh, be quiet! You wear me out.

SEREBRYAKOV. I wear everybody out. Of course I do.

YELENA (*through tears*). This is unbearable. Tell me, what is it you want from me?

SEREBRYAKOV. Nothing.

YELENA. Well then, keep quiet. Please.

SEREBRYAKOV. It's funny. Whenever Vanya or that idiot mother of his has a point to make, everything's fine, everybody listens. But all I have to do is open my mouth and people feel miserable. Even my voice is repulsive. All right, let's say I'm repulsive, self-centered, a despot. But haven't I a right to be self-centered in my old age? Haven't I earned it? Tell me, haven't I the right to a peaceful old age and a little attention?

YELENA. No one's denying you your rights. (*A window bangs in the wind.*) The wind's blowing. I'd better shut the window. (*She shuts it.*) It's going to rain. No one's denying you your rights.

(*Pause. The watchman taps in the garden and sings a song.*)

SEREBRYAKOV. Here I've devoted my whole life to scholarship. I felt at home in my study, my lecture hall, with my distinguished colleagues. And all at once, out of the blue, where do I find myself but in this tomb surrounded by fools spouting inanities day in and day out ... I want to live. I love fame. I love success and excitement. This is like being in exile. It's hard to brood over the past all the time, watching others move ahead and fearing death ... I can't stand it anymore! It's too much for me! And to make matters worse no one will forgive me for being old.

YELENA. Wait. Be patient. In five or six years I'll be old too.

SONYA (*entering*). You were the one who had us send for Dr. Astrov, Father, and now that he's here you won't even see him. It's not very considerate, putting him to all that trouble for nothing.

SEREBRYAKOV. What good is your Astrov to me? He knows as much about medicine as I know about astronomy.

SONYA. You can't very well have the entire Medical School come and look at your gout.

SEREBRYAKOV. Well, I refuse to talk to that fool.

SONYA. Have it your own way. (*She sits.*) I don't care.

SEREBRYAKOV. What time is it?

YELENA. Almost half past twelve.

SEREBRYAKOV. It's so stuffy in here . . . Sonya, bring me my drops from the table.

SONYA. Here you are. (*She hands him the drops.*)

SEREBRYAKOV (*irritated*). Not these! I can't ask anybody for anything.

SONYA. Stop your fussing, will you? Some people may not mind it, but spare me, please. I've got other things on my mind. I've got to be up early in the morning and make sure they get the hay in.

VANYA (*entering in a dressing gown and carrying a candle*). There's a storm brewing. (*Lightning flashes.*) Look at that! Hélène and Sonya, you can go to bed. I'm here to relieve you.

SEREBRYAKOV (*frightened*). No, no! Don't leave me alone with him! He'll talk my head off.

VANYA. But they need their rest. They were up all last night too.

SEREBRYAKOV. Well, let them go to bed, but you go too. Thank you. Please. Don't argue. In the name of our former friendship. We'll talk some other time.

VANYA (*with irony*). Our former friendship . . . *Former* friendship . . .

SONYA. Quiet, Uncle Vanya.

SEREBRYAKOV (*to* YELENA). Don't leave me alone with him, my dear. He'll talk my head off.

VANYA. This is ridiculous.

(*Enter* MARINA *carrying a candle.*)

SONYA. You ought to be in bed, Nanny. It's late.

MARINA. How can I go to bed with the samovar on the table?

SEREBRYAKOV. No one can sleep; everyone's exhausted. I'm the only one having fun.

MARINA (*going up to* SEREBRYAKOV, *affectionately*). There, there. What's wrong? It's the pain, isn't it. I've got one too, down in my legs. Aches something awful. (*She arranges his lap blanket.*) You've had yours a long time. Sonya's mother used to lose a lot of sleep over it. She really loved you . . .

(*Pause.*)

When you're old you're like a child: you need somebody to feel sorry for you. But nobody feels sorry for us old people. (*She kisses* SEREBRYAKOV *on the shoulder.*) Come to bed now, sir . . . Come to bed now . . . I'll make you some nice linden tea and warm your feet . . . Then I'll say a prayer for you . . .

(*Exit* SEREBRYAKOV, SONYA, *and* MARINA.)

YELENA. He wears me out. I can hardly stand.

VANYA. He wears *you* out, and I wear out *myself.* I haven't slept a wink for three nights.

YELENA. There's something wrong with this house. Your mother hates everything but her pamphlets and the professor. The professor's always on edge. He doesn't trust me, and he's afraid of you. Sonya's angry with her father and me both. She hasn't said a word to me for two weeks. You hate my husband and openly despise your mother. I'm on edge all the time. I must have been on the verge of tears twenty times today . . . There's something wrong with this house.

VANYA. Let's drop the philosophy, shall we?

YELENA. You're an intelligent, educated man. You can see it's not thieves or fires that destroy the world; it's hatred, hostility, all this petty squabbling . . . Shouldn't you stop complaining and try to make peace?

VANYA. First help me to make peace with myself. Darling . . . (*He bends over and grabs her hand.*)

YELENA. Leave me alone! (*She takes her hand back.*) Get away!

VANYA. The rain will be over soon, and everything in nature will breathe easy, feel refreshed. Everything but me. The storm won't affect me in the least. Day and night I'm haunted by the thought that my life has gone irrevocably to waste. I have no past—I've wasted it all on trivialities—and my present is impossible, absurd. There they are—my life and love. What shall I do with them? What can I do with them? My passion's dying like a ray of sunlight in a pit. All of me is dying.

YELENA. Whenever you talk about your love, I go numb, I don't know what to say. I'm sorry, I just have nothing to say to you . . . (*She tries to go.*) Good night.

VANYA (*blocking her way*). If you knew how much I suffer from the thought that here, in this house, another life is being wasted— yours. What are you waiting for? What damn philosophy is holding you back? Try to understand me. Try to understand . . .

YELENA (*looking at him closely*). You're drunk, Ivan Petrovich.

VANYA. Maybe I am, maybe I am.

YELENA. Where's the doctor?

VANYA. In there . . . He's sleeping in my room tonight. Maybe I am, maybe I am . . . Anything's possible.

YELENA. So you've been drinking again. What for?

VANYA. It makes me feel alive, if nothing else . . . Don't stop me, Hélène.

YELENA. You never used to drink. You didn't talk so much either . . . Go to bed. You bore me so.

VANYA (*leaning over and seizing her hand*). Darling . . . You're so wonderful!

YELENA (*irritated*). Leave me alone. This is repulsive. (*She exits.*)

VANYA (*alone*). She's gone . . .

(*Pause.*)

Ten years ago I would see her at my sister's. She was seventeen; I was thirty-seven. Why didn't I fall in love with her then and ask her to marry me? It would have been so easy. And now she'd be my wife ... Yes ... The storm would wake us. She'd be frightened by the thunder, and I'd hold her in my arms and whisper, "Don't be afraid. I'm here." What a wonderful thought! It makes me feel so good I'm laughing ... God, I'm confused ... Why am I old? Why won't she understand me? Her rhetoric, her moralizing, her silly, idle thoughts on the destruction of the world—they're so offensive.

(*Pause.*)

I've been made a fool of! I idolized that pitiful, gout-ridden professor. I worked like a dog for him. Sonya and I squeezed every last drop out of his estate. We sold our own curds, peas, and vegetable oil like tightfisted peasants. We begrudged ourselves every scrap of food, hoarding kopeck by kopeck the thousands of rubles we sent him. I took pride in him and his learning. I lived, I breathed him. Every word he wrote or uttered sounded brilliant to me ... Good God, and now? Now that he's retired, I see what his life really amounts to. Not a page of anything he's written will survive him. He's a complete unknown, a nobody, a soap bubble! And he's made a fool of me ... I see it now ... A stupid fool.

(*Enter* ASTROV. *He is wearing a frock coat, but no vest or tie, and is slightly drunk. He is followed by* TELEGIN, *who is carrying his guitar.*)

ASTROV. Play something!

TELEGIN. But everyone's asleep.

ASTROV. Play, I said! (TELEGIN *strums softly. To* VANYA.) Are you by yourself? No ladies? (*He puts his hands on his hips and sings softly.*)

> Dance, my stove, and dance, my sty.
> The master has no place to lie ...[5]

The storm woke me up. Quite a downpour. What time is it?

VANYA. How should I know?

ASTROV. I thought I heard Yelena Andreevna.

VANYA. She was here just now.

ASTROV. A gorgeous woman. (*He looks over the medicine bottles on the table.*) Medicines. Prescriptions of every kind. Prescriptions from Kharkov and Moscow and Tula . . . He's plagued every town in Russia with his gout. Is it serious or is he just pretending?

VANYA. It's serious all right.

(*Pause.*)

ASTROV. What makes you so melancholy today? Don't tell me you're feeling sorry for the professor.

VANYA. Leave me alone.

ASTROV. Or in love with the professor's wife.

VANYA. We're just friends.

ASTROV. So soon?

VANYA. What do you mean "so soon"?

ASTROV. A woman becomes "friends" with a man in a definite sequence: first she's an acquaintance, next a mistress—and only then his friend.

VANYA. That's a pretty crude philosophy.

ASTROV. What? Oh, yes . . . I must admit I've been rather crude lately. See? I'm drunk too. I get drunk like this once a month, and when I'm drunk I'm bold and brazen in the extreme: I don't give a damn about anything. I'll try my hand at the most difficult operations and bring them off brilliantly. I'll draw up the most sweeping plans for the future. When I feel this way, I stop picturing myself as a crackpot. I really believe I'm doing good for mankind . . . Enormous good. When I feel this way, I construct my own philosophical systems, and everyone else—all of you— you're just so many flies to me . . . Flies or microbes. (*To* TELEGIN.) Play, Waffles!

TELEGIN. I'd be only too happy to oblige, dear friend, but you must remember: everyone's asleep.

ASTROV. Play, I said! (TELEGIN *strums softly.*) How about a drink? Come on. We've got some cognac left, I think. And as soon as it's light, we'll drive over to my place. Awright? I've got an assistant who says "awright" for "all right." A real swindler. Well then, awright? (*Seeing* SONYA *enter.*) Sorry. No tie. (*He exits quickly, followed by* TELEGIN.)

SONYA. Drinking with the doctor again, Uncle Vanya. A fine pair you make. He's always been like that, but why you? It's not particularly attractive at your age.

VANYA. What's age got to do with it? When you haven't a real life to live, you live a mirage. It's better than nothing.

SONYA. The hay's mown, it's been raining every day, the crops are rotting, and all you can think of are mirages. You've completely abandoned the estate . . . I do all the work. I'm dead tired. (*Frightened.*) Uncle Vanya, you've got tears in your eyes.

VANYA. Tears? No . . . ridiculous . . . You looked at me just then the way your poor dear mother used to. My sister . . . (*He covers her hands and face with kisses.*) My sister . . . My dear sister . . . Where is she now? If only she knew. Oh, if only she knew.

SONYA. Knew what, Uncle Vanya? If only she knew what?

VANYA. It's so painful, so wrong . . . Never mind . . . I'll tell you later . . . Never mind . . . I'm going. (*He exits.*)

SONYA (*knocking on the door*). Mikhail Lvovich! You're not asleep yet, are you? May I see you for a moment?

ASTROV (*from inside*). I'll be right there. (*He comes out a moment later wearing a vest and tie.*) What can I do for you?

SONYA. Drink all you want if you don't find it repulsive, but please don't encourage my uncle. It's bad for him.

ASTROV. Fine. We'll stop drinking.

(*Pause.*)

I'm going home now. It's all settled. It will be daylight by the time the horses are harnessed.

SONYA. It's raining. Wait till morning.

ASTROV. The storm will pass us by. We'll get only the tail end of it. I'm going. And please don't ask me to look in on your father again. I tell him it's gout; he tells me it's rheumatism. I ask him to lie in bed; he sits in a chair. And today he wouldn't talk to me at all.

SONYA. He's just spoiled. (*She looks in the sideboard.*) Would you like something to eat?

ASTROV. I might. Yes.

SONYA. I love eating in the middle of the night. There's some food in the sideboard . . . They say he was a great ladies' man in his time. The ladies spoiled him. Here, take the cheese. (*They stand at the sideboard and eat.*)

ASTROV. I didn't eat a thing all day; I just drank. Your father's a difficult man. (*He takes a bottle from the sideboard.*) May I? (*He drinks a glass of wine.*) There's nobody here, and I can speak freely. You know, I don't think I'd last a month in your house. I'd suffocate in this atmosphere . . . Your father with nothing in life but his gout and his books. Uncle Vanya with his moods. Your grandmother. Your stepmother . . .

SONYA. What about my stepmother?

ASTROV. Everything in a person should be beautiful: face, clothes, feelings, thoughts. She's a beauty, Heaven knows, but . . . but all she does is eat, sleep, go for walks, and charm us with her looks. She has no obligations. Everyone else works for her . . . Isn't that so? And an idle life can never be pure.

(*Pause.*)

Then again, maybe I'm too hard on her. I'm just as disillusioned with life as your Uncle Vanya, and the two of us are turning into a pair of old grumps.

SONYA. You're disillusioned with life?

ASTROV. I love life per se; it's our life—our provincial, parochial, Russian life—I can't stand. I despise it with all my heart. As for my own private life, believe me there's nothing to recommend it. You know how it is on a black night when you're walking through the woods and far off in the distance you see a speck of light. You don't notice how tired you are or how dark it is, you don't feel the thorny branches lashing out at your face . . . I work harder than anyone in the district. You know that. Fate lashes out at me from all sides, and there are times when I suffer unbearably. But there's no light shining in the distance for me. I don't expect any more out of life. I don't like people . . . and it's a long time since I've loved anyone.

SONYA. You don't love anyone?

ASTROV. No, no one, though I do have a soft spot in my heart for your nanny—for old times' sake. The peasants are all alike—dull-witted and dirty—and I have trouble with intellectuals: they wear me out. So many of our friends have petty thoughts and petty feelings and can't see beyond their noses. They're plain stupid. And the ones who are somewhat brighter, who have something more to offer—they're hysterical and plagued by self-analysis and introspection; they're forever whining, feuding, and maligning one another. They'll sidle up to a person, look him over out of the corner of their eye and state categorically, "A psychopath." "A phony." And when they can't find a label to stick on me, they say, "An odd sort, very odd." I love the woods. That's odd. I don't eat meat. *That's* odd. There's no such thing as a pure, simple, spontaneous way of dealing with nature or people. Not anymore there isn't. (*He is about to take a drink.*)

SONYA (*stopping him*). No, please don't. Don't drink.

ASTROV. Why not?

SONYA. It doesn't become you. You're so distinguished. You have such a gentle voice . . . Not only that. More than anyone I know, you are beautiful. Why should you want to be like ordinary people who drink and gamble? Don't. Please. You're always saying people don't create anything; they only destroy what God has given them. Then why, oh why, are you so bent on destroying yourself? Don't, don't. Please don't. I beg of you.

ASTROV (*holding his hand out to her*). I'll stop drinking.

SONYA. Promise?

ASTROV. I promise.

SONYA (*clasping his hand*). Thank you.

ASTROV. *Basta.*[6] I'm sober now. See? Perfectly sober. And sober I'll remain to the end of my days. (*He glances at his watch.*) Anyway, as I was saying, my time is past, long gone . . . I'm not young anymore. I've worked myself to the bone. I'm crude. My feelings are numb. I'll never feel affection for anyone. I don't love anyone and . . . never will. The only thing that still arouses me is beauty. I can't be indifferent to that. I think Yelena Andreevna could turn my head in a day if she felt like it . . . But that's not love or affection . . . (*He covers his eyes with one hand and shudders.*)

SONYA. What's the matter?

ASTROV. Nothing . . . During Lent a patient of mine died under chloroform.

SONYA. Isn't it time you forgot about it?

(*Pause.*)

Tell me, Mikhail Lvovich . . . If I had a friend or a younger sister, and if you found out that she . . . well, say, loved you, how would you react?

ASTROV (*shrugging his shoulders*). I don't know. I don't think I'd react at all. I'd make it clear that I'd never be able to love her back, that I had other things on my mind . . . Well, I'll be going. If I don't say good-bye now, we'll go on like this till morning. (*He shakes her hand.*) I'll leave through the drawing room if you don't mind. Otherwise your uncle may stop me. (*He exits.*)

SONYA (*alone*). He didn't say anything definite . . . His heart and soul are still a secret . . . Then what makes me so happy? (*She laughs happily.*) "You're so distinguished, so noble. You have such a gentle voice." Was that the wrong thing to say, I wonder? I can still feel his voice in the air—throbbing, caressing . . . And when I said that about a younger sister, he didn't understand . . . (*Wringing her hands.*) Oh, how dreadful it is to be plain! How awful! And I know I am. I know it. I know it . . . Last Sunday as people were coming out of church, I heard them talking about me. "She's kind and generous," one woman said. "A pity she's so plain . . ." Plain . . .

YELENA (*entering and opening the windows*). The storm is over. How good the air feels!

(*Pause.*)

Where's the doctor?

SONYA. He's gone.

(*Pause.*)

YELENA. Sonya!

SONYA. Yes?

YELENA. Why do you keep snubbing me? We've never done anything to hurt each other. Why should we be enemies? Hasn't this gone on long enough? . . .

SONYA. I've been meaning to talk to you too . . . (*She embraces* YELENA.) Let's not be angry anymore.

YELENA. Good.

(*They are both moved.*)

SONYA. Has Father gone to bed?

YELENA. No, he's in the drawing room . . . You and I haven't said a word to each other for weeks on end. Heaven only knows why . . . (*She notices the sideboard is open.*) What's this?

SONYA. The doctor was having some supper.

YELENA. There's wine too . . . Let's drink to our friendship.

SONYA. Yes, let's.

YELENA. From the same glass . . . (*She pours a glass of wine.*) That's better now. Well then, to us?

SONYA. To us. (*They each take a drink, then kiss.*) I've been meaning to make peace with you for ages. It's just that I was so embarrassed . . . (*She begins to cry.*)

YELENA. Why are you crying?

SONYA. Never mind. It's nothing.

YELENA. There, there. That's enough . . . (*She begins to cry.*) Silly girl. Now I'm crying too.

(*Pause.*)

You're angry with me because you think I married your father for selfish reasons . . . I swear to you—if you believe in oaths—I swear I married him for love. I was infatuated with him. He was a scholar, he was famous. It wasn't true love, it was artificial, but it seemed real enough at the time. I have no reason to feel guilty about it. But from the day of our wedding you've been condemning me with those shrewd, suspicious eyes of yours.

SONYA. Peace, peace. Let bygones be bygones.

YELENA. You should never look at anyone like that. It doesn't become you. You should trust everybody. Life is impossible if you don't.

(*Pause.*)

SONYA. Tell me honestly, as a friend . . . Are you happy?

YELENA. No.

SONYA. I knew it. One more question. Frankly, wouldn't you have liked your husband to be young?

YELENA. What a child you are. Of course. (*She laughs.*) Anything else? Go on . . .

SONYA. Do you like the doctor?

YELENA. Yes, very much.

SONYA (*laughing*). I've got a silly look on my face, haven't I? He's gone now, but I keep hearing his voice and footsteps. If I stare into that dark window, I can picture his face. Oh, let me tell you everything . . . But I'm too embarrassed to say it out loud like this. Let's go to my room. We can talk there. You think I'm silly. You do, don't you? . . . Tell me something about him . . .

YELENA. What, for instance?

SONYA. He's so intelligent . . . He can do anything. He can do everything . . . He heals the sick, he plants forests . . .

YELENA. There's more to the doctor than trees and medicine . . . Can't you see, dear? He's a very gifted man. And you know what that means: courage, a free spirit, and breadth of vision . . . Every time he plants a tree, he sees a thousand years into the future. As he works, he envisages the happiness of mankind. People like him are rare. They should be loved . . . Oh, he drinks and he can be a bit crude, but what's wrong with that? In Russia a man with talent can never be pure. Think of the life he leads: roads choked with mud, intense cold, blizzards, vast distances, coarse, primitive people, poverty and disease everywhere . . . Anyone who struggles day after day in conditions like those will have a hard time keeping pure and sober till the age of forty . . . (*She kisses* SONYA.) I wish you the best of everything. You deserve to be happy. (*She stands.*) While I'm just a dull, minor character. In my

music, my husband's house, my loves . . . I've never been anything more. Actually, Sonya, to be honest, I'm terribly, terribly
unhappy. (*She paces restlessly.*) There's no joy for me in life. None.
Why are you laughing?

SONYA (*hiding her face and laughing*). I'm so happy . . . so happy!

YELENA. I feel like playing the piano . . . I think I'll play something.

SONYA. Do. (*She embraces her.*) I can't sleep anyway . . . Go ahead.

YELENA. All right, but your father's still up. Music upsets him when
he's ill. Would you ask him? I'll play if he doesn't object. Would
you?

SONYA. Fine. (*She exits.*)

(*The watchman taps in the garden.*)

YELENA. It's so long since I've played the piano. I'm going to cry
when I play, cry like a baby. (*She calls through the window.*) Is that
you tapping, Yefim?

WATCHMAN'S VOICE. Yes, ma'am.

YELENA. Well, that's enough for now. The master isn't well.

WATCHMAN'S VOICE. Going. (*He whistles.*) Here, Zhuchka! Good
dog! Here, Malchik!

(*Pause.*)

SONYA (*returning*). No.

CURTAIN

ACT THREE

The drawing room of SEREBRYAKOV's *house. There are three doors: right, left, and center. It is shortly past noon.* VANYA *and* SONYA *are seated;* YELENA *paces back and forth, deep in thought.*

VANYA. The Herr Professor has graciously expressed a desire for us to assemble here in the drawing room at one o'clock. (*He looks at his watch.*) A quarter to. He has a message for the world.

YELENA. Some business matter probably.

VANYA. He hasn't got any business other than scribbling, grumbling, and being jealous.

SONYA (*reproachfully*). Uncle Vanya!

VANYA. All right, all right. I apologize. (*He motions towards* YELENA.) Have a look at her, will you? So listless she can hardly put one foot in front of the other. Charming, just charming.

YELENA. And you drone on all day. On and on. And never tire of it! (*In agony.*) I'm bored to death. I don't know what to do with myself.

SONYA (*shrugging*). There's plenty to do if you want to do it.

YELENA. For instance?

SONYA. You could help to run the estate or teach or nurse the sick. And that's only the beginning. Before you and Father came, Uncle Vanya and I would go to market and sell the flour ourselves.

YELENA. I'm no good at those things. Besides, they don't interest me. The only place people teach and nurse peasants is in novels of ideas. How can I start nursing or teaching just like that?

SONYA. I don't see how you can help it. You'd get used to it in time. (*She embraces* YELENA.) It's wrong to be bored, dear. (*She laughs.*) And you're so bored you don't know what to do with yourself.

Boredom and idleness are contagious. Look at Uncle Vanya. All he does is follow you around like a shadow. And I dropped what I was doing so I could run and talk to you. Even I'm lazy now. There's nothing I can do about it. The doctor used to come no more than once a month. It was hard to get him here at all. Now he's here every day and has started neglecting his trees and patients. You must be a sorceress.

VANYA (*to* YELENA). Why so gloomy? (*With spirit.*) Be a good girl now, my beauty, my sweet. You've got the blood of a mermaid in your veins. Why not act like one? Let yourself go for once in your life, get swept off your feet by a sprite, plunge headlong into the deep, leave Herr Professor behind, leave all of us behind in total amazement.

YELENA (*angry*). Leave me alone! How can you be so cruel! (*She tries to go.*)

VANYA (*not letting her past*). There, there, my love. Forgive me . . . I apologize. (*He kisses her hand.*) Peace.

YELENA. You'd try the patience of a saint.

VANYA. Let me bring you a bouquet of roses as a peace offering. I picked them for you this morning . . . They're autumn roses, lovely, melancholy roses . . . (*He exits.*)

SONYA. Autumn roses, lovely, melancholy roses . . .

(SONYA *and* YELENA *gaze out of the window.*)

YELENA. September already. How will we ever get through the winter?

(*Pause.*)

Where's the doctor?

SONYA. In Uncle Vanya's room, painting. I'm glad Uncle Vanya's gone. I've got something to talk to you about.

YELENA. What is it?

SONYA. What is it? (*She puts her head on* YELENA's *breast.*)

YELENA. There, there . . . (*She strokes* SONYA's *hair.*) It's all right . . .

SONYA. I'm so plain.

YELENA. You've got beautiful hair.

SONYA. No. (*She turns and glances at herself in the mirror.*) No. When a woman is plain, people say, "What beautiful eyes you have, beautiful hair." I've loved him for six years. I love him more than I loved my own mother. I never stop hearing his voice or feeling his hand in mine. I keep my eye on the door, waiting, hoping he'll enter any minute. And lately I've been coming to you to talk about him. He visits us every day now, but never looks at me, never even sees me . . . It hurts so much. I have no hope at all, none. (*Desperately.*) O God, give me strength . . . I prayed all night . . . I keep going up to him, trying to start a conversation, look into his eyes . . . I have no pride anymore, no self-control . . . Yesterday I broke down and told Uncle Vanya I loved him . . . All the servants know it too. Everybody knows.

YELENA. What about him?

SONYA. No. He doesn't know I'm here.

YELENA (*pensive*). He's an odd man . . . I'll tell you what. Let *me* talk to him . . . I'll handle it cautiously. I'll just hint . . .

(*Pause.*)

After all, how long can you go without knowing? . . . Let me try. (SONYA *nods in agreement.*) Good. It won't be hard to find out whether he loves you or not. Don't be embarrassed, dear. Don't worry. I'll be discreet about the way I question him. He won't notice a thing. All we need to learn is yes or no.

(*Pause.*)

And if it's no, he should stop coming here, don't you think? (SONYA *nods in agreement.*) It will be easier if you don't see him, and there's no point in putting it off. We'll do it immediately. He's been meaning to show me some maps or something . . . Go and say I want to see him.

SONYA (*extremely agitated*). You'll tell me the whole truth, won't you?

YELENA. Of course I will. No matter how bad, it's better than uncertainty. You can trust me, dear.

SONYA. Yes, yes! I'll say you want to see his maps . . . (*She goes as far as the door, then stops.*) No, it's better not to know . . . At least there's still hope . . .

YELENA. What's that?

SONYA. Nothing. (*She exits.*)

YELENA (*alone*). There's nothing worse than knowing someone else's secret and not being able to help. (*Pensive.*) He's not in love with her—that's obvious—but why shouldn't he marry her? She is plain, but she'd make the perfect wife for a country doctor of his age. She's intelligent and kind and pure . . . No, that's not the point, that's not the point . . .

(*Pause.*)

I understand the poor girl. In the midst of all this excruciating boredom, where gray blotches masquerade as people, where all you hear are crude clichés, where no one does anything but eat, drink, and sleep—in the midst of all this, enter the doctor, so different from the others, so handsome, engaging, fascinating even: a bright moon rising in the darkness . . . It doesn't take much to fall under the spell of a man like that, to be carried away . . . I may be a bit infatuated with him myself. I miss him when he's gone, and here I am smiling just thinking about him . . . Uncle Vanya says I have mermaid blood in my veins. "Let yourself go for once in your life" . . . Well, maybe I should . . . Wouldn't it be wonderful to fly away, free as a bird, away from all of you and your sleepy faces, your endless chatter, and forget you ever existed . . . No, I'm a coward. I'm too timid . . . And my conscience would bother me . . . He's been coming every day now. I can guess why. And already I feel guilty, feel like falling on my knees, weeping and begging Sonya to forgive me . . .

ASTROV (*entering with a map*). Hello. (*He shakes hands with her.*) You wanted to see some of my "artwork"?

YELENA. Yesterday you promised to show me what you've been doing . . . Is this a good time?

ASTROV. Yes, of course. (*He spreads the map out on a card table and fastens it with tacks.*) Where were you born?

YELENA (*helping him*). Petersburg.

ASTROV. And where did you go to school?

YELENA. The Conservatory.

ASTROV. This probably won't interest you.

YELENA. Why not? I may not know life in the country, but I've read a lot.

ASTROV. I have a desk of my own here . . . in Ivan Petrovich's room. When I'm all in, completely exhausted, I drop everything, rush over, and spend an enjoyable hour or two with my maps . . . Ivan Petrovich and Sofya Alexandrovna click away on the abacus; I sit at the desk fiddling with my paints. It's warm and peaceful, the crickets sing. But it's a pleasure I don't indulge in very often—once a month . . . Now look at this. (*He points to a spot on the map.*) This is the way our district looked fifty years ago. Green, light and dark, stands for woodlands. They cover half the area. The parts crosshatched in red were inhabited by elk and wild goats. I show both flora and fauna. This lake had swans, geese, ducks, and—as the old people say—a "power" of birds, all kinds and great numbers of them, whole clouds of them flying overhead. As you can see, in addition to the towns and villages there were isolated settlements, farms, small monasteries, and water mills . . . Horses and cattle were in abundance. They're in blue. In this region, for instance, there's a strong concentration of blue. It had whole herds of horses, three horses to every household.

(*Pause.*)

Now let's look lower down, the way things were twenty-five years ago. By then only one third of the total area was wooded. The wild goats are gone, but there are still some elk. Both green and blue are paler. And so it goes, on and on. If we move to part three—the way the district looks today—we find an occasional patch of green, but nothing solid. Elk and swans and grouse—they've all disappeared . . . And there's not a trace of those settlements, farms, monasteries, or mills. What we have here is basically a picture of gradual but unmistakable decay, and the way things are going it won't take another ten or fifteen years to complete. You might say it's just civilization at work, the old naturally giving way to the new, and I agree: if road and railways had replaced the ravaged woods, if factories and schools had been built, then people would be healthier, better off, better educated. But that's not what's happened. The district is plagued with the same swamps and mosquitoes, the same terrible roads, the same poverty, typhus and diphtheria, fires ... The decay we see here is the result of a struggle for existence man is losing. It's the result of inertia, ignorance, and an utter lack of awareness. A man who is shivering, hungry, and diseased grabs instinctively, unconsciously at anything that can fill his belly and keep him warm. Since his only interest is to preserve what is left of his own life and protect the lives of his children, he destroys everything without thinking of the future ... Nearly everything has been destroyed, and nothing has been created to take its place. (*Coldly.*) But I can see from your face you're not interested.

YELENA. There's so much I don't understand ...

ASTROV. There's nothing to understand. You're just not interested.

YELENA. To be perfectly frank, my thoughts were elsewhere. I'm sorry. I have to put you through a brief interrogation, and I'm embarrassed. I don't quite know how to go about it.

ASTROV. An interrogation?

YELENA. Yes, but ... a fairly harmless one. Shall we sit? (*They sit.*) It's about a young woman of my acquaintance. We can have an honest talk, can't we? Between friends, no beating about the bush. And when it's over, we'll forget all about it. Agreed?

ASTROV. Agreed.

YELENA. It's about my stepdaughter Sonya. Do you like her?

ASTROV. Yes, I respect her.

YELENA. Do you like her as a woman?

ASTROV (*after a brief pause*). No.

YELENA. A few more words and I'm through. Have you noticed anything?

ASTROV. Nothing.

YELENA (*takes him by the hand*). You don't love her. I can see it in your eyes ... She's suffering ... Try to understand and ... stop coming here.

ASTROV (*standing*). I'm too old for that sort of thing . . . And too busy . . . (*He shrugs his shoulders.*) Where would I find the time? (*He is embarrassed.*)

YELENA. What an unpleasant conversation. I'm so overwhelmed I feel I've been carrying a great weight on my back. Thank goodness it's over. Let's forget we ever had it and . . . and please go . . . You're an intelligent man. You can understand . . .

(*Pause.*)

I'm blushing all over.

ASTROV. If you'd told me all this a month or two ago, I might have given it some thought, but now . . . (*He shrugs.*) And if she's suffering, well then of course . . . There's just one thing I don't understand: why did you need the interrogation? (*He looks her in the eye and shakes his finger at her.*) You're a sly one.

YELENA. What is that supposed to mean?

ASTROV (*laughing*). Very sly. Granted Sonya is suffering. I can accept that. But why your interrogation? (*He stops her from answering and continues with great animation.*) Don't look surprised. You know very well what brings me here every day . . . You know very well why I come, who I come to see . . . Don't look at me like that, you sweet beastie. I'm a wise old owl. You won't catch me.

YELENA. Beastie? I don't know what you're talking about.

ASTROV. A fluffy little weasel, that's what you are . . . You need victims. I haven't done a stitch of work all month, I've let everything slide. I'm greedy for every glimpse of you. And you love it, don't you? You just love it . . . Well, what can I do? You've got me where you want me. But you knew that before your interrogation. (*He crosses his arms over his chest and bows his head.*) I surrender. Here I am. Eat me up.

YELENA. Have you gone out of your mind?

ASTROV (*laughing sardonically*). How timid you are . . .

YELENA. I am better, more worthy than you think. I swear it. (*She starts to go.*)

ASTROV (*barring her way*). I'll leave today. I won't come back. But . . . (*He takes her hand and looks around.*) Where can we meet? Tell me quickly. Where? Someone may be coming. Tell me quickly. (*Passionately.*) You're so gorgeous, so magnificent ... One kiss ... Just let me kiss your fragrant hair ...

YELENA. I swear to you ...

ASTROV (*stopping her from talking*). Why swear? There's no need. No need for words ... Oh, how beautiful you are! What hands! (*He kisses her hands.*)

YELENA. That's enough now ... Get away ... (*She takes her hands back.*) You're forgetting yourself.

ASTROV. First tell me, tell me where we can meet tomorrow. (*He puts his arms around her waist.*) See? We can't fight it. We've got to meet. (*He kisses her just as* VANYA *enters with a bouquet of roses.* VANYA *stops in the doorway.*)

YELENA (*not seeing* VANYA). Stop torturing me, will you ... Let me go ... (*She puts her head on* ASTROV's *chest.*) No! (*She starts to go.*)

ASTROV (*holding on to her by the waist*). Come to the woods tomorrow ... At two ... Will you? Will you? Will you be there?

YELENA (*seeing* VANYA). Let me go! (*She goes over to the window in great embarrassment.*) This is awful.

VANYA (*laying his bouquet on the table and wiping his face and neck with a handkerchief in dismay*). Never mind ... Yes ... Never mind ...

ASTROV (*sulking*). Lovely weather we're having, dear Ivan Petrovich. Oh, we had a few clouds this morning. It even looked like rain. But now the sun is out. As a matter of fact, we've been having good weather all autumn ... The winter crops are coming along. (*He rolls up the map.*) The only thing is, the days are getting shorter ... (*He exits.*)

YELENA (*quickly goes up to* VANYA). You must do everything you can, use all your influence to see to it that my husband and I leave today. Today, do you hear?

VANYA (*wiping his face*). What was that? Oh, yes ... Fine ... I saw everything, Hélène, everything ...

YELENA (*tensely*). I must leave here today!

(*Enter* SEREBRYAKOV, SONYA, TELEGIN, *and* MARINA.)

TELEGIN. I'm not feeling too well myself, Your Excellency. It's been going on for two days now. Something to do with my head.

SEREBRYAKOV. Where is everybody? I hate this house. It's a regular labyrinth. Twenty-six enormous rooms and people wandering off in all directions. You can never find anybody. (*He rings a bell.*) Tell my wife and Maria Vasilyevna I want to see them.

YELENA. I'm here.

SEREBRYAKOV. Please be seated, everybody.

SONYA (*going up to* YELENA, *impatiently*). What did he say?

YELENA. I'll tell you later.

SONYA. You're trembling. You're all upset. (*She looks searchingly into her face.*) I see . . . He said he wouldn't be coming anymore . . . Didn't he?

(*Pause.*)

Well, didn't he? (YELENA *nods.*)

SEREBRYAKOV (*to* TELEGIN). I can put up with poor health if need be. There's one thing I can't stand, though, and that's the routine of country life. It's like landing on another planet. Please be seated, everyone . . . Sonya!

(*Pause.*)

She doesn't hear me. (*To* MARINA.) You sit too, Nanny. (MARINA *sits and starts knitting.*) Now, my friends, hang your ears on the hook of attention, to coin a phrase. (*He laughs.*)

VANYA (*upset*). Perhaps you won't be needing me. May I go?

SEREBRYAKOV. No, we need you more than anyone.

VANYA. In what capacity, if I may be so bold?

SEREBRYAKOV. Why so formal? You're not angry, I hope.

(*Pause.*)

Do accept my apologies if I've done anything to offend you.

VANYA. You needn't adopt such a tone . . . Well, what are we waiting for? What's on your mind?

(*Enter* MARIA VASILYEVNA.)

SEREBRYAKOV. Good, there's *maman*. Let me begin.

(*Pause.*)

I've invited you here, gentlemen, to inform you that an Inspector General is on his way.[7] But joking aside, this is a serious matter. I've called you together to ask for assistance and advice, and acquainted as I am with your customary benevolence, I trust I shall receive them. I am a scholar, a man of letters. I am now and have always been a stranger to the realm of practical matters. I cannot manage without the guidance of those better informed than I, and so I turn to you, Ivan Petrovich, and you, Ilya Ilyich, and you, *maman* . . . The fact is, *manet omnes una nox*, that is, we are all mortal.[8] I am old and ailing and therefore feel the time has come for me to settle my worldly affairs insofar as they pertain to my family. My own life is over—I'm not thinking of myself—but I have a young wife and an unmarried daughter.

(*Pause.*)

I cannot go on living in the country. We are not cut out for country living. But neither can we live in town, at least not on the income we receive from the estate. Now suppose we sold the forest. That would be an extraordinary measure, one that could not be repeated year after year. What we are after is a method of guaranteeing ourselves a constant and more or less stable income. I have hit upon such a method, and I hereby submit it for your consideration. I shan't go into detail. My idea, in broad terms, is this. Our estate yields an average of not more than two percent. I propose to sell it. If we invest the proceeds in securities, we'll receive between four and five percent. There may even be a few thousand to spare, enough to purchase a cottage in Finland.

VANYA. Wait . . . I don't think I heard you quite right. Say that again.

SEREBRYAKOV. We'll buy securities with the money and, if anything is left over, a cottage in Finland.

VANYA. No, not Finland . . . You said something else.

SEREBRYAKOV. I propose to sell the estate.

VANYA. That's it. Sell the estate. Fine. A brilliant idea . . . And what do you intend to do with me and my aging mother. And Sonya here?

SEREBRYAKOV. We'll discuss that in good time. We can't settle everything at once.

VANYA. Wait. It's obvious I've been laboring under a misapprehension. All along I've been stupid enough to believe the estate belongs to Sonya. My father bought it as a dowry for my sister. All along I've been naïve enough to believe that, since we are under Russian and not Turkish law, the estate has passed from my sister to Sonya, her daughter.

SEREBRYAKOV. The estate does belong to Sonya. Nobody's denying that. I should never presume to sell it without Sonya's consent. Indeed, I am making the proposal for her own good.

VANYA. I can't believe it. I can't believe it. Either I've lost my mind or . . . or . . .

MARIA VASILYEVNA. Don't contradict Alexander, Jean. Believe me, he knows right from wrong better than we do.

VANYA. No. Give me some water. (*He drinks the water.*) Say what you like, whatever you like.

SEREBRYAKOV. I don't see why you're upset. I don't claim my plan is ideal. I shan't insist if you find it unsuitable.

(*Pause.*)

TELEGIN (*embarrassed*). Not only do I maintain deep bonds of reverence for learning, Your Excellency, but deep bonds of kinship as well. My brother, Grigory Ilyich, has a brother-in-law, Konstantin Trofimovich Lakademonov—perhaps you know him—who has a Master of Arts degree . . .

VANYA. Wait, Waffles. We're talking business . . . You can tell us that later . . . (*To* SEREBRYAKOV.) Why not ask him? The estate was purchased from his uncle.

SEREBRYAKOV. What for? Where would that get us?

VANYA. The estate was originally purchased for ninety-five thousand rubles. My father paid only seventy, which left a debt of twenty-five thousand. Now listen carefully . . . The estate would never have been bought in the first place if I hadn't given up my inheritance to my sister, whom I dearly loved. On top of that I worked like a dog for ten years to pay off the debt ...

SEREBRYAKOV. I'm sorry I ever started this discussion.

VANYA. My personal efforts alone have kept the estate out of debt and in working condition, and now that I'm old they want to kick me out.

SEREBRYAKOV. I fail to see what you're driving at.

VANYA. For twenty-five years I've run this estate, working to send you money like a devoted bailiff, and not once have you thanked me for it. All that time—when I was young and now—you paid me a salary of five hundred a year, a pittance, and never thought of adding so much as a ruble to it.

SEREBRYAKOV. But how could I have known, Ivan Petrovich? I'm no businessman, I have no head for such things. You could have helped yourself to as much as you pleased.

VANYA. Why didn't I steal? I suppose you all look down on me for not stealing. It would have been justified, after all. And then I wouldn't be a pauper now.

MARIA VASILYEVNA (*sternly*). Jean!

TELEGIN (*upset*). Stop, Vanya, stop ... I'm trembling all over ... Why spoil good relations? (*He kisses him.*) Stop now.

VANYA. For twenty-five years I've been cooped up in this place like a mole with Mother here ... All our thoughts and feelings were with you. Not a day went by when we didn't talk about you and your work. We were proud of you, we uttered your name in awe. And we wasted our nights reading journals and books I now hold in the utmost contempt.

TELEGIN. Stop, Vanya, stop! ... I can't bear it!

SEREBRYAKOV (*angrily*). I don't understand what you want.

VANYA. You were a superior being to us. We knew your articles by heart ... But now my eyes are wide open! I see everything! You write on art, but you don't know the first thing about it! All those books and articles I loved so much aren't worth a thing! You made fools out of us!

SEREBRYAKOV. Stop him, somebody, or I'm leaving!

YELENA. Ivan Petrovich, I insist you be quiet! Do you hear?

VANYA. I refuse. (*Barring* SEREBRYAKOV's *way.*) Stay where you are. I haven't finished! You've ruined my life! I haven't lived, haven't lived at all! Thanks to you I've wasted, squandered the best years of my life! You're my worst enemy!

TELEGIN. I can't bear it anymore ... I can't stand it ... I'm going ... (*He exits in great distress.*)

SEREBRYAKOV. What do you want from me? And what right have you to talk to me like this? You nobody! Take the estate if it's yours! I don't need it!

YELENA. I'm getting out of this hellhole at once! (*She shouts.*) I've had as much of this as I can stand!

VANYA. My life's gone to waste! I'm gifted, daring, intelligent ... If I'd had a normal life, I could have been a Schopenhauer, a Dostoevsky ... What am I saying! I'm going out of my mind ... Mother, I'm desperate! Mother!

MARIA VASILYEVNA. Do as Alexander tells you.

SONYA (*kneeling at* MARINA's *feet and nestling up to her*). Nanny, Nanny!

VANYA. What should I do, Mother? No, no! Don't tell me! I know what to do! (*To* SEREBRYAKOV.) You won't forget me! (*He exits through the center door followed by* MARIA VASILYEVNA.)

SEREBRYAKOV. Can anyone tell me what is going on here? Keep that maniac away from me! I can't live under the same roof with him! (*He points to the center door.*) Look, his room is practically next to mine. See to it he moves into the village or the lodge, or I shall move out myself. I cannot stay in the same house with him ...

YELENA (*to* SEREBRYAKOV). We're leaving today. The arrangements must be made immediately.

SEREBRYAKOV. That nobody!

SONYA (*still on her knees, turning to her father, tense, through tears*). Do try and show some compassion, Father! Uncle Vanya and I are so miserable! (*She attempts to control her despair.*) Do try and show some compassion! Remember when you were younger and Uncle Vanya and Grandmother sat up night after night translating books for you and making fair copies of your manuscripts ...

Night after night. Uncle Vanya and I never stopped working. We were afraid to spend a kopeck on ourselves. We sent everything to you . . . We earned every piece of our daily bread! I'm saying it all wrong, all wrong, but you've got to understand us, Father. You must show some compassion.

YELENA (*very upset, to* SEREBRYAKOV). For God's sake, Alexander! Try and talk to him . . . Please!

SEREBRYAKOV. All right, I shall . . . I'm not accusing him of anything. I'm not angry. Though you must admit his behavior has been—to put it mildly—peculiar. Very well, I'll go to him. (SEREBRYAKOV *exits through the center door.*)

YELENA. Be as gentle with him as you can. Try and calm him down . . . (*She follows him out.*)

SONYA (*nestling up to* MARINA). Nanny, Nanny!

MARINA. It's all right, child. The geese will have their cackle and stop . . . Cackle and stop.

SONYA. Nanny!

MARINA (*stroking her hair*). Shivering like it was freezing. There, there, little orphan. God is merciful. A sip of linden or raspberry tea and you'll be just fine . . . Nothing to fret about . . . (*She looks up at the center door, angrily.*) There go the geese again, drat them! (*There is a shot offstage.* YELENA *screams.* SONYA *gives a start.*) Curse them!

SEREBRYAKOV (*staggering with fright*). Stop him! Stop him! He's out of his mind!

YELENA (*struggling with* VANYA *in the doorway for his revolver*). Give it to me! Give it to me, I tell you!

VANYA. Let me go, Hélène! Let me go! (*He wrenches himself free and looks around for* SEREBRYAKOV.) Where is he? Ah, there he is! (*He fires at him.*) Bang!

(*Pause.*)

Missed him? Missed again?! (*Angrily.*) Damn it! Damn it! . . . Damn it to hell! . . . (*He flings the revolver to the floor and drops exhausted into a chair.* SEREBRYAKOV *is stunned.* YELENA *is leaning against the wall about to faint.*)

YELENA. Get me away from here. Take me away. I'd rather die than stay.

VANYA (*in despair*). Oh, what am I doing? What have I done?

SONYA (*softly*). Nanny, Nanny!

CURTAIN

ACT FOUR

VANYA's *room, which is both a bedroom and the estate office. By the window stands a large table with ledgers and assorted papers. The room also contains a bookkeeper's desk, cupboards, and a pair of scales. A smaller table, covered with drawing materials and paints for* ASTROV, *has a portfolio leaning against it. There is a birdcage with a starling. A map of Africa, obviously of no use to anyone, is hanging on the wall over an enormous oilcloth sofa. To the left is a door leading to the rest of the house, to the right—a door leading to the entrance hall. At the right-hand door is a mat for peasants to wipe their boots on.*

It is an autumn evening, and everything is quiet. TELEGIN *and* MARINA *sit facing each other, winding wool.*

TELEGIN. Hurry, Marina Timofeevna. They'll be calling us to say good-bye any minute now. The carriage has been sent for.
MARINA (*trying to speed up her winding*). There's just a little left.
TELEGIN. They're going to Kharkov. They're going to live there.
MARINA. A good thing too.
TELEGIN. Some scare they had . . . "I won't spend another hour in this house," Yelena Andreevna keeps saying. All she talks about is leaving. "We're going to Kharkov," she says. "We'll send for our things once we've had a look round." They're taking almost nothing. So they're not going to live here after all, Marina. Fate has decreed otherwise.
MARINA. A good thing too. The racket they made this afternoon, the shooting—disgraceful!
TELEGIN. Yes, a scene for the brush of an Aivazovsky.[9]
MARINA. I never thought I'd see the day.

(*Pause.*)

Now things will be like they were: tea every morning at seven, a solid meal at twelve, and supper in the evening. Everything in order, like normal people live, the Christian way. It's ages since I've had a good bowl of noodles.

TELEGIN. True. Nobody has made noodles in a long time.

(*Pause.*)

A long time . . . I was walking through the village this morning, and you know what the grocer shouted out after me? "Sponger!" That's what. And it hurt.

MARINA. Don't you go listening to them now. We're all spongers off the Lord. But you and Sonya and Ivan Petrovich—none of you sit with your arms folded. Everyone works around here. Everybody . . . Where's Sonya?

TELEGIN. In the garden. She and the doctor are looking all over for Ivan Petrovich. They're afraid he'll try to do away with himself.

MARINA. Where's his pistol?

TELEGIN (*whispering*). I hid it in the cellar.

MARINA (*with a scornful smile*). The goings-on in this house.

(*Enter* VANYA *and* ASTROV *from outside.*)

VANYA. Leave me alone. (*To* MARINA *and* TELEGIN.) Go away. Can't you leave me by myself for even an hour? I can't stand being watched over.

TELEGIN. I was just leaving, Vanya. (*He exits on tiptoe.*)

MARINA. The goose goes cackle, cackle. (*She gathers her wool and exits.*)

VANYA. Leave me alone!

ASTROV. I'd be only too glad to go. I should have left long ago. But I repeat: I'm not leaving till you give me back what you've taken.

VANYA. I haven't taken anything from you.

ASTROV. I'm not joking. And don't keep me waiting. I'm long overdue.

VANYA. I haven't taken a thing. (*He sits down.*)

ASTROV (*sitting*). Really? Well then, I'll just wait a little longer. But soon, I'm sorry, I'll have to use force. We'll tie you up and search you. I mean it.

VANYA. That's fine with me.

(*Pause.*)

How could I be such a fool? Shooting twice and missing both times. I'll never forgive myself.

ASTROV. Why didn't you blow your own brains out if you were so intent on shooting?

VANYA (*shrugging*). Funny. Here I've tried to commit murder and no one arrests me, no one takes me to court. They must think I'm insane. (*With a nasty laugh.*) So I'm insane. And what about people who hide their incompetence, their stupidity, their monumental heartlessness behind the mask of a learned seer? They're not insane. No. Or people who marry old men and then deceive them in full view. I saw you with your arms around her. I saw you.

ASTROV. Yes, I did put my arms around her. So there. (*He thumbs his nose at him.*)

VANYA (*looking at the door*). The whole world must be insane if it suffers the likes of you.

ASTROV. What a stupid thing to say.

VANYA. Well, what of it? If I'm insane, I'm not responsible for my actions. I have every right to say stupid things.

ASTROV. Don't expect me to fall for that. You're not insane; you're a crackpot, a clown. I used to think all crackpots were crazy, sick, but now I believe that being a crackpot is the normal human condition. You're perfectly normal.

VANYA (*covering his face with his hands*). I'm so ashamed. If only you knew how ashamed I feel. It hurts more than any pain. (*In anguish.*) It's unbearable! (*He bends over the table.*) What can I do? What can I do?

ASTROV. Nothing.

VANYA. Give me something! God! . . . I'm forty-seven years old. Suppose I live to be sixty. Thirteen more years! It's too long. How can I get through thirteen years? What can I do with them? What can I fill them with? Don't you see? . . . (*He grabs* ASTROV'*s hand convulsively.*) Don't you see? If only we could live out our lives in some new way. Wake up one clear, quiet morning to find we'd started life all over again and the past had been forgotten, blown away like smoke. (*He starts crying.*) If I could start a new life . . . Tell me how to begin . . . Where to begin . . .

ASTROV (*irritated*). New life! You can't be serious! Our situation's hopeless, yours and mine.

VANYA. It is?

ASTROV. I'm convinced of it.

VANYA. Give me something . . . (*He points to his heart.*) I've got a burning pain here.

ASTROV (*shouting angrily*). Stop it! (*He relents.*) The people who come a hundred, two hundred years after us and look down on us for living such stupid, tasteless lives—they may find a way to be happy. As for us . . . You and I have one hope and one hope alone: that as we lie in our graves we may be visited by dreams, maybe even sweet dreams. (*He sighs.*) Yes, my friend. Our whole district had only two decent, cultured men: you and me. But ten years of this despicable provincial existence has dragged us down. Its noxious fumes have poisoned our blood, and now we're as petty and narrow-minded as the rest of them. (*With sudden animation.*) But stop trying to talk your way out of it. Give it back.

VANYA. I haven't taken anything.

ASTROV. You took a bottle of morphine from my medicine bag.

(*Pause.*)

Look, if you're determined to kill yourself, then go out into the woods and shoot. But give me back my morphine or else people will start suspecting things, and before you know it they'll be saying I *gave* it to you . . . Isn't it enough I'll have to do the post-mortem? . . . Think I'll enjoy it?

(*Enter* SONYA.)

VANYA. Leave me alone.

ASTROV (*to* SONYA). Your uncle has stolen a bottle of morphine from my bag and won't give it back. Tell him it's . . . not very bright. I can't waste any more time. I've got to go.

SONYA. Did you take that morphine, Uncle Vanya?

(*Pause.*)

ASTROV. He took it, all right.

SONYA. Give it back. Why do you want to frighten us? (*Tenderly.*) Give it back, Uncle Vanya. Believe me, I'm just as unhappy as you and I don't despair. I bear my burden and I'll go on bearing it until my life comes to a natural end ... You do the same ...

(*Pause.*)

Give it back. (*She kisses his hands.*) Dear Uncle Vanya, sweet Uncle Vanya, give it back. (*She starts to cry.*) You're so good. You'll take pity on us and give it back, won't you? Bear your burden, Uncle Vanya.

VANYA (*taking the bottle out of a desk drawer and handing it to* ASTROV). Here. Take it. (*To* SONYA.) We've got to go back to work immediately. We've got to hurry and do something or I can't go on.

SONYA. Back to work. Yes, yes. As soon as we've seen them off, we'll get right down to work ... (*She shuffles through the papers on the table nervously.*) Everything's been so neglected.

ASTROV (*putting the bottle into his bag and pulling the strap*). Well, now I can be on my way.

YELENA (*entering*). Ivan Petrovich, are you here? We're leaving ... Go and see Alexander. He has something to tell you.

SONYA. Do go, Uncle Vanya. (*She takes* VANYA *by the arm.*) Come on. You and Father need to make peace. You must. (*She and* VANYA *exit.*)

YELENA. I'm leaving. (*She gives* ASTROV *her hand*). Good-bye.

ASTROV. So soon?

YELENA. The carriage is waiting.

ASTROV. Good-bye.

YELENA. You promised me today you would leave.

ASTROV. I remember. I'm going.

(*Pause.*)

You were scared, weren't you? (*He takes her by the hand.*) Is it that terrifying?

YELENA. Yes, it is.

ASTROV. Why not stay? How about it. Tomorrow in the woods . . .

YELENA. No . . . It's all settled . . . The only reason I can face you un-
afraid is that we're definitely leaving . . . I have a favor to ask of
you: don't think too badly of me. I want you to respect me.

ASTROV. Oh! (*With a gesture of annoyance.*) Please stay . . . Please.
Admit it: you've got nothing else to do, no goal in life, nothing to
occupy your mind, and sooner or later your feelings are going to
get the better of you. It's inevitable. Doesn't it make more sense
for it to happen here, in the lap of nature, rather than in Kharkov
or a place like Kursk? . . . At least it's romantic and has its own
beauty: the woods, tumbledown manors out of Turgenev . . .

YELENA. You're strange, you know . . . Here I am, annoyed with you,
but still . . . I'll always enjoy thinking of you. You're interesting,
original. We'll never see each other again so . . . Why hide it? I
was a trifle infatuated with you. Well, let's shake hands and part
friends. No hard feelings.

ASTROV (*after shaking her hand*). Yes, you'd better go . . . (*Thoughtfully.*)
You seem so sincere and good, but everything about you is somehow strange as well. The moment you and your husband arrived,
we all dropped the constructive things we were running about
doing and spent the whole summer taking care of your husband's
gout and you. You infected all of us with your idleness—yours
and his. I was infatuated with you and didn't do a thing all month.
And meanwhile people have been falling ill, the peasants have let
their cattle graze in the woods I was planting . . . So you see, you
and your husband wreak havoc wherever you go . . . I'm only joking, of course, and yet . . . it is strange. And I'm convinced that if
you'd stayed on, the destruction would have been enormous. I'd
never have survived, and . . . you wouldn't have escaped either. So
go. *Finita la commedia.*[10]

YELENA (*picking up a pencil from his desk and hiding it quickly*). I'm taking this pencil to remember you by.

ASTROV. Funny, isn't it . . . We were friends, and suddenly, for no
reason . . . we'll never see each other again. It's like everything in
life . . . Before anybody comes, before Uncle Vanya brings in his

bouquet, let me . . . kiss you . . . good-bye . . . May I? (*He kisses her on the cheek.*) There . . . Now everything's fine.

YELENA. All the best. (*She looks around.*) Well, here goes, for once in my life! (*She embraces him impulsively. They separate quickly.*) I've got to go.

ASTROV. Then go, go quickly. Leave if the carriage is ready.

YELENA. I think I hear them coming. (*She and* ASTROV *listen.*)

ASTROV. *Finita.*

(*Enter* SEREBRYAKOV, VANYA, MARIA VASILYEVNA, *with a book,* TELEGIN, *and* SONYA.)

SEREBRYAKOV (*to* VANYA). Let bygones be bygones. So much has happened. I've been through and thought through so much in the past few hours I feel I could write an entire treatise on the art of living for the edification of posterity. I willingly accept your apology and hope you will accept mine. Good-bye. (*He and* VANYA *kiss three times.*)

VANYA. You'll be receiving the same amount in the same regular installments. Everything will be as before.

(YELENA *embraces* SONYA.)

SEREBRYAKOV (*kissing* MARIA VASILYEVNA's *hand*). Have your picture taken again, Alexander, and send me a copy. You know how much you mean to me.

TELEGIN. Good-bye, Your Excellency. Don't forget us.

SEREBRYAKOV (*after kissing* SONYA). Good-bye . . . Good-bye, everybody. (*He shakes hands with* ASTROV.) Thank you for the pleasure of your company . . . I respect your point of view, your enthusiasm, and your impulses, but allow an old man to interject one last observation. It's what you do that counts, ladies and gentlemen, what you do that counts. (*He bows all around.*) Good-bye. (*He exits, followed by* MARIA VASILYEVNA *and* SONYA.)

VANYA (*pressing* YELENA's *hand to his lips*). Good-bye . . . Forgive me . . . We'll never meet again.

YELENA (*moved*). Good-bye, dear Ivan Petrovich. (*She kisses him on the forehead and exits.*)

ASTROV (*to* TELEGIN). Waffles, tell them to get my carriage ready while they're at it, will you?

TELEGIN. At your service, my friend. (*He exits.*)

(*Only* ASTROV *and* VANYA *remain.*)

ASTROV (*picking up his paints from the desk and packing them in a case*). Aren't you going to see them off?

VANYA. Let them go. I can't. I'm so miserable. I'd better find something to do at once ... Work, work! (*He rummages through the papers on the table.*)

(*Pause followed by harness bells.*)

ASTROV. They're gone. The professor's happy, that's for sure. Nothing in the world could drag him back here.

MARINA (*entering*). They're gone. (*She sits in an armchair and starts knitting her stocking.*)

SONYA (*entering*). They're gone. (*She wipes her eyes.*) God grant them a safe journey. (*To* VANYA.) Well, Uncle Vanya, let's get to work.

VANYA. Work, work ...

SONYA. It's a long, long time since we sat together at this table. (*She lights the lamp.*) There doesn't seem to be any ink ... (*She takes the inkwell over to the cupboard and fills it with ink.*) I'm sad they're gone.

MARIA VASILYEVNA (*entering slowly*). They're gone. (*She sits and immerses herself in her reading.*)

SONYA (*sitting at the table and leafing through a ledger*). First we'll do the accounts, Uncle Vanya. Everything's been so neglected. There was another call for a bill today. Here, you start. You do one; I'll do the next.

VANYA (*writing*). "Re: the account of ..." (*He and* SONYA *go on writing in silence.*)

MARINA (*yawning*). Time for my bed.

ASTROV. It's so quiet with the pens scratching and the crickets chirping. Warm and cozy ... I hate to leave. (*Harness bells ring out.*) There's my carriage ... So the only thing left for me to do is say good-bye to you, friends, say good-bye to my table, and—I'm off. (*He puts his maps in the portfolio.*)

MARINA. What's your hurry? Why not sit a while?

ASTROV. I can't.

VANYA (*writing*). "Plus two hundred and seventy-five from the previous bill ..."

WORKMAN (*entering*). Your carriage is ready, sir.

ASTROV. Yes, I heard. (*He hands him his medicine bag, case, and portfolio.*) Here, take these. And be careful not to crush the portfolio.

WORKMAN. Yes, sir. (*He exits.*)

ASTROV. Well ... (*He goes over to them to say good-bye.*)

SONYA. When will we see you again?

ASTROV. Not before summer, I imagine. Certainly not all winter ... Let me know if anything happens, of course, and I'll come straight over. (*He shakes everyone's hand.*) Thanks for your hospitality, for your kindness, for everything. (*He goes over to* MARINA *and kisses her on the head.*) Good-bye.

MARINA. You're not going to leave without tea, are you?

ASTROV. I don't feel like any, Nanny.

MARINA. A little vodka, then?

ASTROV (*hesitating*). Well ...

(MARINA *exits.*)

ASTROV (*after a pause*). My trace horse seems to have gone lame. I noticed it yesterday when Petrushka was taking him to water.

VANYA. Needs reshodding.

ASTROV. I'll have to stop at the blacksmith's on my way home. I've no choice. (*He goes up to the map of Africa and looks at it.*) Must be sweltering down there in Africa.

VANYA. Probably is.

MARINA (*returning with a glass of vodka and a piece of bread on a tray*). Here you are.

(ASTROV *drinks the vodka.*)

MARINA. Your health, Mikhail Lvovich. (*She makes a low bow.*) Have a little bread with it.

ASTROV. No, that's all right ... Well then, good-bye. (*To* MARINA.) Don't bother to see me out, Nanny. There's no need. (ASTROV *exits.* SONYA *follows him with a candle to see him out.* MARINA *sits in her armchair.*)

VANYA (*writing*). "February the second: vegetable oil, twenty pounds... February the sixteenth: vegetable oil again, twenty pounds ... Buckwheat ..."

(*Pause followed by harness bells.*)

MARINA. He's gone.

(*Pause.*)

SONYA (*entering and putting the candle on the table*). He's gone.

VANYA (*adding up some figures on the abacus*). Which makes ... fifteen ... twenty-five ...

(SONYA *sits and starts writing.*)

MARINA (*yawning*). Dear me, dear me!

(*Enter* TELEGIN *on tiptoe. He sits and softly tunes his guitar.*)

VANYA (*to* SONYA, *passing his hand once over her hair*). I'm so miserable, my child. You don't know how miserable I am.

SONYA. What can we do? We must live.

(*Pause.*)

And live we shall, Uncle Vanya. We shall live through a long, long line of days and endless nights. We shall patiently bear the trials fate has in store for us. We shall work for others— now and in our old age—and know no rest. And when our time comes, we shall die a humble death. And there, beyond the grave, we shall say we suffered and wept; we shall say our days were bitter. And God will have mercy on us. And you and I, dear Uncle, we shall find a life that is bright and beautiful and fine. We shall rejoice and look back on our present misfortunes with tenderness and smiles. And we shall rest. This I believe ... fervently, passionately believe ... (*She kneels down before him and places her head on his hands, then goes on in a weary voice.*) We shall rest.

(TELEGIN *begins to play softly.*)

We shall rest. We shall hear the angels, we shall see the heavens
sparkling with diamonds. All the ills of the world and all our sufferings will be drowned in a flood of mercy, which will fill the
earth. And our lives will be as soft, gentle, and sweet as a caress.
I believe, I believe ... (*She wipes his tears with a handkerchief.*) Poor,
poor Uncle Vanya. You're crying ... (*Through tears.*) You've had
no joy in life, Uncle Vanya, but wait, wait ... We shall rest ... (*She
embraces him.*) We shall rest ...

(*The watchman is heard tapping.* TELEGIN *plays his guitar.* MARIA
VASILYEVNA *jots something in the margins of her pamphlet.* MARINA
knits her stocking.)

We shall have rest.

THE CURTAIN SLOWLY FALLS

THREE SISTERS

A PLAY IN FOUR ACTS

CHARACTERS[1]

ANDRÉI SERGÉEVICH PRÓZOROV.

NATÁLYA IVÁNOVNA (NATÁSHA). His fiancée, later his wife.

ÓLGA (ÓLYA), MÁSHA, IRÍNA. His sisters.

FYÓDOR ILYÍCH KULÝGIN. A schoolmaster and Masha's husband.

ALEXÁNDER IGNÁTYEVICH VERSHÍNIN. Lieutenant colonel, battery
     commander.

NIKOLÁI LVÓVICH TUSENBACH. Baron, lieutenant.

VASÍLY VASÍLYEVICH SOLYÓNY. Captain.

IVÁN ROMÁNOVICH CHEBUTÝKIN. Army doctor.

ALEXÉI PETRÓVICH FEDÓTIK. Second lieutenant.

VLADÍMIR KÁRLOVICH RODET. Second lieutenant.

FERAPÓNT. A watchman at the District Council,[2] an old man.

ANFÍSA. The Prozorovs' eighty-year-old nursemaid.

The action takes place in a provincial town.

ACT ONE

The PROZOROV *house. A drawing room with columns. A ballroom is visible in the background. Noon. It is sunny and cheerful outside. A table in the ballroom is being set for lunch.* OLGA, *in the dark-blue uniform of a girls' secondary-school teacher, is correcting exercise books, first standing still, then pacing back and forth.* MASHA, *in a black dress, is sitting with a hat in her lap, reading a book.* IRINA, *in a white dress, is standing lost in thought.*

OLGA. Father died exactly a year ago today, May the fifth. Your name day, Irina.[3] It was so cold then. Snowing. I never thought I'd survive. You lay there in a dead faint. But now a year's gone by, and it scarcely bothers us to think about it. You're wearing white, your face is radiant . . . (*The clock strikes twelve.*) The clock struck then too.

(*Pause.*)

I remember the band playing as they carried Father to the cemetery. And the salute they fired. He was a general, he had his own brigade, yet very few people came. Of course, it was raining. A heavy rain, mixed with snow.

IRINA. Why look back?

(TUSENBACH, CHEBUTYKIN, *and* SOLYONY *appear near the table in the ballroom behind the columns.*)

OLGA. It's warm today. We can keep the windows wide open. But the birch trees are still bare. We all left Moscow eleven years ago: Father had been given a brigade here. And—I remember it perfectly—at this time of year in Moscow, early May, everything is in bloom, it's warm, everything is bathed in sunlight.

Eleven years have gone by, and I remember it all as if we'd left yesterday. Dear God! I woke up this morning, saw all that light, saw it was spring, and my heart nearly burst with joy. Suddenly I couldn't wait to be home again.

CHEBUTYKIN. Not a chance in hell!

TUSENBACH. Of course. It's nonsense.

(MASHA, *lost in thought, softly whistles a song.*)

OLGA. Don't whistle, Masha. How can you?

(*Pause.*)

Teaching at the school every day and tutoring into the evening has given me a permanent headache and the thoughts of an old woman. In fact, through these four years at the school I've felt my energy and youth draining out of me, day by day, drop by drop. The only thing in me that grows and gains strength is the dream of . . .

IRINA. . . . . going to Moscow. Selling the house, settling our affairs here, and off to Moscow . . .

OLGA. Yes. To Moscow, as soon as possible.

(CHEBUTYKIN *and* TUSENBACH *laugh.*)

IRINA. Andrei will be a professor most likely. There's nothing to keep him here. The only problem is poor Masha.

OLGA. Masha will come to Moscow for the whole summer, every year.

(MASHA *softly whistles her song.*)

IRINA. I pray to God it all works out. (*She looks out of the window.*) What a beautiful day! I wonder why I'm in such a good mood. I felt so happy this morning when I realized it was my name day and I remembered my childhood and Mother being alive. Such wonderful thoughts kept running through my mind, wonderful thoughts!

OLGA. You look radiant today, exceptionally lovely. Masha's looking lovely too. Andrei would be handsome except he's put on so much weight. It doesn't become him. And I'm older and much thinner. It comes from losing my temper with the girls at school, I suppose. But today I'm free, at home, and my headache's gone. I feel younger than yesterday. I'm only twenty-eight, after all. It's just that ... All's well in God's world, of course, but I do have the feeling that if I'd married and could have stayed at home all day things would have been better.

(*Pause.*)

I'd have loved my husband.

TUSENBACH (*to* SOLYONY). Everything you say is so ridiculous I can't listen anymore. (*He enters the drawing room.*) Oh yes, I forgot to tell you. Vershinin, our new battery commander, is coming to call today. (*He sits at the piano.*)

OLGA. He is? That's nice.

IRINA. Is he old?

TUSENBACH. No, not particularly. Forty, forty-five at most. (*He plays softly.*) Seems nice enough, and nobody's fool, that's for sure. Though he does talk a lot.

IRINA. Is he attractive?

TUSENBACH. I suppose so, but he has a wife, a mother-in-law, and two little girls. His second marriage, incidentally. He makes social calls and tells everybody he's got a wife and two girls. He'll tell you too. His wife isn't all there. She wears her hair in a long, maidenlike braid, specializes in grandiloquent pronouncements and philosophizing, and tries to commit suicide every so often, obviously to spite her husband. I'd have left her long ago, but he puts up with it. He just complains.

SOLYONY (*entering the drawing room from the ballroom with* CHEBU-TYKIN). Whereas with one hand I can lift only fifty pounds, with two I can lift a hundred and fifty, even two hundred. From which I conclude that two men are stronger than one not by a factor of two but by a factor of three or more.

CHEBUTYKIN (*reading a newspaper while entering*). To prevent loss of hair ... dissolve ten grams of naphthalene in half a bottle of alcohol ... and apply daily ... (*He jots it down in his notebook.*) Let's make a note of that. (*To* SOLYONY.) Now, as I was saying, you cork the bottle and stick a glass tube through the cork ... Then you take a pinch of alum—plain, ordinary alum ...

IRINA. Ivan Romanovich! Dear Ivan Romanovich!

CHEBUTYKIN. What is it, my little girl, my sweet?

IRINA. Tell me. Why am I so happy today? I feel I've set sail under a vast blue sky with huge white birds soaring through it. Why is that?

CHEBUTYKIN (*kissing both her hands tenderly*). You're my white bird ...

IRINA. I woke up this morning, got out of bed, washed, and all at once everything in the world seemed clear to me. I seemed to know how to live. I know everything, dear Ivan Romanovich. We must work, work by the sweat of our brow, no matter who we are. In that alone is the meaning, the purpose of our lives—our happiness, our ecstasy. How good to be a workman, who rises with the sun and breaks stones in the road, or a shepherd, or a teacher, who teaches children, or an engine driver ... Good Lord, I'd rather be an ox or a common everyday horse—anything that works—than a young woman who awakes at noon, takes coffee in bed, and then spends two hours dressing. It's dreadful! You know how thirsty you are on a hot day? Well, that's how thirsty I am for work. And if I don't start getting up early and going to work, you won't be friends with me anymore, will you?

CHEBUTYKIN (*tenderly*). Of course I won't, of course I won't ...

OLGA. Father trained us to get out of bed at seven. Irina still wakes up at seven, but then she lies in bed until at least nine—thinking. And how serious she looks! (*She laughs.*)

IRINA. You're so used to seeing me as a little girl you think it's odd for me to look serious. I'm twenty years old!

TUSENBACH. The longing for work—good Lord, how I understand it. I haven't done a stroke of honest work all my life. I was born in Petersburg—cold, idle Petersburg—into a family that didn't know what work is, never had a care in the world. I remember coming home from cadet school and having my boots pulled off by the footman. I always made a fuss, but my mother would look on adoringly, amazed when others saw me in a different light.

They tried to shelter me from work, but they don't seem to have succeeded. The time has come. A colossus is upon us, a mighty, health-giving storm. It's on its way, moving closer, and soon it will sweep our society clean of sloth, indifference, of prejudice against work, of putrefying boredom. I will work, and in twenty-five or thirty years' time everyone will work. Everybody.

CHEBUTYKIN. I won't work.

TUSENBACH. You don't count.

SOLYONY. Twenty-five years from now you won't be around, thank God. In two or three you'll kick the bucket or I'll lose my temper and put a bullet through your head, my pet. (*He takes a bottle of scent from his pocket and sprinkles his chest and hands.*)

CHEBUTYKIN (*laughing*). I haven't done a thing all my life. From the day I left university I haven't lifted a finger. Or even read a book. Nothing but newspapers ... (*He takes another newspaper from his pocket.*) Here ... The newspaper says there's a man named Dobrolyubov, but what he wrote I don't know ...[4] God only knows... (*There is a knock on the floor from below.*) Oh! They're calling me downstairs. Someone must have come to see me. I'll be right back. Wait for me ... (*He rushes out combing his beard.*)

IRINA. He's got something up his sleeve.

TUSENBACH. Yes. He left with a festive look on his face. He's obviously coming back with a present for you.

IRINA. I wish he wouldn't.

OLGA. So do I. It's terrible. He's always doing silly things like that.

MASHA.

> A green oak stands upon a firth,
> A chain of gold hangs round its trunk ...

A chain of gold hangs round its trunk ...[5] (*She stands and starts humming softly.*)

OLGA. Not very cheerful today, are you, Masha. (MASHA, *still humming, puts on her hat.*) Where are you going?

MASHA. Home.

IRINA. That's odd.

TUSENBACH. Walking out on your sister's name day?

MASHA. Don't worry. I'll be back tonight. Good-bye, my sweet. (*She kisses* IRINA.) I wish you all the best again. Be well, be happy . . . In the old days, when Father was alive, we had thirty or forty officers here every time there was a name day. Now we're down to a man and a half, and it's quiet as a tomb . . . Well, I'll be going . . . I'm depressed today. I've got melancholera. Don't pay any attention to me. (*She laughs through her tears.*) Good-bye for now, Irina. We'll talk later. I'm off.

IRINA (*displeased*). How can you? . . .

OLGA (*in tears*). I know how you feel, Masha.

SOLYONY. When a man philosophizes, you get philosophistry or—what do they call it?—sophistry; when a woman philosophizes, you get out of her way.

MASHA. What do you mean by that, you horrible, awful man!

SOLYONY. Nothing at all.

> He ne'er had time to say a prayer,
> When he was sat on by the bear.[6]

(*Pause.*)

MASHA (*to* OLGA, *angrily*). Stop your bawling.

(*Enter* ANFISA *and* FERAPONT *with a cake.*)

ANFISA. This way, this way. Come on in. Your feet are clean. (*To* IRINA.) From Mikhail Protopopov at the District Council . . . It's a cake.

IRINA. Thank you. And thank him for us. (*She accepts the cake.*)

FERAPONT. What's that?

IRINA (*louder*). Thank him.

OLGA. Anfisa dear, give him a piece of meat pie. Go with Anfisa, Ferapont. She'll give you a piece of pie.

FERAPONT. What's that?

ANFISA. Let's go. Come with me . . . (*She exits with* FERAPONT.)

MASHA. I don't like that bear of a Protopopov. He shouldn't have been invited.

IRINA. I didn't invite him.

MASHA. That's good.

(*Enter* CHEBUTYKIN *followed by an orderly holding a silver samovar. There is a hum of astonishment and displeasure.*)

OLGA (*covering her face with her hands*). A samovar! Oh, how could you! (*She goes over to the table in the ballroom.*)

IRINA. Dear Ivan Romanovich, what a thing to do!

TUSENBACH (*laughing*). I told you so.

MASHA. You ought to be ashamed of yourself, Ivan Romanovich.

CHEBUTYKIN. My dear, sweet girls. You're all I've got. You're more precious to me than anything in the world. I'm nearly sixty, an old man, lonely and good-for-nothing . . . There's nothing good in me but my love for you, and if it weren't for you I'd have long since breathed my last . . . (*To* IRINA.) My dear child, I've known you since the day you were born . . . I carried you in my arms . . . I loved your mother, may she rest in peace.

IRINA. But why such expensive gifts?

CHEBUTYKIN (*through tears, angrily*). Expensive gifts . . . Really now. You're impossible, all of you! (*To the orderly.*) Put the samovar down over there. (*He mimics* IRINA.) Expensive gifts . . .

(*The orderly takes the samovar into the ballroom.*)

ANFISA (*on her way across the drawing room*). There's a colonel out there I've never seen before, dears. He's taken his coat off. He'll be here any minute now. You be nice to him, Irina my sweet. On your best behavior . . . (*She exits.*) Goodness me! It's long past lunchtime . . .

TUSENBACH. That must be Vershinin. (*Enter* VERSHININ.) Lieutenant Colonel Vershinin.

VERSHININ (*to* MASHA *and* IRINA). Allow me to introduce myself. My name is Vershinin. I'm very, very happy to be here with you at last. My, my, how you've grown!

IRINA. Won't you sit down? We're very pleased to meet you.

VERSHININ (*cheerfully*). And I'm so happy to be here! So, so happy!

But aren't there *three* sisters? Three girls. I remember it well. I
can't remember the faces anymore, but I do remember that your
father, Colonel Prozorov, had three little girls. I saw them with
my own eyes. How time flies. How time does fly.

TUSENBACH. The lieutenant colonel is from Moscow.

IRINA. Moscow? You're from Moscow?

VERSHININ. Why, yes. I am. Your father, may he rest in peace, was a
battery commander there, and I was an officer in the brigade. (*To*
MASHA.) Now, your face I seem to remember slightly.

MASHA. I don't remember you.

IRINA. Olya, Olya! (*She calls into the ballroom.*) Olya, come quickly!
(OLGA *enters from the ballroom.*) Guess what! Lieutenant Colonel
Vershinin is from Moscow!

VERSHININ. You must be Olga Sergeevna, the eldest... And you are
Maria... And you—Irina, the youngest...

OLGA. You're from Moscow?

VERSHININ. Yes. I went to school in Moscow and entered the service in Moscow. I was stationed there for a long time, and now
I've got my own battery. As you can see, here I am. I don't remember each of you separately. All I remember is that there
were three sisters. Your father, though—he's deeply engraved in
my memory. If I close my eyes, I can see him plain as day. I used
to visit you in Moscow.

OLGA. I thought I remembered everyone, and suddenly...

VERSHININ. My full name is Alexander Ignatyevich Vershinin...

IRINA. Alexander Ignatyevich. So you're from Moscow... What a
surprise!

OLGA. We're moving there soon.

IRINA. We plan to be there by autumn. We're natives of Moscow. We
were born there... Old Basmannaya Street... (*She and* OLGA
laugh joyfully.)

MASHA. Isn't this a nice surprise! Someone from home. (*Excitedly.*)
Now I remember! Remember, Olya? "The lovesick major"
everyone called him. You were a lieutenant then and in love with
somebody, and to tease you they called you major for some reason...

VERSHININ. That's it . . . The lovesick major. That's right . . .

MASHA. You had only a mustache then . . . My, how you've aged! (*Through tears.*) How you've aged!

VERSHININ. Yes, I was young when they called me the lovesick major. Young and in love. That's all over now.

OLGA. But you don't have a single gray hair. You may have aged, but you're not old.

VERSHININ. I *am* nearly forty-three. Have you been away from Moscow for long?

IRINA. Eleven years. Why are you crying, Masha silly? . . . (*Through tears.*) You'll make me cry too . . .

MASHA. I'm all right. Where did you live in Moscow?

VERSHININ. Old Basmannaya Street.

OLGA. So did we . . .

VERSHININ. And German Street for a time. I would walk from there to the Red Barracks. On the way I'd pass a gloomy-looking bridge with water flowing under it. It gives a lonely man a heavy heart.

(*Pause.*)

But what a broad, rich river you have. A magnificent river.

OLGA. Yes. Only it's cold here. Cold and full of mosquitoes . . .

VERSHININ. What do you mean? You have a fine, healthy, Russian climate. The woods, the river . . . and all those birch trees. Those dear, modest birch trees. I love them more than any other. A fine place to live. Though isn't it odd? The station is twelve miles out of town . . . And no one knows why.

SOLYONY. I know why. (*They all look at him.*) Because if the station were nearby, it wouldn't be far away, and if it's far away it can't be nearby. (*Awkward silence.*)

TUSENBACH. Quite the wit, aren't you, Solyony!

OLGA. Now I've placed you. I remember.

VERSHININ. I knew your late mother.

CHEBUTYKIN. A good woman, bless her soul.

IRINA. Mama is buried in Moscow.

OLGA. In the New Virgin Cemetery . . .

MASHA. Can you imagine? I'm beginning to forget her face. People won't remember us either. We'll all be forgotten.

VERSHININ. Yes, we'll be forgotten. That's the way things are. There's nothing we can do about it. Things that appear serious, significant, so very important—the time will come when they're forgotten or seem unimportant.

(Pause.)

And interestingly enough, we, living now, can't have the faintest idea of what will actually be considered lofty, important, and what will seem pitiful or ridiculous. Didn't the discoveries of a Copernicus or, say, Columbus seem pointless, ridiculous at first, while the empty blatherings of some crackpot or other seemed to hold the truth? It may be that the life we now lead, the life we simply take for granted, will in time seem strange, awkward, unwise, impure, even sinful perhaps . . .

TUSENBACH. Who can tell? Maybe people will call our life lofty and think back on it with respect. There's no more torture, there are no public executions, no invasions. Yet the suffering, that remains.

SOLYONY (*in a high-pitched voice*). Here chicky, chicky, chicky . . . Nothing the baron likes more than a bit of philosophizing.

TUSENBACH. Leave me alone, will you . . . (*He moves to another seat.*) I'm getting sick and tired of this.

SOLYONY (*in a high-pitched voice*). Here chicky, chicky, chicky . . .

TUSENBACH (*to* VERSHININ). Still, the suffering we see around us nowadays—and there's plenty of it—is a sign that society has reached a certain level of moral development . . .

VERSHININ. Yes, yes. Of course.

CHEBUTYKIN. You've just said, Baron, that someday our life may be called lofty. But people are still pretty low . . . (*He stands.*) Look how low I am. Really now. Anyone who tells me my life is lofty is only trying to make me feel better.

(A violin starts playing offstage.)

MASHA. That's Andrei playing. Our brother.

IRINA. He's the scholar of the family. He's going to be a professor, we think. Father was a military man; his son has chosen a scholarly career.

MASHA. Which is how Father wanted it.

OLGA. We've been teasing him today. He seems a bit in love.

IRINA. With a young lady from town. She'll be coming today most likely.

MASHA. You ought to see the way she dresses! It's not even unattractive or unfashionable; it's pitiful, that's all. An odd, gaudy, yellowish skirt with a cheap-looking fringe topped by a red blouse. And those cheeks: always freshly scrubbed—scrubbed! Andrei's not in love. I refuse to believe it. He's got taste, after all. It's just a game he's playing to tease us. Yesterday I heard she was going to marry Protopopov, the chairman of the District Council. Well, let her . . . (*In the direction of a side door.*) Andrei, come here. Please, Andrei. Just for a minute!

(*Enter* ANDREI.)

This is my brother, Andrei Sergeevich.

VERSHININ. Vershinin.

ANDREI. Prozorov. (*He wipes the sweat off his face.*) Are you the new battery commander?

OLGA. Guess what! The lieutenant colonel is from Moscow.

ANDREI. Really? Congratulations. Now my sisters won't give you a moment's peace.

VERSHININ. I've bored them already, I'm sure.

IRINA. Look at the little picture frame Andrei gave me today. (*She shows him the frame.*) He made it himself.

VERSHININ (*looking at the frame without knowing what to say*). Yes . . . It's quite . . . something.

IRINA. And the frame over the piano—he made that too. (ANDREI *makes a gesture of impatience and walks away from them.*) He's the family scholar, he plays the violin, he's handy with a saw—in other words, he's a jack-of-all-trades. Don't walk off like that, Andrei. He has a habit of walking off. Come here. (MASHA *and* IRINA *lock arms with him and drag him back, laughing.*)

MASHA. Come on, come on.

ANDREI. Leave me alone. Please!

MASHA. Isn't he silly! People used to call Alexander Ignatyevich the lovesick major, and *he* never lost his temper.

VERSHININ. Never.

MASHA. The lovesick fiddler. That's what I'll call you.

IRINA. Or the lovesick professor . . .

OLGA. He's in love! Andrei's in love!

IRINA (*clapping*). Bravo, bravo! Encore! Andrei's in love!

CHEBUTYKIN (*coming up behind* ANDREI *and putting both arms around his waist*). "Nature put us on this earth for love and love alone."[7] (*He laughs loudly. He is still carrying a newspaper.*)

ANDREI. That's enough now, that's enough . . . (*He wipes his face.*) I didn't sleep a wink all night, and I'm not quite myself, so to speak. I read until four, then lay down, but it was no use. I kept thinking about this and that, and the next thing I knew it was light. The sun comes straight into my room. There's an English book I mean to translate this summer while I'm here.

VERSHININ. You read English?

ANDREI. Yes. Father, may he rest in peace, overloaded us with education. It's ridiculous, absurd, but I must admit that since his death I've been putting on weight—I'm fat now, a year later— as though my body had been freed of an oppressive burden. Thanks to Father my sisters and I know French, German, and English. Irina knows Italian too. But at what a price.

MASHA. Knowing three languages in a town like this is an expendable luxury. No, not even a luxury; it's an expendable appendage, like a sixth finger. We've got a lot of useless knowledge.

VERSHININ. What a thing to say! (*He laughs.*) Useless knowledge. As far as I'm concerned, there can't be anyplace so dismal and dull that it has no use for someone intelligent and well educated. Suppose that among the hundred thousand inhabitants in this town, which is clearly backward and uncivilized, there are only three like you. Naturally you're not going to overcome the mass ignorance surrounding you. Little by little, as you live out your lives, you'll be forced to retreat and lose your identity to that crowd of a hundred thousand. Life will stifle you. Still, you won't disappear; you'll have your influence. You may be followed by six more of your kind, then twelve, and so on, until people like yourselves are in the majority. In two or three hundred years life on earth will be indescribably beautiful, wonderful, the life the human race was meant to live. And if it doesn't yet exist, we must prophesy it, dream about it, count upon it, make way for it. And to do that we must see and know more than our fathers and grandfathers saw and knew. (*He laughs.*) And you complain about useless knowledge.

MASHA (*taking off her hat*). I'm staying for lunch.

IRINA (*with a sigh*). Someone really ought to take all that down . . .

(ANDREI *has left the room unnoticed.*)

TUSENBACH. You say that many years from now life on earth will be beautiful, wonderful. True enough. But if we wish to take part in it now, even at a distance, we must make the necessary preparations, we must work . . .

VERSHININ (*standing*). Yes. My, what a lot of flowers you have. (*He looks around.*) And what a fine house. I envy you. All my life I've flitted from one furnished room to the next: two chairs, a sofa, and stoves that never stop smoking. Flowers like these— that's what I've missed all my life . . . (*He rubs his hands together.*) Oh well . . .

TUSENBACH. Yes, we must work. I bet you think I'm just another of those maudlin Germans. But believe me, I'm Russian. I don't even speak German. My father is Russian Orthodox . . .

(*Pause.*)

VERSHININ (*walking back and forth*). I often wonder what it would be like to live life over again, fully conscious of what it entails. What if the life we now live were only a rough draft, so to speak, and the second one the fair copy. I don't think any of us would want to repeat ourselves. The very least we'd do is create new sur- roundings, a house like this with flowers and plenty of light, for instance . . . I have a wife and two little girls, my wife is not well, and so on and so forth. And well, if I had my life to live over, I'd never marry. No, no.

(*Enter* KULYGIN *in regulation dress.*)

KULYGIN (*going up to* IRINA). Dearest sister-in-law! Allow me to wish you the very best on the feast of your saint. I sincerely hope, I pray from the bottom of my heart, that you will be granted good health and everything one may wish a girl of your age. And allow me to present you with this small book. (*He hands her a book.*) The history of our school for the past fifty years. I wrote it myself. A paltry little thing, written only because I had nothing better to do. Still, be sure to read it. Good afternoon, ladies and gentlemen. (*To* VERSHININ.) Kulygin is my name. I teach at the local school. Civil servant, rank seven. (*To* IRINA.) The book contains the names of everyone who has completed the course of study at our school during the past fifty years. *Feci quod potui, faciant melior potentes.*[8] (*He kisses* MASHA.)

IRINA. But you gave me a copy for Easter.

KULYGIN (*laughing*). Did I? In that case give it back. Or even better, give it to the colonel. Take it, Colonel Vershinin. You can read it sometime when you're bored.

VERSHININ. Thank you. (*He makes ready to go.*) It's been a great pleasure . . .

OLGA. Leaving? No, no!

IRINA. Stay and have lunch with us. Please.

OLGA. Yes, do.

VERSHININ (*bowing*). I seem to have broken in on your name-day party. Forgive me. I didn't know. I haven't offered my best wishes. (*He goes into the ballroom with* OLGA.)

KULYGIN. Today, my friends, is Sunday, the day of rest. Let us rest then and enjoy ourselves, each in accordance with his age and station. The rugs will have to be taken up for the summer and stored till winter . . . treated with insect powder or naphthalene . . . The Romans were healthy because they knew how to work and how to relax. They had a *mens sana in corpore sano.*[9] Their lives had structure. Our headmaster says the most important thing in any life is structure. Take away the structure and there's nothing left. The same holds for our day-to-day existence. (*He puts his arm around* MASHA'*s waist, laughing.*) Masha loves me. My wife loves me. The curtains will have to be stored together with the rugs . . . I'm so happy today. I'm in such a good mood. We're due at the headmaster's at four, Masha. There's a picnic for the teachers and their families.

MASHA. I'm not going.

KULYGIN (*chagrined*). Why not, Masha darling?

MASHA. I'll tell you later . . . (*Angrily.*) Oh, all right. I'll go. Only please leave me alone . . . (*She walks away.*)

KULYGIN. And then we're spending the evening at the headmaster's. Despite his poor health he does everything he can to be sociable. A shining light. A splendid man. Yesterday after our meeting he said to me, "I'm tired, Kulygin. Tired." (*He glances at the clock, then at his watch.*) Your clock is seven minutes fast. "Yes," he said, "tired."

(*A violin starts playing offstage.*)

OLGA. Do come and sit down, everybody. Lunch is ready. Meat pie.

KULYGIN. Dear, dear Olga. Yesterday I worked from morning till eleven at night. I was so tired. And today I feel happy. (*He goes over to the table in the ballroom.*) Dear Olga . . .

CHEBUTYKIN (*putting his newspaper in his pocket and combing his beard*). Meat pie? Splendid!

MASHA (*to* CHEBUTYKIN, *sternly*). Just don't drink today, do you hear? Drinking is bad for you.

CHEBUTYKIN. What do you mean? I stopped long ago. Haven't been on a binge in two years. (*Impatiently.*) What's the difference anyway?

MASHA. Still, no drinking. No drinking. (*Angrily, but softly enough so* KULYGIN *cannot hear.*) Another whole evening of boredom at the headmaster's, damn it.

TUSENBACH. I wouldn't go if I were you . . . It's very simple.

CHEBUTYKIN. Don't go, my sweet.

MASHA. What do you mean "Don't go"! . . . Damn this life! It's unbearable . . . (*She goes into the ballroom.*)

CHEBUTYKIN (*following her*). Come on . . .

SOLYONY (*on his way into the ballroom*). Here chicky, chicky, chicky . . .

TUSENBACH. Enough is enough, Solyony.

SOLYONY. Here chicky, chicky, chicky . . .

KULYGIN (*lightheartedly*). Your health, Colonel! I'm a pedagogue, and I feel at home in this house. I'm Masha's husband . . . And Masha is kind, so kind . . .

VERSHININ. I think I'll have some of that dark vodka . . .[10] (*He drinks.*) Your health! (*To* OLGA.) How nice it is to be here with all of you . . .

(*Only* IRINA *and* TUSENBACH *are left in the drawing room.*)

IRINA. Masha's out of sorts today. She married him at eighteen, when she thought he was the most intelligent man in the world. Things have changed now. He's very kind, but not very intelligent.

OLGA (*impatiently*). Andrei! Where *are* you!

ANDREI (*offstage*). Coming. (*He enters and goes over to the table.*)

TUSENBACH. What are you thinking about?

IRINA. Nothing much. I don't like your Solyony. I'm afraid of him. He says such stupid things.

TUSENBACH. He's a strange man. Sometimes I'm sorry for him, sometimes annoyed, but more often sorry than annoyed. I think he's shy . . . He can be quite clever and affectionate when we're alone, but in company he's rude and picks fights. Don't go yet. Not till they've all sat down. Let me be near you a while. What are you thinking about?

(*Pause.*)

You're twenty; I'm not thirty yet. Picture all the years ahead of us. A long, long procession of days full of my love for you . . .

IRINA. Don't talk to me about love, Nikolai Lvovich.

TUSENBACH (*not listening*). I have a passionate longing for life. I long to struggle, to work, and deep inside me that longing has merged with my love for you, Irina. And then, you're so beautiful that life seems beautiful too! . . . What are you thinking about?

IRINA. You say that life seems beautiful. Yes, but what if it no more than seems so? Life hasn't been so beautiful for my sisters and me. It's stifled us, like a weed . . . Now I'm crying. I mustn't . . . (*She quickly wipes away her tears and smiles.*) <u>Work</u>—that's what I need. Work. <u>The reason we're so unhappy and take such a gloomy view of life is that we don't know what work</u> is. We come from people who had nothing but contempt for work . . .

(*Enter* NATASHA. *She is wearing a pink dress and a green sash.*)

NATASHA. Oh, they're sitting down to lunch . . . I'm late . . . (*She glances at herself in the mirror and tidies her hair.*) My hair looks all right . . . (*She sees* IRINA.) Many happy returns, Irina Sergeevna. (*She gives her a vigorous and prolonged kiss.*) All those guests! It makes me so uncomfortable. Really . . . How do you do, Baron.

OLGA (*entering the drawing room*). Oh, there you are, Natalya Ivanovna. How are you, my dear? (*They kiss.*)

NATASHA. Best wishes. What a crowd! I'm terribly nervous.

OLGA. Don't be. They're only family and friends. (*In an undertone, alarmed.*) That's a green sash you're wearing. It's not right, you know.

NATASHA. You mean it's bad luck?

OLGA. No, it just doesn't match your dress . . . And it looks so odd . . .

NATASHA (*tearfully*). It does? But it's not really green. It's not shiny enough.

(*She follows* OLGA *into the ballroom. They sit down to lunch. No one is left in the drawing room.*)

KULYGIN. I hope you find yourself a nice young man, Irina. It's time you married.

CHEBUTYKIN. I hope you find one too, Natalya Ivanovna.

KULYGIN. Natalya Ivanovna *has* one.

MASHA (*tapping her fork on her plate*). Join me in a shot of vodka, everybody! Eat, drink, and be merry! Don't let life get you down.

KULYGIN. That's zero minus for conduct.

VERSHININ. Delicious vodka. What's it flavored with?

SOLYONY. Cockroaches.

IRINA (*tearfully*). Ugh! Disgusting!

OLGA. We'll be having roast turkey and apple tart tonight. Thank God I'll be at home all day. Come again tonight, everybody . . .

VERSHININ. May I come too?

IRINA. Oh, please do.

NATALYA. They're very informal.

CHEBUTYKIN. "Nature put us on this earth for love and love alone."

ANDREI (*angrily*). Not again! Won't you ever stop?

(FEDOTIK *and* RODET *enter with a large basket of flowers.*)

FEDOTIK. You see? They're eating.

RODET (*loudly, with a slight* r *defect*). Eating already? So they are . . .

FEDOTIK. Wait a minute. (*He takes a picture.*) That's one. Wait just a second more . . . (*He takes another picture.*) That's two. All done.

(*They pick up the basket and go into the ballroom, where they are greeted noisily.*)

RODET (*loudly*). Many happy returns. The best of everything to you, the best of everything. What beautiful weather we're having today. Absolutely perfect. I spent all morning out walking with the students. I've been teaching gymnastics at the school . . .

FEDOTIK. You can move now if you like, Irina Sergeevna. Go ahead. (*He takes a picture.*) You look so attractive today. (*He takes a top out of his pocket.*) Oh, by the way, here's a top . . . It makes a wonderful hum . . .

IRINA. Delightful!

MASHA.

> A green oak stands upon a firth,
> A chain of gold hangs round its trunk . . .

A chain of gold hangs round its trunk . . . (*In a whining voice.*) Why do I keep saying that? I haven't been able to get it out of my head since morning.

KULYGIN. Thirteen at table!

RODET (*loudly*). Don't tell me you're superstitious, all of you!

(*Laughter.*)

KULYGIN. Whenever thirteen people sit at a table, it means one of them is in love. It isn't you by any chance, Ivan Romanovich? ...

(*Laughter.*)

CHEBUTYKIN. Oh, I'm an old reprobate, but what I can't understand is why Natalya Ivanóvna here is blushing so.

(*Loud laughter.* NATASHA *runs out of the ballroom into the drawing room with* ANDREI *at her heels.*)

ANDREI. Stop ... Don't pay any attention to them. Wait ... Stand still a minute, please ...

NATASHA. I'm so ashamed ... I don't know what's wrong with me, but I'm always the butt of their laughter. It's bad manners to leave the table like that, but I can't help it ... I can't help it ... (*She covers her face with her hands.*)

ANDREI. Darling, please, listen to me. Don't be upset. Believe me, they're only joking. They don't mean any harm. Natasha darling, they're kind, good-hearted people, all of them. They're fond of us both. Come over here to the window. They can't see us here ... (*He looks around.*)

NATASHA. I'm not used to society like this.

ANDREI. How young you are, Natasha. How wonderful and marvelous and young! Don't be upset, Natasha darling. Trust me. Trust me, please ... I feel so wonderful, so in love, so ecstatically happy ... Oh, nobody can see us. Nobody at all. Why I fell in love with you, when I fell in love with you—I haven't the faintest idea. My darling, my sweet, my innocent Natasha, be my wife. I love you ... I've never been in love like this before ... (*They kiss.*)

(*Two officers enter. They stop and stare in amazement when they notice the couple kissing.*)

CURTAIN

ACT TWO

The setting is the same as in Act One. It is eight o'clock in the evening. The barely audible strains of an accordion come from outside. The stage is dark. Enter NATASHA *wearing a dressing gown and holding a candle. She crosses the stage, stopping at the door to* ANDREI'*s room.*

NATASHA. What are you doing, Andrei? Reading? No, nothing's wrong. I just . . . (*She goes over to another door, opens it, looks in, then shuts it.*) Has anyone left a light burning? . . .

ANDREI (*entering with a book in his hand*). What are you doing, Natasha?

NATASHA. Just making sure nobody's left a light burning . . . The servants are impossible now that carnival is here. I've got to keep an eye on things. You never know what might happen. Yesterday at midnight on my way through the dining room I saw a candle burning. I still haven't been able to find out who lit it. (*She sets down the candle.*) What time is it?

ANDREI (*glancing at his watch*). A quarter past eight.

NATASHA. And Olga and Irina aren't home yet. Still slaving away, poor things. Olga at her staff meeting, Irina at the telegraph office . . . (*She sighs.*) Just this morning I told your sister, "Irina darling," I said, "you take care of yourself, now." But she won't listen. A quarter past eight, you say? I'm worried. Little Bobik isn't well. Why does he get so cold? Yesterday he had a fever, and today he's cold all over . . . I'm so worried.

ANDREI. It's nothing, Natasha. The boy's fine.

NATASHA. Still, I think he needs a special diet. I'm worried. And the carnival people are due tonight at nine. I wish they'd stay away.

ANDREI. I don't know what to tell you. They were invited, after all.

NATASHA. This morning the little darling woke up and looked at me, and all at once he smiled. Don't you see? He recognized me. "Hello there, Bobik," I said. "Hello, my sweet." And he laughed. Babies understand, they understand perfectly. So I'll order the servants not to let the carnival people in, all right, dear?

ANDREI (*indecisively*). But isn't that up to Olga and Irina? This is *their* house.

NATASHA. Theirs *too*. I'll tell them. They're so kind . . . (*She starts walking off.*) I've ordered yogurt for your supper. The doctor says you're to eat nothing but yogurt or you'll never lose weight. (*She stops.*) Bobik gets so cold. I'm afraid it's the room. We should find another room for him until the weather turns warm. Irina's room, for instance. It's just right for a baby: dry, and sunny all day. We'll have to tell her. She can move in with Olga for a while . . . She's never at home in the daytime anyway; she just sleeps here . . .

(*Pause.*)

Why don't you say something, Andrei?

ANDREI. I was thinking . . . Besides, there's nothing to say . . .

NATASHA. I see . . . Now, what was I going to tell you? . . . Oh yes. Ferapont is here from the District Council. He wants to see you.

ANDREI (*yawning*). Send him in. (*Exit* NATASHA. ANDREI *hunches over the candle she has left behind and starts reading his book. Enter* FERAPONT *wearing a shabby overcoat with the collar turned up. He has a scarf wound round his ears.*) What's on your mind, old friend? How are you?

FERAPONT. A book and some papers from the chairman. Here they are . . . (*He hands him a book and a package.*)

ANDREI. Good. Thank you. But why so late? It's after eight.

FERAPONT. What's that?

ANDREI (*louder*). I said it's late. It's after eight o'clock.

FERAPONT. Yes, sir. It was still light when I got here, but they wouldn't let me in. The master was busy, they told me. So I said to myself, I said, "If he's busy, he's busy. I'm not rushing any-place." (*He thinks* ANDREI *has asked him something.*) What's that?

ANDREI. Nothing. (*He glances through the book.*) Tomorrow's Friday.

The office is closed. But I'll go in anyway . . . It'll keep me busy. I'm so bored at home . . .

(*Pause.*)

Funny—isn't it, old man—how life changes, how it strings us along. Today out of sheer boredom I picked these up again—my old lecture notes. What a joke . . . Good Lord, here I am secretary of the District Council, the Council headed by Protopopov. Secretary of the District Council, and the most I can look forward to is becoming a member. A member of the District Council. And I still dream every night of being a professor at Moscow University, a famous scholar, the pride of all Russia!

FERAPONT. I wouldn't know, sir . . . I'm a little hard of hearing.

ANDREI. Do you think I'd be telling you all this if you weren't? I've got to talk to somebody. My wife doesn't understand me, and I'm afraid of my sisters. Afraid they'll laugh at me and make me ashamed of myself . . . I don't drink and I don't like taverns, but what a treat to spend even an hour at Testov's or the Grand Muscovite in Moscow.

FERAPONT. There were some merchants eating pancakes in Moscow—a contractor at the District Council told us about it the other day—and one of them, he ate forty of them and, sort of, died. Forty or fifty, I can't rightly remember.

ANDREI. In Moscow you can sit in a huge restaurant without knowing anyone or being known and still not feel a stranger. Here you know everyone and everyone knows you, but you're a stranger, an utter stranger . . . A stranger and all alone.

FERAPONT. What's that?

(*Pause.*)

The same contractor, he also said—only he may've been lying—there's a rope stretched straight across Moscow.

ANDREI. What for?

FERAPONT. I wouldn't know, sir. That's what the contractor said.

ANDREI. Well, it's nonsense. (*He starts reading again.*) Have you ever been to Moscow?

FERAPONT (*after a pause*). No. Wasn't God's will.

(*Pause.*)

Can I go now?

ANDREI. Yes. Good-bye. (*Exit* FERAPONT.) Good-bye. (*Reading.*)
Come back tomorrow morning for the papers . . . You may go
now . . .

(*Pause.*)

He's gone. (*A bell rings.*) It never stops . . . (*He stretches and exits slowly
to his room.*)

(*Offstage a nursemaid is singing a lullaby to the baby. Enter* MASHA
and VERSHININ. *A maid lights a lamp and candles as they talk.*)

MASHA. I don't know.

(*Pause.*)

I don't know. Habit is important, of course. After Father's death, for
instance, it took us a long time to get used to living without or-
derlies. But even if we forget about habit, I'm being only fair, I
think. It may not be the same everywhere, but here in our town
the most decent, noble, and cultured people belong to the military.

VERSHININ. I'm thirsty. I wish I could have some tea.

MASHA (*glancing at her watch*). They'll be serving it soon. I was married off when I was eighteen. I was afraid of my husband because
he was a schoolmaster and I'd just finished school. He seemed
oh so learned then, so clever and dignified. Not anymore, sorry
to say.

VERSHININ. Yes . . . I see.

MASHA. I don't mean my husband—I'm wed to him—but civilians
as a whole are so often coarse, disagreeable, and ill-mannered.
Anything coarse upsets and offends me; it makes me suffer to see
a person lacking refinement, lacking sensitivity, manners. Whenever I'm with those teachers, my husband's colleagues, I simply
suffer . . .

VERSHININ. Yes ... Though I don't think it makes much difference if they're soldiers or civilians. One's as boring as the next, in this town at least. No, no difference. Sit down with any educated person—soldier or civilian—and the first thing you'll hear is he's tired of his wife, tired of his house, tired of his estate, tired of his horses ... A Russian likes nothing better than to think lofty thoughts, but why, when it comes to life, does he aim so low? Why?

MASHA. Why?

VERSHININ. Why is he tired of his children, tired of his wife? And why are his wife and children tired of him?

MASHA. You're a little out of sorts today.

VERSHININ. Maybe I am. I haven't eaten a thing since morning. One of my daughters isn't feeling well, and whenever my daughters are ill I take it terribly to heart and agonize at the thought of having inflicted such a mother on them. Oh, if you could have seen her this morning. She's beneath contempt. We started quarreling at seven, and at nine I slammed the door and left.

(*Pause.*)

I never talk about these things. It's odd: you're the only one I complain to. (*He kisses her hand.*) Don't be angry. I have no one but you, nobody ...

(*Pause.*)

MASHA. What a din the stove's making. The chimney made the same howling noise just before Father died. The very same.

VERSHININ. Are you superstitious?

MASHA. Yes.

VERSHININ. That's odd. (*He kisses her hand.*) You're a wonderful, marvelous woman. Wonderful, marvelous. It's dark in here, but I can see your eyes sparkling.

MASHA (*moving to another chair*). There's more light over here.

VERSHININ. I love you, love you, love you ... I love your eyes, the way you move. I dream about it ... You wonderful, marvelous woman.

MASHA (*laughing softly*). For some reason it makes me laugh to hear you talk to me like that, though it scares me too. Don't do it again, please … (*In a low voice.*) No, go ahead. I don't care … (*She covers her face with her hands.*) I don't care. Somebody's coming. Change the subject …

(*Enter* IRINA *and* TUSENBACH *through the ballroom.*)

TUSENBACH. I have a triple-barreled name: Baron Tusenbach-Krone-Altschauer, but I'm Russian and Russian Orthodox just like you. There isn't much of the German left in me, except the patience and persistence I keep boring you with. Walking you home every evening …

IRINA. I'm so tired.

TUSENBACH. And I'll go on calling for you at the telegraph office and walking you home, night after night, for ten years or twenty, until you chase me away. (*Noticing* MASHA *and* VERSHININ. *Happily.*) Oh, it's you. Greetings.

IRINA. Home at last. (*To* MASHA.) Just now a woman came to the office to send her brother in Saratov a telegram saying that her son had died today, but she couldn't remember his address. So she addressed it Saratov, nothing else, no street. There she stood, crying, and I was rude to her and told her I was busy. It was all so stupid. Are the carnival people coming tonight?

MASHA. Yes.

IRINA (*sitting down in an armchair*). I need to rest. I'm tired.

TUSENBACH (*with a smile*). You look so tiny and forlorn when you come home from work.

(*Pause.*)

IRINA. I'm tired. I don't like working at the telegraph office. Not one bit.

MASHA. You've lost weight … (*She starts to whistle.*) You look younger too. Your face looks like a little boy's.

TUSENBACH. It's the hair.

IRINA. I've got to find another job. This one's not right for me. It has none of the things I'd hoped for, dreamt about. It's work with no poetry or ideas . . . (*There is a knock on the floor.*) That's the doctor knocking. (*To* TUSENBACH.) Knock back, Baron dear, will you? . . . I'm too tired . . . (TUSENBACH *knocks on the floor.*) He'll be right up. We've got to do something about Andrei and the doctor. Yesterday they went to the club and lost again. Andrei lost two hundred rubles, I hear.

MASHA (*apathetically*). What can we do about it now?

IRINA. He lost two weeks ago, he lost in December. I wish he'd lose it all. Then maybe we'd get out of this place. Dear God in Heaven, I dream about Moscow every night. I'm obsessed with it. (*She laughs.*) We're moving there in June. Let's see, that leaves February, March, April, May—nearly half a year.

MASHA. We'd better make sure Natasha doesn't find out how much he's lost.

IRINA. I don't think it makes any difference to her.

(*Enter* CHEBUTYKIN, *who has just awoken from an afternoon nap. He comes into the ballroom combing his beard, sits down at the table, and takes a newspaper out of his pocket.*)

MASHA. Here he is . . . Has he paid his rent?

IRINA (*laughing*). No, not a kopeck for eight months. Must have forgotten.

MASHA. Doesn't he look grand sitting there?

(*Everyone laughs. Pause.*)

IRINA. Why so quiet, Alexander Ignatyevich?

VERSHININ. I don't know. I wish I had some tea. My kingdom for a glass of tea. I haven't had a thing to eat since morning . . .

CHEBUTYKIN. Irina.

IRINA. What is it?

CHEBUTYKIN. Come over here, please. *Venez ici.* (IRINA *goes and sits at the table.*) I need you.

(IRINA *lays out cards for a game of patience.*)

VERSHININ. Well, if we're not going to have any tea, let's at least have some philosophizing.

TUSENBACH. Yes, let's. What about?

VERSHININ. What about? Let's dream a little . . . About life after we're gone, for instance. Two or three hundred years from now.

TUSENBACH. All right. After we're gone, people will fly in balloons, their jackets will be different, they'll discover a sixth sense, perhaps, and develop it, but life will remain the same: hard, full of mystery, and happy. Even a thousand years from now people will sigh "Life is hard," yet be as frightened of death and unwilling to die as we are.

VERSHININ (*after a moment's thought*). How shall I put it? To my mind, all things on earth must change gradually and are in fact changing before our very eyes. In two or three hundred years, in a thousand years perhaps—time is not of the essence—a new and happy life will dawn. We won't be part of that life, of course, but we're living for it now, working for it, yes, and suffering for it. We are its creators, and therein lies the sole reason for our existence and, if you will, our happiness.

(MASHA *laughs softly.*)

TUSENBACH. Why are you laughing?

MASHA. I don't know. I haven't stopped since morning.

VERSHININ. I had the same schooling as you. I didn't go on to the Academy. I do a lot of reading, but I'm no good at choosing books and may be reading all the wrong things. Still, the longer I live, the more I want to know. My hair's turning gray—I'll be an old man soon—and how little I know, how little I know! But what I feel I do know, really know, is what matters. Matters most. I'd give anything to make you see that happiness doesn't exist for us, that it will not, should not exist for us . . . All we can do is work and go on working. Happiness is for our remote descendants.

(*Pause.*)

If not for me, then for my children's children.

(FEDOTIK *and* RODET *appear in the ballroom. They sit down and sing softly, accompanying themselves on the guitar.*)

TUSENBACH. So you feel we shouldn't even dream of happiness. Well, what if I *am* happy.

VERSHININ. You're not.

TUSENBACH (*throwing up his hands and laughing*). We obviously don't understand each other. Let's see. How can I convince you? (MASHA *laughs softly.* TUSENBACH *shakes his finger at her.*) Go ahead and laugh. (*To* VERSHININ.) Not only two or three hundred years from now, a million years from now life will be the same as always. Life doesn't change; it remains constant, following its own laws, which are no concern of yours or which at least you'll never learn. Migratory birds—cranes, for instance—they fly on and on, and for all the great thoughts or small thoughts going round in their heads, they'll keep flying without knowing why or where. On and on they'll fly no matter what philosophers join their ranks. Let them philosophize all they please, so long as they go on flying . . .

MASHA. Still, it all has a meaning.

TUSENBACH. Meaning . . . Look, it's snowing. What's the meaning of that?

(*Pause.*)

MASHA. I think a person should have faith or be searching for it. Otherwise life is empty, empty . . . How can you live without knowing why cranes fly, why children are born, why there are stars in the sky . . . Either you know what you're living for, or everything's nonsense, nothing matters.

(*Pause.*)

VERSHININ. Still, I'm sorry I'm not young anymore.

MASHA. As Gogol said, "Life on earth's an awful bore, my friends."[11]

TUSENBACH. Well, I say, "Arguing with you is hard to take, my friends." I've had enough.

CHEBUTYKIN (*reading his paper*). Balzac was married in Berdichev.[12] (IRINA *starts singing softly.*) I'd better write that down. (*He writes it down.*) Balzac was married in Berdichev. (*He goes on reading.*)

IRINA (*lost in thought, laying out the cards for patience*). Balzac was married in Berdichev.

TUSENBACH. The die is cast. Did you know, Maria Sergeevna? I've handed in my resignation.

MASHA. So I hear. And I can't say I approve. I don't like civilians.

TUSENBACH. What's the difference. (*He stands.*) I'm so plain. What good am I as a soldier? And anyway, what's the difference . . . I'm going to work. For once in my life I'm going to put in an honest day's work, come home at night, drop into bed exhausted, and fall asleep instantly. (*He goes into the ballroom.*) Workmen sleep soundly, I'm sure.

FEDOTIK (*to* IRINA). I've just been to Moscow Street. I bought you some colored pencils at Pyzhikov's. And this penknife . . .

IRINA. You treat me like a little girl. I'm grown up, you know . . . (*She accepts the pencils and penknife. Gleefully.*) How lovely!

FEDOTIK. I bought a penknife for myself too . . . Here, have a look at it . . . One blade, another blade, a third: this one to clean out your ears, this one a tiny pair of scissors, this one to trim your nails . . .

RODET (*loudly*). Doctor, how old are you?

CHEBUTYKIN. Me? Thirty-two.

(*Laughter.*)

FEDOTIK. Here, let me show you another way to play . . . (*He lays out the cards.*)

(*The samovar is brought in, and* ANFISA *takes charge of it. Shortly thereafter* NATASHA *enters and starts fussing about at the table. Then* SOLYONY *enters, greets everyone, and takes a seat.*)

VERSHININ. Listen to that wind!

MASHA. Yes. I'm tired of winter. I've forgotten what summer is like.

IRINA. It's going to come out. We're going to Moscow.

FEDOTIK. No, it's not. See? The eight is on the two of spades. (*He laughs.*) So you're not going to Moscow.

CHEBUTYKIN (*reading his newspaper*). "Tsitsihar. There is a smallpox epidemic raging."

ANFISA (*going up to* MASHA). Time for your tea, Masha dear. (*To* VERSHININ.) You too, Your Excellency . . . Excuse me, sir. I've forgotten your name . . .

MASHA. Bring it out here, Nanny. I'm not going in there.

IRINA. Nanny!

ANFISA. Coming, coming.

NATASHA (*to* SOLYONY). Babies understand perfectly well. "Hello there, Bobik," I said to him. "Hello, sweetheart." And he looked up at me with a special kind of look. Don't think it's only the mother in me talking. Oh no! Believe me, he's an extraordinary child.

SOLYONY. If that child were mine, I'd fry him in oil and eat him. (*He goes into the drawing room with his tea and takes a seat in the corner.*)

NATASHA (*covering her face with her hands*). Oh you rude, uncultured man!

MASHA. Happy are they who take no note of summer or winter. If I were in Moscow, I wouldn't care about the weather.

VERSHININ. The other day I was reading the prison diary of a French cabinet member convicted for his part in the Panama Affair. He goes into raptures, ecstasies over the birds he sees through the prison window and never noticed when he was a cabinet member. Now that he's free, of course, he takes no more notice of them than before. The same thing will happen to you. You won't notice Moscow when you live there. We're not happy. We've never been happy. We only long to be.

TUSENBACH (*picking a box up from the table*). What happened to the chocolates?

IRINA. Solyony ate them.

TUSENBACH. All of them?

ANFISA (*serving tea*). A letter for you, sir.

VERSHININ. For me? (*He takes it.*) It's from my daughter. (*He reads it.*) Yes, of course . . . You'll excuse me, Maria Sergeevna. I'll slip away quietly. No tea for me. (*He stands, agitated.*) The same old story . . .

MASHA. What is it? Is it a secret?

VERSHININ (*softly*). My wife's taken poison again. I've got to go. I'll just slip out. It's all terribly unpleasant. (*He kisses* MASHA's *hand.*) Darling. You wonderful, marvelous woman . . . I'll just slip out here . . . (*He exits.*)

ANFISA. Now where's he off to? After I give him his tea . . . What a way to behave!

MASHA (*losing her temper*). Get away from here. You're always underfoot. Never give anyone a moment's peace. (*She goes over to the table with her cup.*) I'm sick and tired of you, you old busybody . . .

ANFISA. Now what's got you so upset? Darling!

ANDREI (*calling out from his room*). Anfisa!

ANFISA (*mimicking him*). Anfisa! Sitting there doing nothing . . . (*She exits.*)

MASHA (*at the table in the ballroom, angrily*). Give me a place to sit. (*She messes up the cards on the table.*) Taking up the whole table with your cards. Why don't you drink your tea?

IRINA. You *are* in a foul mood, Masha.

MASHA. Don't talk to me if I'm in such a foul mood. Don't bother me.

CHEBUTYKIN (*laughing*). Don't bother her. Don't bother her.

MASHA. Sixty years old and still a brat, blurting out every damned thing that comes into your head.

NATASHA (*sighing*). Really, Masha dear. Must you use that sort of language in public? A beauty like you would charm the best society—take my word for it—you'd be simply enchanting, if only you watched your language. *Je vous prie, pardonnez-moi, Marie, mais vous avez des manières un peu grossières.*[13]

TUSENBACH (*trying to control his laughter*). Give me some . . . Give me some . . . Isn't that cognac over there?

NATASHA. *Il paraît que mon Bobik déjà ne dort pas.* He's awake. He's not well today. Excuse me. I'd better go and look in on him . . .

IRINA. Where did Alexander Ignatyevich go?

MASHA. Home. It's his wife again.

TUSENBACH (*going over to* SOLYONY *with a small decanter of cognac*). You're always sitting by yourself, brooding over one thing or another. Come on, let's make peace. Let's have a drink together. (*They drink.*) Now I'll have to play the piano all night. The same old rubbish, I suppose . . . Well, why not.

SOLYONY. What do we need to make peace for? We haven't quarreled, you and I.

TUSENBACH. You keep making it seem as though something had gone wrong between us. You must admit you have a strange temperament.

SOLYONY (*reciting*). "I may be strange, but then who is not? ... Aleko, be not wroth!"[14]

TUSENBACH. What's Aleko got to do with it? ...

(*Pause.*)

SOLYONY. I'm all right when I'm alone with a person: I'm like everybody else. But in company I'm gloomy, shy, and ... I spout the worst rubbish. But even so I'm more honest and noble than many, a great many people ... And I can prove it.

TUSENBACH. You get on my nerves, picking on me when other people are around, but somehow I still like you. I think I'll get drunk tonight, damn it. Come on, let's have another.

SOLYONY. Fine. (*They drink.*) I've never had anything against you, Baron. It's just that I have the temperament of a Lermontov.[15] (*Softly.*) I even look a bit like Lermontov ... Or so I'm told ... (*He takes a bottle of scent from his pocket and sprinkles some over his hands.*)

TUSENBACH. I've handed in my resignation. I've had enough. I've been thinking it over for five years now, and I've finally made up my mind. I'm going to work.

SOLYONY (*reciting*). "Aleko, be not wroth . . . Forget, forget thy dreams ..."

(*While they are talking,* ANDREI *enters quietly with a book and sits down by a candle.*)

TUSENBACH. I'm going to work.

CHEBUTYKIN (*on his way into the drawing room with* IRINA). And the food they served was authentic Caucasian: an onion soup and chekhartma for the meat course.

SOLYONY. Cheremsha isn't meat; it's a plant in the onion family.

CHEBUTYKIN. Oh no, my dear man. Chekhartma is no onion; it's roast lamb.

SOLYONY. And I tell you cheremsha is an onion.

CHEBUTYKIN. Well, I tell you chekhartma is lamb.

SOLYONY. And I tell you cheremsha is an onion.

CHEBUTYKIN. Why am I arguing with you anyway? You've never even been to the Caucasus.[16] You've never eaten chekhartma.

SOLYONY. I've never eaten it because I detest it. It smells like garlic.

ANDREI (*beseechingly*). Enough, gentlemen! Please!

TUSENBACH. When are the carnival people due?

IRINA. They promised to come by nine. They should be here any minute.

TUSENBACH (*putting his arm around* ANDREI). "O my porch, my porch, my brand-new porch, my porch of maple fine . . ."[17]

ANDREI (*singing and dancing*). "O my brand-new porch, my grand new porch . . ."

CHEBUTYKIN (*dancing*). ". . . of latticework design!"

(*Laughter.*)

TUSENBACH (*hugging* ANDREI). Let's drink, damn it! Let's drink, drink to friendship everlasting! You and me—we'll go to Moscow together, to the university.

SOLYONY. Which one? Moscow has two universities.

ANDREI. Moscow has one university.

SOLYONY. It has two, I tell you.

ANDREI. Why not three while you're at it? The more the merrier.

SOLYONY. Moscow has two universities.

(*Murmurs of protest, hushing noises.*)

Moscow has two universities: the old and the new. But if you don't wish to listen to me, if what I say upsets you, I can stop talking altogether. I can leave the room, for that matter . . . (*He exits through one of the doors.*)

TUSENBACH. Bravo! Bravo! (*He laughs.*) Ready, everybody? I'm about to begin. He's a funny fellow, that Solyony. (*He sits at the piano and plays a waltz.*)

MASHA (*waltzing by herself*). The baron's drunk, the baron's drunk, the baron's drunk.

NATASHA (*entering, to* CHEBUTYKIN). Ivan Romanovich! (*She says something to* CHEBUTYKIN, *then exits quietly.* CHEBUTYKIN *touches* TUSENBACH *on the shoulder and whispers something to him.*)

IRINA. What is it?

CHEBUTYKIN. It's time we were off. Good night.

TUSENBACH. Good night. Time to go.

IRINA. But why? ... What about the carnival people? ...

ANDREI (*embarrassed*). They won't be coming. You see, Irina, Natasha says Bobik's not feeling very well, so it ... Actually, I don't know and couldn't care less.

IRINA (*shrugging her shoulders*). Bobik isn't well.

MASHA. Well, I'm not going to let it bother me. We'll go somewhere else if they kick us out. (*To* IRINA.) It's not Bobik who's sick; it's Natasha ... And here. (*She taps her forehead.*) The small-town nobody.

(ANDREI *exits to his room, followed by* CHEBUTYKIN. *People in the ballroom start taking leave of one another.*)

FEDOTIK. What a shame. Here I was, looking forward to a nice party. Of course if the baby's not well ... I'll bring him some toys tomorrow ...

RODET (*loudly*). I specially took a nap this afternoon, thought I'd be dancing all night. And it's only nine.

MASHA. Let's go outside. We can talk things over there and decide what to do.

(*They say,* "Good-bye. Good night." TUSENBACH *laughs gaily. They exit.* ANFISA *and a maid clear the table and put out the lights. A nursemaid is singing offstage.* ANDREI, *wearing a coat and hat, and* CHEBUTYKIN *enter quietly.*)

CHEBUTYKIN. I never found time to get married. My life has flashed by like lightning. Besides, I was madly in love with your mother, and she was married ...

ANDREI. There's no reason to get married. None. It's a bore.

CHEBUTYKIN. Maybe so. But what about loneliness? You can philosophize all you like, my boy, but loneliness is a terrible thing ...

Though when all is said and done . . . what difference does it make?

ANDREI. Come on. Let's go.

CHEBUTYKIN. What's the rush. We've got plenty of time.

ANDREI. I'm afraid Natasha will stop me.

CHEBUTYKIN. Oh.

ANDREI. I won't gamble tonight. I'll just sit and watch. I'm not feeling too well . . . I've been short of breath lately. What should I do for it, Ivan Romanovich?

CHEBUTYKIN. Don't ask me. I don't remember, my boy. I don't know . . .

ANDREI. Let's go out through the kitchen.

(*They exit. A bell rings, then rings again. Voices and laughter come from offstage.*)

IRINA (*entering*). What's that?

ANFISA (*in a whisper*). The carnival people.

(*The bell rings.*)

IRINA. Tell them there's no one at home, Nanny. Tell them we're sorry.

(*Exit* ANFISA. IRINA *walks back and forth, deep in thought. She is upset. Enter* SOLYONY.)

SOLYONY (*puzzled*). There's nobody here . . . Where have they gone?

IRINA. Home.

SOLYONY. That's odd. Are you alone?

IRINA. Yes.

(*Pause.*)

Good night.

SOLYONY. I lost control of myself just now. It was tactless of me. But you're not like the others. You're high-minded and pure. You see the truth . . . You're the only one who can understand me. I love you. I love you deeply, boundlessly . . .

IRINA. Please go. Good night.

SOLYONY. I can't live without you. (*He follows her.*) O my joy! (*In tears.*)
My happiness! What marvelous, glorious, breathtaking eyes you
have. Never have I seen such eyes in a woman ...

IRINA. Stop it, Captain.

SOLYONY. I've never talked to you of love before. It's like leaving earth
for another planet. (*He rubs his forehead.*) Well, what difference does
it make. I can't make you love me, of course ... But I will have no
successful rivals ... None ... I swear to you by everything that's
holy. I will kill all rivals ... Oh, how wonderful you are!

(*Enter* NATASHA *carrying a candle.*)

NATASHA (*peering in at one door, then another, and walking past the door
that leads to* ANDREI's *study*). Andrei's in there reading. Well, let
him ... Oh, excuse me, Captain. I didn't realize you were here.
I'm not dressed ...

SOLYONY. What difference does it make. Good-bye. (*He exits.*)

NATASHA. You're tired, darling, you poor little girl. (*She kisses*
IRINA.) You should go to bed earlier.

IRINA. Is Bobik asleep?

NATASHA. Yes, but not sound asleep. Which reminds me, Irina dear.
I've been meaning to talk to you, but either you've been out
or I've been busy ... Bobik's nursery seems awfully cold and
damp to me. Your room would be just right for him. Irina precious, move in with Olga for a while, will you?

IRINA (*not understanding*). Where?

(*The sound of sleigh bells comes from offstage as a troika drives up to the
house.*)

NATASHA. You and Olga will share a room for the time being, and
your room will go to Bobik. He's such a sweet little thing. Today
I said to him, "Bobik," I said, "you're mine, all mine." And he
looked straight up at me with those adorable little eyes of his.
(*The doorbell rings.*) That must be Olga. How late she is. (*The maid
goes up to* NATASHA *and whispers something in her ear.*) Protopopov?
What a funny man. That's Protopopov outside inviting me for a
ride in his troika. (*She laughs.*) Aren't men funny? ... (*The doorbell*

rings.) There's somebody else at the door. Why not take a fifteen-minute spin? . . . (*To the maid.*) Tell him I'll be there in a minute. (*The doorbell rings.*) The doorbell's ringing . . . It must be Olga . . . (*She exits.*)

(*The maid runs out.* IRINA *sits deep in thought. Enter* KULYGIN *and* OLGA, *followed by* VERSHININ.)

KULYGIN. How do you like that! And they said there'd be a party.

VERSHININ. That's odd. I didn't leave more than a half hour ago. They were expecting the carnival people.

IRINA. They've all gone.

KULYGIN. Masha too? Where did she go? And why is Protopopov waiting down there in his troika? Who's he waiting for?

IRINA. Don't ask questions . . . I'm tired.

KULYGIN. Naughty, naughty.

OLGA. The meeting lasted all this time. I'm exhausted. The head-mistress is ill, and I'm taking her place. Oh, my head, my head, my aching head . . . (*She sits down.*) Andrei lost two hundred rubles at cards yesterday . . . The whole town's talking about it.

KULYGIN. Yes. The meeting wore me out too. (*He sits down.*)

VERSHININ. My wife just wanted to give me another scare. She almost did herself in this time, but everything's under control now, thank God, and I can relax . . . So we have to leave. Well then, good-bye, everybody. Let's go out somewhere, Fyodor Ilyich. I can't stay at home tonight, I just can't . . . What do you say?

KULYGIN. I'm too tired. I couldn't. (*He stands.*) I'm much too tired. Has my wife gone home?

IRINA. I think so.

KULYGIN (*kissing* IRINA's *hand*). Good-bye. I'm going to rest all day tomorrow and the day after. Good night. (*He starts to go.*) I'd have liked some tea. I was looking forward to an evening in pleasant company, and—*O fallacem hominum spem!*[18] Accusative of exclamation . . .

VERSHININ. I'll have to go alone then. (*He exits with* KULYGIN, *whistling.*)

OLGA. Oh, my head, my aching head . . . Andrei losing at cards . . .

The whole town talking... I'm going to lie down. (*She starts to go.*) Tomorrow I'm free... Dear God, won't that be nice! Tomorrow and the day after... Oh, my head, my aching head... (*She exits.*)

IRINA (*alone*). They've all gone. There's no one left.

(*An accordion is playing outside. The nursemaid is singing a song.*)

NATASHA (*crossing the ballroom in a fur coat and cap, followed by the maid*). I'll be back in half an hour. I'm just off for a spin.

IRINA (*alone, longingly*). To Moscow. Moscow. Moscow.

CURTAIN

ACT THREE

The bedroom shared by OLGA *and* IRINA. *The beds, left and right, are behind screens. It is past two in the morning. A fire alarm bell is ringing offstage: a fire has been raging for some time. Clearly no one in the house has gone to bed yet.* MASHA, *as usual in black, is lying on the sofa. Enter* OLGA *and* ANFISA.

ANFISA. They're down there now, under the stairs . . . "Come on up," I tell them. "You can't just sit there." They're in tears. "But we don't know where Papa is," they say. "He may have burned to death, God forbid." The idea! . . . There's some other people outside. They're half naked too.

OLGA (*taking dresses out of the wardrobe*). Here, take this nice gray one . . . And this one . . . The blouse as well . . . And this skirt, Nanny . . . Dear God, what a thing to happen! Kirsanov Lane has burnt to the ground, apparently . . . Take this . . . And this . . . (*She throws the clothes into* ANFISA's *arms.*) The poor Vershinins had quite a scare . . . Their house nearly caught fire. They'd better stay with us tonight . . . We can't send them home . . . Poor Fedotik's lost everything to the fire. He hasn't a stick left . . .

ANFISA. Would you call Ferapont, Olga dear? I can't carry all this myself . . .

OLGA (*ringing*). Nobody answers . . . (*Through the door.*) Come in, anyone who's out there! (*Through the open door comes the glare of a window red from the fire. The sound of the fire brigade riding by comes from offstage.*) How awful it all is, and how sick of it I am! (*Enter* FERAPONT.) Here, take these downstairs . . . You'll find the Kolotilin girls under the staircase . . . Give them this . . . and this . . .

FERAPONT. Yes, Miss. Back in 1812 Moscow went up in flames too. Good God in Heaven, those Frenchies were surprised!

OLGA. Go on now, get along.

FERAPONT. Yes, Miss. (*Exit* FERAPONT.)

OLGA. Give it all away, Anfisa dear. We don't need anything. Give it all away . . . I'm so tired I can hardly stand . . . Don't let the Vershinins leave . . . The girls can sleep in the drawing room, and we'll send the lieutenant colonel downstairs to the baron . . . Fedotik can go in with the baron too, or else downstairs in the ballroom . . . Wouldn't you know it! The doctor's drunk, dead drunk. We can't move anybody in with him. Vershinin's wife will have to stay in the drawing room too.

ANFISA (*in a weary voice*). Don't send me away, Olga dearest. Please don't.

OLGA. What a silly thing to say, Nanny. Nobody's sending you away.

ANFISA (*laying her head on* OLGA*'s breast*). Olga darling, precious Olga. I do my work. I work hard . . . When I'm too weak to work, they'll say, "Get out!" But where can I go? Where can I go? I'm eighty years old . . . eighty-one . . .

OLGA. Sit down a while, Nanny . . . You're all tired out, poor thing . . . (*She helps her to sit down.*) Rest a while, Nanny dearest. You look so pale.

NATASHA (*entering*). There's talk in town of starting a relief committee for the victims. And why not? A splendid idea. The rich have an obligation to help the poor. Bobik and baby Sophie are asleep, sound asleep, as if nothing had happened. The house is full of people. You can't take a step without bumping into somebody. And influenza's going round. I'm afraid the children will catch it.

OLGA (*not listening to her*). You can't see the fire from this room. It's quiet here . . .

NATASHA. Yes . . . I must look a mess. (*In front of a mirror.*) People say I've put on weight . . . It's not true. Not in the least. Oh, Masha's asleep. Worn out, poor thing . . . (*To* ANFISA, *coldly.*) How dare you sit in my presence! Get up! Leave at once! (*Exit* ANFISA.)

(*Pause.*)

Why you keep that old woman I'll never understand.

OLGA (*taken aback*). I'm sorry, I don't see . . .

NATASHA. There's no need for her here. She's a peasant. She belongs in the country. And look how you spoil her! I like order in a house. A house should have no unnecessary servants. (*She strokes her cheek.*) You're tired, poor thing. Our headmistress is tired. I'll be scared of you when baby Sophie grows up and starts going to your school.

OLGA. I'm not going to be headmistress.

NATASHA. You're everybody's choice. It's all settled.

OLGA. I'll turn it down. I can't . . . I haven't the strength . . . (*She takes a drink of water.*) You were awfully rude to Nanny just now . . . I'm sorry, I'm in no condition to tolerate that kind of thing. I nearly fainted . . .

NATASHA (*disturbed*). Forgive me, Olga, forgive me. (*She kisses her.*)

OLGA. Anything the least bit coarse, a brusque remark upsets me . . .

NATASHA. I tend to talk too much, true, but you must agree, Olga darling, she could live in the country.

OLGA. She's been with us for thirty years.

NATASHA. But don't you see? She can't do any work. Either I don't understand you or you refuse to understand me. She's too old to work. All she does is sleep or sit.

OLGA. Well, let her.

NATASHA (*astonished*). Let her? She's a servant, isn't she? (*Through tears.*) I just can't understand you, Olga. I've got a wet nurse, a nanny; we've got a maid, a cook . . . What do we need that old woman for? Tell me.

(*The fire alarm bell rings offstage.*)

OLGA. I've aged ten years tonight.

NATASHA. It's time we set things straight, Olga, once and for all. Your place is at school, mine in the home. You teach; I run the household. And when I say something about the servants, I know what I'm talking about. *I know what I'm talking about* . . . Now, I want that old hag, that old thief, out of here by tomorrow!... (*She stamps her feet.*) The witch!... How dare you upset me like this! How dare you! (*She regains her self-control.*) Really, if you don't move downstairs, we'll never stop quarreling. It's awful.

KULYGIN (*entering*). Where's Masha? We should be getting home. They say the fire's dying down. (*He stretches.*) Only one street has actually burnt to the ground. The wind was so strong that at first the whole town seemed on fire. (*He sits.*) I'm exhausted. Olga dear... I often think that if it hadn't been for Masha I'd have married you. You're such a fine person... I'm completely worn out. (*He pricks up his ears.*)

OLGA. What is it?

KULYGIN. Wouldn't you know the doctor would pick tonight for a binge. He's roaring drunk. (*He stands.*) That must be him now... Do you hear? Yes, here he comes... (*He laughs.*) What a character... I think I'll hide... (*He goes and stands in the corner next to the wardrobe.*) The rascal!

OLGA. Two years without a drop, and suddenly he's drunk... (*She walks to the back of the room with* NATASHA.)

(*Enter* CHEBUTYKIN. *He crosses the room without staggering, as if sober. He stops, looks around, then goes up to the washstand and starts washing his hands.*)

CHEBUTYKIN (*morose*). Damn them all . . . Damn them one and all . . . Thinking I'm a doctor and can cure all ills. I don't know a thing. Forgotten everything I knew. Don't remember a damned thing, not a thing. (*Exit* OLGA *and* NATASHA *without his noticing.*) Damn them. Last Wednesday a village woman I was treating upped and died on me, and it was my fault she died. Yes . . . Twenty-five years ago I knew a thing or two, but I can't remember any of it. Not a thing... My head is empty, my heart is cold. Maybe I'm not even human. Maybe I only pretend to have arms and legs and a head. Maybe I don't exist at all and only imagine that I walk, eat, and sleep. (*He begins to cry.*) If only I could cease to exist. (*He stops crying and continues morosely.*) Damn it all . . . A couple of days ago I heard them going on at the club about

Shakespeare, Voltaire . . . I've never read a word of either, no, but I did my best to look as if I had. And so did the others. Isn't that low? Isn't it cheap? And then that woman I killed on Wednesday came back to me . . . It all came back, and I felt twisted, rotten, foul all over . . . So I went and had a few snorts . . .

(*Enter* IRINA, VERSHININ, *and* TUSENBACH. TUSENBACH *is wearing fashionable new civilian clothes.*)

IRINA. Let's sit here a while. No one will come in.

VERSHININ. If it hadn't been for the soldiers, the whole town would have burnt down. They're good men. (*He rubs his hands together with pleasure.*) Salt of the earth. Good men.

KULYGIN (*going up to them*). What's the time, gentlemen?

TUSENBACH. Well after three. It's getting light.

IRINA. They're all in the ballroom. Nobody's leaving. Your Solyony's there too . . . (*To* CHEBUTYKIN.) You should go to bed, Doctor.

CHEBUTYKIN. I'm all right, thank you. (*He combs his beard.*)

KULYGIN (*laughing*). Feeling no pain, eh, Doctor? (*He gives him a slap on the shoulder.*) Good for you. *In vino veritas*,[19] the ancients used to say.

TUSENBACH. People have been asking me to organize a benefit concert for the fire victims.

IRINA. But who could we get to . . .

TUSENBACH. *We* could *ourselves* if we wanted to. Maria Sergeevna, for instance. She's an excellent pianist.

KULYGIN. An excellent pianist.

IRINA. She's forgotten her music. She hasn't played a note for three years. Or is it four?

TUSENBACH. Nobody in this town understands music. Not a soul. Except for me, and I give you my word: Maria Sergeevna is a superb pianist. Extremely gifted.

KULYGIN. Yes, right, Baron. I love her very much, my Masha. A fine woman she is.

TUSENBACH. It must be awful to play so exquisitely, knowing all the while that nobody but nobody understands.

KULYGIN (*sighing*). Yes . . . But is it proper for her to take part in a public concert?

(*Pause.*)

I don't know about these things. Maybe there's nothing wrong with it. No one can deny that our headmaster's a fine man, a very fine man—and most intelligent. But his views do tend towards the . . . Of course it doesn't concern him directly. Still I'd better talk it over with him first.

(CHEBUTYKIN *picks up a porcelain clock and examines it.*)

VERSHININ. I got filthy at the fire. What a sight I am.

(*Pause.*)

I heard a rumor yesterday that they were transferring the brigade somewhere a long way off. Some say Poland, others Siberia.

TUSENBACH. I've heard the same thing. The town will be completely deserted.

IRINA. We're leaving too.

CHEBUTYKIN (*dropping the clock, which breaks*). Smashed to smithereens!

(*Pause. Everyone is upset and embarrassed.*)

KULYGIN (*picking up the pieces*). Imagine breaking such a valuable piece. Ivan Romanovich, Ivan Romanovich. Zero minus for conduct.

IRINA. That was Mother's clock!

CHEBUTYKIN. Maybe . . . Well, what if it was? But maybe I didn't break it; maybe it only seems I did. Maybe it only seems we exist when we don't exist at all. What do I know? What does anybody know? (*At the door.*) What are you all staring at? Natasha's having an affair with Protopopov, and you don't even notice. You sit there with your eyes shut while Natasha has her fling with Protopopov . . . (*He sings.*) "Please eat this date at my behest . . ."[20]

VERSHININ. Yes . . . (*He laughs.*) How strange it all is, really.

(*Pause.*)

The fire breaks out. I run straight home, and what do I see? The house is untouched, out of danger, but my two little girls are standing in the doorway in their underwear, their mother nowhere to be found. There are people rushing by, horses and dogs running wild, and the girls' faces are the picture of anguish, terror, pleading, and heaven knows what else. It broke my heart to look at them. Good Lord, I thought, imagine the suffering their long lives hold in store for them. I snatched them up, and as I ran I couldn't stop thinking of the suffering that lay ahead of them.

(*A fire alarm bell rings. Pause.*)

When I got here, I found their mother screaming, furious. (*Enter* MASHA *with a pillow. She sits on the sofa.*) And while my little girls stood there in the doorway barefoot, in their underclothes—the street red with flames, the racket appalling—I thought to myself, "This is how it must have been many years ago when an enemy pounced upon a town, looting and setting fire to it." Though actually, what a difference there is between the way things are and the way they used to be. And it won't be long now—another two or three hundred years—before people look back on our present way of life with the same horror and contempt, and the way we do things today will seem clumsy and stodgy and oh, so disagreeable and strange. My, what a life that's bound to be, what a life. (*He laughs.*) Sorry. There I go—philosophizing again. But please don't stop me, friends. I can't tell you how much I need to philosophize. I'm in just the mood for it.

(*Pause.*)

Looks like they're all asleep. Anyway, as I was saying... What a life it will be. Try and picture it... The town may have only three of your kind at present, but in generations to come it will gain more—more and more—until there comes a time when everything changes and people act like you, live like you. And then even you will grow obsolete. People better than you will be born... (*He laughs.*) I'm in an odd mood today. I want so much to live... (*He sings.*)

> True love knows neither age nor station.
> Its pangs are pure invigoration . . .[21]

(*He laughs.*)

MASHA. Dum-de-dum . . .

VERSHININ. Dum-dum . . .

MASHA. Trum-ta-ta?

VERSHININ. Tra-la-la. (*He laughs.*)

FEDOTIK (*dancing as he enters*). Ashes, ashes! Everything's in ashes! (*He laughs.*)

IRINA. What are you laughing about? Did the fire get it all?

FEDOTIK. Absolutely everything. There's not a stick left. The guitar—burnt, the camera—burnt, all my letters . . . Everything down to the little notebook I'd been meaning to give you.

(*Enter* SOLYONY.)

IRINA. No, please go away, Captain. You can't come in.

SOLYONY. Tell me, why may the baron stay and not I?

VERSHININ. Actually, it's time we were all on our way. What's the fire like?

SOLYONY. It's dying down, they say. No, I find it highly peculiar that the baron may stay and not I. (*He takes out his bottle of scent and sprinkles it over himself.*)

VERSHININ. Dum-de-dum?

MASHA. Dum-dum.

VERSHININ (*laughing, to* SOLYONY). Let's go into the ballroom.

SOLYONY. Very well, but I won't forget this.

> Our moral might be made a bit more clear,
> But that would only tease the geese, I fear.[22]

(*He looks over at* TUSENBACH.) Here chicky, chicky, chicky . . . (*He exits with* VERSHININ *and* FEDOTIK.)

IRINA. The smoke Solyony leaves behind . . . (*Bewildered.*) The baron's asleep. Baron! Baron!

TUSENBACH (*waking up*). So tired . . . Brickyard . . . No, I'm not delirious. I really am leaving to start work at a brickyard soon . . . It's all settled. (*To* IRINA, *tenderly.*) You're so pale and beautiful and fascinating . . . Your pallor brightens the darkness like a ray of light . . . You look sad, you look dissatisfied with your life here . . . Come away with me. Come away with me and we'll work together . . .

MASHA. Please leave, Baron.

TUSENBACH (*laughing*). You're here? I didn't see you. (*He kisses* IRINA's *hand.*) Good-bye. I'm going . . . Looking at you now, I can't help thinking how once a long time ago—it was your name day—you talked about the joys of work, all bright and cheerful . . . The happy life I dreamt of then. Where has it gone? (*He kisses her hand.*) You've got tears in your eyes. Go to bed. It's getting light . . . It's nearly morning. If only I had the chance to give my life for you.

MASHA. Do leave, Baron. Really now . . .

TUSENBACH. I'm going . . . (*He exits.*)

MASHA (*lying down*). Fyodor, are you asleep?

KULYGIN. What?

MASHA. Why don't you go home?

KULYGIN. Darling Masha, precious Masha . . .

IRINA. She's exhausted. Let her rest.

KULYGIN. I'll be off in a minute . . . What a fine, wonderful wife I have . . . And oh, how I love you, you and you alone . . .

MASHA (*angrily*). Amo, amas, amat; amamus, amatis, amant.[23]

KULYGIN (*laughing*). No, really, she's amazing. Here I've been married to you for seven years, and it seems like only yesterday. Honestly it does. No, really, you're an amazing woman. I'm so pleased, pleased, pleased.

MASHA. I'm so bored, bored, bored . . . (*She sits up.*) And there's something I can't get out of my mind . . . Something disgraceful. It's like a nail in my head. I can't keep it to myself any longer. It's Andrei . . . He's mortgaged the house to the bank, and Natasha's grabbed all the money. The house doesn't belong to him alone; it belongs to the four of us! He must know that if he has any decency left in him.

KULYGIN. Why bring it up, Masha? Why even mention it? So he's in debt up to his ears. That's his business.

MASHA. Still, it's disgraceful. (*She lies down.*)

KULYGIN. You and I aren't poor. I work. I have my position at the school and give private lessons too . . . I'm an honest man, a simple man . . . *Omnia mea mecum porto*, as the saying goes.[24]

MASHA. I don't need anything for myself. It's the injustice of it all that infuriates me.

(*Pause.*)

Why don't you go home, Fyodor?

KULYGIN (*kissing her*). You're tired. Rest here for half an hour or so. I'll wait for you downstairs. Get some sleep now . . . (*He starts to leave.*) I'm so pleased, pleased, pleased. (*He exits.*)

IRINA. You're right. That woman has taken our Andrei and turned him into a shallow, petty old fogy. He had hopes of being a professor once, and yesterday I heard him boasting about joining the District Council. Andrei a member, Protopopov the chairman . . . The whole town's talking about it, laughing about it. He's the only one who refuses to see or hear what's going on . . . Just now, when everyone ran off to the fire, he sat alone in his room, not taking the slightest notice, playing away on his violin. (*Upset.*) It's so awful, awful, awful. (*She starts crying.*) I can't stand it! . . . I can't take it anymore! . . . I can't . . . I can't . . .

(*Enter* OLGA. *She straightens up her bedside table.*)

IRINA (*sobbing*). Throw me out, throw me out! I can't stand it anymore!

OLGA (*frightened*). What's the matter, Irina? What's wrong?

IRINA (*sobbing*). Where has it all gone to? Where? Where? O my God, my God. I've forgotten everything, everything. Everything's jumbled up inside my head . . . I can't remember how to say "window" in Italian . . . or . . . "ceiling." I'm forgetting everything. I forget something every day. And life moves on and will never come back, never. We'll never get to Moscow . . . I just know we won't . . .

OLGA. Darling . . . Darling . . .

IRINA (*trying to control herself*). I'm so miserable . . . I can't work, I

won't work. I've had enough, enough! First the Telegraph Office,
now the Town Council. I hate and despise everything they give
me to do . . . I'll be twenty-four soon. I've been working forever.
My brain has dried up. I'm getting thinner, plainer, older by the
day, with nothing, nothing to show for it. As time goes by, I find
myself pulling away from what makes life beautiful and real,
pulling farther and farther away, into an abyss. I'm desperate.
How can I still be alive? Why haven't I killed myself? . . .

OLGA. Don't cry, little one, don't cry . . . It makes me suffer so.

IRINA. I'm not crying, I'm not crying . . . See? I've stopped. I'm not
crying anymore . . . I've stopped . . . I've stopped.

OLGA. Let me give you a piece of advice, Irina dear. As a sister and
a friend. Marry the baron. (IRINA *cries softly.*) You respect him,
after all. You think highly of him . . . He's not handsome, it's true,
but he's decent and pure . . . People don't marry for love, you
know; they marry out of duty. That's how I see it anyway, and I'd
marry without love. I'd marry anyone who asked me so long as
he was decent. I'd even marry an old man.

IRINA. I'd been waiting for us to move to Moscow, thinking I'd meet
my true love there. I dreamt about him, loved him . . . But now I
see it's just nonsense, pure nonsense.

OLGA (*embracing* IRINA). I understand, Irina. Dear, wonderful Irina.
When the baron left the military and came to see us in civilian
clothes, he looked so plain it brought tears to my eyes . . . He
asked me what I was crying for and I couldn't tell him of course,
but it would make me happy if the good Lord meant him to
marry you. That's different, you know, very different.

(NATASHA, *carrying a candle, crosses the stage in silence from a door
stage right to a door stage left.*)

MASHA (*sitting up*). The way she walks you'd think she was the one
who started the fire.

OLGA. You're so silly, Masha. You're the silliest one in the family.
Forgive me for saying so.

(*Pause.*)

MASHA. Olga, Irina—I've a confession to make. I've got to get it off my chest, and once I do I'll never tell anyone else, ever ... But let me tell you now. (*Softly.*) It's a secret, but I want you both to know ... I can't keep it to myself anymore ...

(*Pause.*)

I love him ... I love him ... I'm in love with that man ... The man you saw just now ... Oh, what's the use ... What I mean is, I'm in love with Vershinin.

OLGA (*going behind her screen*). Don't say it. I refuse to hear it.

MASHA. But what can I do? (*She clutches her head.*) At first I found him strange, then I felt sorry for him ... Then I fell in love ... in love with his voice, his words, his misfortunes, his two little girls ...

OLGA (*behind the screen*). I can't hear a word you're saying. I can't hear any of the silly things you're saying.

MASHA. You're the silly one, Olga. If I'm in love, it's my fate, that's all. The way it had to be ... He loves me too ... It's all so terrifying, isn't it? But is it wrong? (*She takes* IRINA's *hand and draws her to herself.*) Dear Irina ... How are we going to live out our lives? What will become of us? In a novel it all seems so obvious and trite. Then you fall in love yourself, and you realize nobody knows a thing, we each have to make our own decisions. Dear sisters, sweet sisters ... Now that I've made my confession, I won't say another word ... I'll be like the madman in Gogol's story ... Silence ... Silence ...[25]

(*Enter* ANDREI *followed by* FERAPONT.)

ANDREI (*angry*). What do you want? I don't understand.

FERAPONT (*in the doorway, impatient*). But I've told you ten times, sir.

ANDREI. In the first place, I am not "sir"; I am Your Excellency.

FERAPONT. The firemen, Your Excellency, they want permission to go through the garden on their way to the river. Otherwise they've got to take the long way round, and it's very hard on them.

ANDREI. All right. Tell them it's all right. (*Exit* FERAPONT.) They're driving me crazy. Where's Olga? (OLGA *comes out from behind the screen.*) I've been looking for you. Give me the key to the strong-box. I've lost mine. It's one of the small ones. (OLGA *gives him the key without a word.* IRINA *goes behind her screen.*)

(*Pause.*)

Quite a fire, isn't it? Starting to die down though. That Ferapont made me lose my temper, damn it. What a stupid thing to say . . . Your Excellency . . .

(*Pause.*)

Why don't you say something, Olga?

(*Pause.*)

Isn't it time you stopped being so silly, sulking and pouting for no reason at all? Masha, you're here. Irina's here. Fine. Let's bring it out into the open, once and for all. What have you got against me? Tell me.

OLGA. Not now, Andrei. We can talk it over tomorrow. (*Upset.*) What a dreadful night.

ANDREI (*very embarrassed*). Don't get upset now. I'm asking you perfectly calmly what it is you have against me, and I want a straight answer.

VERSHININ (*calling from offstage*). Dum-de-dum.

MASHA (*standing, in a loud voice*). Dum-dum. (*To* OLGA.) Good night, Olga. God bless you. (*She goes behind the screen and kisses* IRINA.) Sleep well. Good night, Andrei. Leave them alone now. They're exhausted . . . You can talk it over tomorrow . . . (*She exits.*)

OLGA. Yes, Andrei. Let's put it off till tomorrow . . . (*She goes behind her screen.*) It's time for bed.

ANDREI. Let me have my say and I'll go . . . First, you've all got something against Natasha. I've felt it from the day we were married. Natasha is a fine, upstanding person, sincere and noble. In my opinion. I love my wife and respect her—respect her, understand?—and I demand that others should do the same. I repeat, she is upstanding and noble, and all your objections to her, I'm sorry, they're simply infantile.

(Pause.)

Second, you seem to be annoyed with me for not being a professor or writing scholarly articles. But I'm a civil servant, a member of the District Council, and I consider my work there every bit as holy and sublime as scholarship. I'm a member of the District Council and, for your information, proud of it . . .

(Pause.)

Third . . . There's something else . . . I've mortgaged the house without your permission . . . It was wrong, I admit it, and I apologize . . . I did it to pay off my debts . . . thirty-five thousand rubles. I've stopped gambling. I gave it up long ago. The most I can say in my defense is that each of you girls receives an income from Father's pension, while I've had no . . . earnings, so to speak . . .

(Pause.)

KULYGIN (*at the door*). Isn't Masha here? (*Troubled.*) Where can she be? That's odd . . . (*He exits.*)

ANDREI. They're not listening. Natasha is a fine, upstanding woman. (*He paces in silence, then stops.*) When I married her, I thought we'd be happy . . . All of us . . . But good Lord . . . (*He starts weeping.*) Dear sisters, dearest sisters, don't believe me, don't believe me . . . (*He exits.*)

KULYGIN (*at the door, troubled*). Where is Masha? Isn't she here? This is most peculiar. (*He exits.*)

(The fire alarm bell rings. The stage is empty.)

IRINA (*behind the screen*). Olya, who's that knocking on the floor?

OLGA. The doctor. He's drunk.

IRINA. What an exhausting night this has been.

(Pause.)

Olga! (*She looks out from behind the screen.*) Have you heard? They're taking the brigade from us and sending it far away.

OLGA. It's only a rumor.

IRINA. We'll be left here by ourselves . . . Olya!

OLGA. What is it?

IRINA. Olya dear. I respect the baron. I admire him. He's a fine man. I'll marry him. I consent. Only let's go to Moscow. Please let's go! There's nothing in the world like Moscow. Let's go, Olya! Do let's go.

CURTAIN

ACT FOUR

The old garden of the Prozorovs' house. A long fir-lined path with a view of the river at the other end. Woods along the far bank. To the right a terrace and a table strewn with bottles and glasses. People have obviously been drinking champagne. It is noon. Now and then someone cuts through the garden from the street on his way to the river. Five or six soldiers walk briskly past. CHEBUTYKIN, *in a genial mood that remains with him throughout the act, is seated in an armchair in the garden, waiting to be called. He is wearing his army cap and holding a walking stick.* IRINA, KULYGIN—*who has a medal hanging around his neck and no longer wears a mustache—and* TUSENBACH *are standing on the terrace bidding farewell to* FEDOTIK *and* RODET, *who are coming down the steps. Both are in full uniform.*

TUSENBACH (*exchanging kisses with* FEDOTIK). You're a fine man. We've had some good times together. (*He exchanges kisses with* RODET.) Once more . . . A last farewell, my boy.

IRINA. But we'll be seeing you again.

FEDOTIK. No, never. We'll never meet again.

KULYGIN. Who can tell? (*He wipes his eyes and smiles.*) There, I've stopped crying.

IRINA. We'll meet again sometime.

FEDOTIK. In ten years, fifteen? By then we'll hardly recognize each other, at most exchange a cool hello . . . (*He takes a picture.*) Hold it . . . One last time.

RODET (*hugging* TUSENBACH). We'll never meet again. (*He kisses* IRINA*'s hand.*) Thank you for everything, everything.

FEDOTIK (*annoyed*). Hold still!

TUSENBACH. We'll meet again, God willing. Don't forget to write. Be sure to write.

RODET (*looking round the garden*). Good-bye, trees. (*He shouts.*) Yoo-hoo!

(*Pause.*)

Good-bye, echo.

KULYGIN. Better watch out or you'll get married there in Poland . . .
   And your Polish wife will throw her arms around you and call
   you "*kochane*"![126] (*He laughs.*)

FEDOTIK (*glancing at his watch*). We've got less than an hour left.
   Solyony's the only one from the battery taking the barge; the rest
   of us are going with the troops. A division of three batteries
   leaves today; another three go tomorrow. And then the town will
   settle down once more.

TUSENBACH. To unspeakable boredom.

RODET. Where's Masha?

KULYGIN. In the garden.

FEDOTIK. Let's go and say good-bye to her.

RODET. Good-bye. We'd better go. I'll start crying if we don't. (*He
   quickly hugs* TUSENBACH *and* KULYGIN *and kisses* IRINA's *hand.*)
   We've had wonderful times here . . .

FEDOTIK (*to* KULYGIN). Here's something to remember me by . . . A
   notebook with its own little pencil . . . We'll be going down to the
   river this way . . . (*They both move off, glancing back from time to time.*)

RODET (*calling*). Yoo-hoo.

KULYGIN (*calling*). Good-bye.

(FEDOTIK *and* RODET *meet* MASHA *at the back of the stage and say
   good-bye to her. She exits with them.*)

IRINA. They're gone . . . (*She sits down on the lowest step of the terrace.*)

CHEBUTYKIN. Without saying good-bye to me.

IRINA. Did you say good-bye to them?

CHEBUTYKIN. Well no, I suppose I didn't. I'll be seeing them soon
   enough anyway. I'm leaving tomorrow myself. Yes . . . Only one
   more day. A year from now I'll retire, start drawing my pension,
   and come back here to live out the rest of my days near you . . .
   Only one short year to pension. (*He puts one newspaper in his pocket
   and takes out another.*) I'm going to turn over a new leaf when I

come back ... I'll be as quiet as can be, well- ... behaved, and oh so respectable ...

IRINA. You really should turn over a new leaf. I mean it. And soon.

CHEBUTYKIN. I know. (*He sings softly.*)

> Ta-ra-ra boom-de-ay, Ta-ra-ra boom-de-ay.
> Sat on a tomb all day, ta-ra-ra boom-de-ay.[27]

KULYGIN. You're incorrigible, Doctor. Simply incorrigible.

CHEBUTYKIN. With you as a teacher I'm sure I'd make progress.

IRINA. Fyodor's shaved off his mustache. I can't bear to look at him.

KULYGIN. Why? What's wrong?

CHEBUTYKIN. I could tell you what that face of yours looks like now, but I don't dare.

KULYGIN. Well, that's our way, our modus vivendi. The headmaster shaved off his mustache, so as soon as I became his assistant I shaved off mine. No one likes me this way, but I don't mind. I'm happy. Mustache or no, I'm happy. (*He sits.*)

(ANDREI *wheels a pram with a sleeping baby in it across the back of the garden.*)

IRINA. Be a dear, Ivan Romanovich. I'm all upset. Tell me what happened on the boulevard yesterday. You were there.

CHEBUTYKIN. What happened? Nothing. Nothing to speak of. (*He starts reading his newspaper.*) What's the difference.

KULYGIN. People are saying that Solyony and the baron met on the boulevard near the theater ...

TUSENBACH. Stop it! I mean, really ... (*He exits into the house with a dismissive wave of the hand.*)

KULYGIN. Near the theater ... Solyony started picking on the baron, and the baron lost his temper and said something insulting ...

CHEBUTYKIN. I don't know. It's all a lot of hokum.

KULYGIN. A teacher in a seminary once wrote "hokum" at the top of a composition, and the pupil read it as a Latin word: "ho-kum." (*He laughs.*) Isn't that funny? They say Solyony's in love with Irina and hates the baron ... I can understand that. Irina's a fine girl.

She's even a bit like Masha—always lost in thought. Except that you're more easygoing, Irina. Though Masha's perfectly good-natured herself. I love her, my Masha.

(*Offstage a "Yoo-hoo, yoo-hoo" comes from the back of the garden.*)

IRINA (*with a start*). Everything seems to be frightening me today.

(*Pause.*)

My things are all packed. I'm sending them off this afternoon. After the wedding tomorrow the baron and I leave for the brickyard immediately, the day after tomorrow I start work at the school, and with God's help a new life begins. I felt so happy taking the teachers' exam, so elated, I actually wept . . .

(*Pause.*)

The cart should be coming for my things any minute now . . .

KULYGIN. That's all well and good, but there's not much substance to it somehow. All idea and no substance. Still, I wish you every happiness.

CHEBUTYKIN (*deeply moved*). Dearest, darling . . . precious Irina . . . You're so far ahead there's no catching up with you. You've left me behind like a bird too old to fly south. Fly on, my dears, fly on, and God bless you.

(*Pause.*)

You know, Kulygin, you never should have shaved off that mustache.

KULYGIN. That's enough out of you. (*He sighs.*) Well, the soldiers are leaving today, and everything will be as it was. No matter what anyone says, Masha is a fine, upstanding woman. I love her very much and thank my lucky stars for her . . . We're not all so lucky . . . There's a clerk in the Tax Office—a man named Kozyrev. We were at school together. He was expelled in the fifth year because he could never quite grasp the *ut consecutivum.*[28] Now he's terribly poor and ailing to boot, and whenever I run into him I say, "Hello there, *ut consecutivum.*" And he says, "Right, *consecutivum,*" coughing away . . . No, I've been lucky all my life. I'm very fortunate. I even have a Stanislas medal, second class.[29] And now I'm teaching others the *ut consecutivum.* Of course, I'm intelligent, more intelligent than many, but that's not what makes me happy . . .

(*Someone starts playing "A Maiden's Prayer" on the piano inside.*)[30]

IRINA. By tomorrow night I'll no longer have to listen to that "Maiden's Prayer" or run into Protopopov . . .

(*Pause.*)

He's in the drawing room. Even today.

KULYGIN. Is the headmistress here yet?

IRINA. No. We've sent for her. You can't imagine how hard it's been for me to live here alone, without Olga . . . Now that she's headmistress and so busy she has to live at school, I sit here alone, bored, with nothing to do, hating even the room I live in. So I've made up my mind. If I wasn't meant to live in Moscow, it can't be helped. It's my fate. That's all there is to it. Thy will be done, O Lord. When the baron asked for my hand, well, I thought it over and decided to say yes. He's a good man, very good, extraordinarily good . . . And suddenly I felt my soul had wings. I brightened up, breathed easy, felt ready to work again, work . . . Then something happened yesterday. There's a mystery hanging over me . . .

CHEBUTYKIN. Hokum. Ho-kum.

NATASHA (*through the window*). The headmistress!

KULYGIN. The headmistress is here. Let's go in. (*He exits with* IRINA *into the house.*)

CHEBUTYKIN (*reading his newspaper and singing softly*).

Ta-ra-ra boom-de-ay, ta-ra-ra boom-de-ay.
Sat on a tomb all day, ta-ra-ra boom-de-ay.

(MASHA *comes up to him.* ANDREI *crosses the back of the stage wheeling the pram.*)

MASHA. There he sits, not a care in the world.

CHEBUTYKIN. What of it?

MASHA (*sitting down*). Nothing . . .

(*Pause.*)

Did you love my mother?

CHEBUTYKIN. Very much.

MASHA. Did she love you?

CHEBUTYKIN (*after a pause*). I don't remember.

MASHA. Is my man around? That's what our cook Marfa used to call her policeman: my man. Is my man around?

CHEBUTYKIN. Not yet.

MASHA. When you take your happiness in snatches, in bits and pieces, and lose it, as I'm about to, you gradually turn hard and malicious. (*She points to her breast.*) I'm burning inside . . . (*She looks over at her brother* ANDREI, *who is again wheeling the pram across the stage.*) There goes Andrei, our darling brother . . . All our hopes—smashed. Once there was a bell that thousands helped to hoist. Money was no object, no effort was spared. And suddenly it fell and shattered. All at once, just like that. That's how it was with Andrei . . .

ANDREI. Will we never have a moment's peace in this house? What a racket!

CHEBUTYKIN. It won't be long now. (*He looks at his watch.*) I have an old-fashioned watch. It strikes the hour. (*He winds the watch, and it strikes the hour.*) Batteries One, Two, and Five depart at one o'clock sharp . . .

(*Pause.*)

And I go tomorrow.

ANDREI. For good?

CHEBUTYKIN. I'm not sure. I may come back next year. Though damn it all . . . What's the difference.

(*Somewhere in the distance a harp and violin are playing.*)

ANDREI. The town will be deserted, dead to the world.

(*Pause.*)

Something happened yesterday near the theater. I don't know what, but everybody's talking about it.

CHEBUTYKIN. Oh, nothing. A lot of nonsense. Solyony started picking on the baron, and the baron lost his temper and insulted him. It went so far that Solyony had to challenge him to a duel. (*He looks at his watch.*) Looks like the time has come ... Half past twelve in the Imperial Woods ... You can see the spot from here, across the river ... Bang, bang. (*He laughs.*) Solyony fancies himself a Lermontov. He actually writes poetry! All joking aside, though, this is his third duel.

MASHA. Whose?

CHEBUTYKIN. Solyony's.

MASHA. And the baron?

CHEBUTYKIN. What about the baron?

(*Pause.*)

MASHA. I'm all mixed up ... Still, I don't think they should be allowed to fight. Solyony might wound the baron or even kill him.

CHEBUTYKIN. The baron's a good man all right, but a baron more, a baron less—what's the difference. Let them go ahead with it. What's the difference. (*A call of "Yoo-hoo" comes from beyond the garden.*) Hold your horses! That's Skvortsov, the second. See him in the boat?

(*Pause.*)

ANDREI. Fighting a duel or just taking part, even as a doctor, is downright immoral, if you ask me.

CHEBUTYKIN. It only seems that way ... We're not real. Nothing on earth is real. It's all an illusion. We don't exist; we only seem to exist ... So what's the difference.

MASHA. Talk, talk, talk. All day long ... (*She starts going off.*) As if the weather weren't bad enough—snow at a moment's notice—no, you've got to talk all the time ... (*She stops.*) I won't set foot in that house. I can't go in there anymore ... Tell me when Vershinin

comes ... (*She walks down the path.*) The birds are flying south ...
(*She looks up.*) Are they swans or geese? ... How precious you are,
how lucky ... (*She exits.*)

ANDREI. The house will be deserted. The soldiers are going, you're
going, Irina's getting married, and I'll be left here by myself.

CHEBUTYKIN. What about Natasha?

(*Enter* FERAPONT *with some papers.*)

ANDREI. What about her? She's fine, upstanding, and, well, kind-
hearted, but there's something about her that reduces her to the
level of a petty, blind, scruffy little animal. At any rate, she's not
human. I'm telling you this because you're my friend, the only
person I can really talk to. I love Natasha, really I do, but there
are times when I find her impossibly vulgar, and then I flounder
and can't understand why I love her so much—or did, anyway.

CHEBUTYKIN (*standing*). I'm leaving tomorrow, Andrei. We may
never meet again. Let me give you a piece of advice. Put on your
hat, grab your walking stick, and go ... Go, keep going, and don't
look back. The further the better.

(SOLYONY *crosses the back of the stage with two officers. Seeing*
CHEBUTYKIN, *he turns to him. The other officers continue on
their way.*)

SOLYONY. The time has come, Doctor. Half past twelve. (*He greets*
ANDREI.)

CHEBUTYKIN. I'll be right there. You make me sick, the lot of you.
(*To* ANDREI.) If anyone asks for me, say I'll be right back ... (*He
sighs.*)

SOLYONY.

> He ne'er had time to say a prayer
> When he was sat on by the bear.

(*He starts off with* CHEBUTYKIN.) What are you groaning about, you
old codger?

CHEBUTYKIN. Me?

SOLYONY. How do you feel?

CHEBUTYKIN (*angrily*). Fit as a fiddle.

SOLYONY. Now, now . . . No need to get upset. I won't overdo it; I'll just wing him, like a woodcock. (*He takes out his scent and sprinkles some on his hands.*) I've used up a whole bottle today, and they still smell. Like a corpse.

(*Pause.*)

Yes, they do . . . Remember the lines:

> And he, the rebel, seeks the tempest
> As if in tempests there were peace . . . ?[31]

CHEBUTYKIN. Yes.

> He ne'er had time to say a prayer
> When he was sat on by the bear.

(*He exits with* SOLYONY.)
(*Cries of "Yoo-hoo!" Enter* ANDREI *and* FERAPONT.)

FERAPONT. Some papers to sign . . .

ANDREI (*irritated*). Get away from me! Get away, will you! (*He exits with the pram.*)

FERAPONT. What are papers for if not to be signed? (*He goes to the back of the stage.*)

(*Enter* IRINA *and* TUSENBACH, *who is wearing a straw hat.* KULYGIN *crosses the stage shouting, "Yoo-hoo! Masha! Yoo-hoo!"*)

TUSENBACH. He's probably the only person in town who's glad to see the soldiers go.

IRINA. That's understandable.

(*Pause.*)

The town will be deserted now.

TUSENBACH (*glancing at his watch*). I'll be right back, darling.

IRINA. Where are you going?

TUSENBACH. I've got to go into town, and then . . . see some friends off.

IRINA. That's not true . . . Why are you so distracted today, Nikolai?

(*Pause.*)

What happened yesterday near the theater?

TUSENBACH (*with a gesture of impatience*). I'll be back in an hour. I'll see you then. (*He kisses her hands.*) My love . . . (*He looks into her eyes.*) It's five years now since I fell in love with you, and I still can't get used to it. You seem more beautiful to me every day. That wonderful, lovely hair. Those eyes. Tomorrow I'll be taking you away. We'll work, we'll be rich, all my dreams will come alive. You'll be happy. There's only one thing missing, one thing. You don't love me.

IRINA. I haven't got it in me. I'll be your wife, your faithful, obedient wife, but I don't feel any love, and there's nothing I can do about it. (*She starts crying.*) I've never been in love. I've dreamt of it day and night, but my heart is like a fine piano no one can play because the key is lost.

(*Pause.*)

You look worried.

TUSENBACH. I didn't close my eyes all night. There's nothing so frightening to me in life as that lost key. It tortures me and won't let me sleep . . . Say something . . .

(*Pause.*)

Anything . . .

IRINA. What? What? Suddenly everything's so mysterious. The old trees standing there, silent . . . (*She leans her head on his chest.*)

TUSENBACH. Say something.

IRINA. What? What do you want me to say?

TUSENBACH. Anything.

IRINA. No more of this, please. No more.

(*Pause.*)

TUSENBACH. Funny how all at once silly, trivial details can take on such importance. You laugh at them as you always have, still find them trivial, but somehow you're powerless to stop yourself. Let's not talk about it, though. I'm happy. I feel I'm seeing these firs and maples and birches for the first time. I feel all of them watching me and wondering what's going to happen. What beautiful trees and how beautiful life under them ought to be.

(*Someone shouts, "Yoo-hoo!"*)

I've got to go. The time has come . . . Look, that tree may have withered, but it still sways in the wind with the others. That's how I think I'll be if I die: still part of life in one way or another. Goodbye, my darling . . . (*He kisses her hands.*) The papers you gave me are on my desk, underneath the calendar.

IRINA. I'm coming with you.

TUSENBACH (*alarmed*). No, no! (*He starts off quickly, but pauses at the path.*) Irina . . .

IRINA. What?

TUSENBACH (*not knowing what to say*). I didn't have any coffee this morning. Ask them to make some for me, will you? . . . (*He exits quickly.*)

(IRINA *stands lost in thought, then goes to the back of the stage and sits on a swing. Enter* ANDREI *with the pram.*)

FERAPONT (*entering*). They're not my papers, sir; they're from the office. I didn't invent them.

ANDREI. Where has it gone? Where is my youth, when I was bright and cheerful, when I thought beautiful thoughts and dreamt beautiful dreams, when both present and past were radiant with hope? Why is it that almost before we've really begun to live, we turn into boring, gray, uninteresting, lazy, indifferent, useless, and unhappy people? . . . Our town has been in existence for two hundred years now. It has a hundred thousand inhabitants. And not one of them is any different from the next, not one of them, past or present, has done anything heroic. There's no scholar among them, no artist, no one who stands out and might make the others envious or inspire them to imitate him ... All they do is eat, drink, sleep, and die ... And when others are born, they eat, drink, and sleep too, and to keep from going numb with boredom, they fill out their lives with rotten gossip, vodka, cards, and lawsuits. Wives deceive husbands; husbands lie and make believe they see nothing, hear nothing. And the brutal insensitivity of it all weighs so heavily on the children that the divine spark in them dies and they turn into pitiful, corpselike imitations of one another like their mothers and fathers before them. (*To* FERAPONT, *angrily.*) What do you want?

FERAPONT. What's that? Papers for you to sign.

ANDREI. Will you stop pestering me!

FERAPONT (*handing him the papers*). The doorkeeper at the Tax Office was just saying ... he said that Petersburg had temperatures of two hundred below last winter.

ANDREI. The present is so awful, but when I think of the future I feel good again. I feel open, I can breathe. I see a light glimmering in the distance, I see freedom, I see me and my children freed from lethargy, kvass,[32] goose with cabbage, after-dinner naps, from this foul parasitic way of life ...

FERAPONT. Two thousand people froze to death, he said. People were scared out of their wits. Either Petersburg or Moscow. I can't remember which.

ANDREI (*in a rush of tenderness*). What dear, dear sisters I have! (*Through tears.*) Dear Masha ... Dear sisters ...

NATASHA (*at the window*). Who's that talking so loud out there? Is it you, Andrei? You'll wake up baby Sophie. *Il ne faut pas faire du bruit, la Sophie est dormée déjà. Vous êtes un ours.*[33] (*She flares up.*) Find someone else to take the baby if you have to talk. Ferapont, take over the pram from your master.

FERAPONT. Yes, ma'am. (*He takes the pram.*)

ANDREI (*embarrassed*). I wasn't talking loud.

NATASHA (*from behind the window, petting her son*). Bobik's been a bad boy. Naughty Bobik.

ANDREI (*looking over the papers*). All right, I'll go through them and sign what needs to be signed. Then you can take them back to the office . . . (*He goes into the house reading the papers.*)

(FERAPONT *pushes the pram to the rear of the garden.*)

NATASHA (*from behind the window*). Bobik, tell Mama her name. There's a darling! And who's this? It's Auntie Olya. Say hello to Auntie Olya. Say, "Hello, Olya."

(*Two wandering musicians, a man and a girl, enter playing a violin and a harp.* VERSHININ, OLGA, *and* ANFISA *come out of the house and listen to the music for a moment in silence.* IRINA *joins them.*)

OLGA. Our garden is like a public thoroughfare. People walk through it, drive through it . . . Give the musicians something, Nanny . . .

ANFISA (*handing them some coins*). Good-bye now. God bless you. (*The musicians bow and go off.*) Poor things. They wouldn't play a note if they had enough to eat. (*To* IRINA.) Hello, Irina dear. (*She kisses her.*) Mmm, child. Oh, the life I'm living! Rooms over at the school, darling. Just Olga and me. And paid for by the government. God has blessed me in my old age. I never dreamed I'd live like this, sinner that I am . . . So big, and paid for by the government. I've got my own little room, my own little bed. All paid for by the government. Sometimes I wake up at night and think how lucky I am. O Lord, Mother of God, there's no one luckier than me.

VERSHININ (*glancing at his watch*). We'll be leaving any minute, Olga Sergeevna. It's time for me to go.

(*Pause.*)

I wish you all the . . . all the . . . Where is Maria Sergeevna?

IRINA. In the garden somewhere . . . I'll go and find her.

VERSHININ. Please do. I'm in a hurry.

ANFISA. I'll go. I'll find her. (*She shouts.*) Yoo-hoo! Masha. (*She and* IRINA *go off to the other end of the garden.*) Yoo-hoo! Yoo-hoo!

VERSHININ. All things come to an end. Now we must say good-bye too. (*He glances at his watch.*) The town gave us a sort of going-away lunch: we drank champagne, the mayor made a speech . . .

But while I ate and listened, my heart was here, with you . . . (*He looks round the garden.*) I feel at home with you.

OLGA. Will we ever meet again?

VERSHININ. Not likely.

(*Pause.*)

My wife is staying on another month or two with the girls. If anything happens or they need anything, please . . .

OLGA. Yes, yes, of course. Don't worry.

(*Pause.*)

There won't be a single soldier left in town tomorrow. It will all be a memory, and we'll start life all over again . . .

(*Pause.*)

Nothing happens the way we want it to. I didn't want to be headmistress, and here I am. Now I'll never get to Moscow . . .

VERSHININ. Well . . . Thank you for everything . . . Forgive me if there's been anything amiss. I've talked a lot, much too much, in fact. Forgive me that too. Remember what was good.

OLGA (*wiping her eyes*). Why hasn't Masha come yet? . . .

VERSHININ. What else can I say by way of farewell? What can I philosophize about? . . . (*He laughs.*) Life is hard. To many of us it seems stagnant and hopeless. But we must admit it's getting clearer and brighter, and in all probability the time is not far off when it will be absolutely radiant. (*He glances at his watch.*) Time for me to go. Mankind used to spend all its energy making war. Life was just one campaign, one invasion, one victory after the next. That's all over now, but it's left behind a tremendous void, and so far nothing's come along to fill it. Mankind is trying as hard as it can to find something and it will of course. I only hope it won't be long now.

(*Pause.*)

You know, if we could combine education with hard work and hard work with education . . . (*He glances at his watch.*) I really must be going . . .

OLGA. Here she comes.

(*Enter* MASHA.)

VERSHININ. I've come to say good-bye.

(OLGA *moves slightly to one side so as not to intrude.*)

MASHA (*looking into his eyes*). Good-bye . . . (*A long kiss.*)
OLGA. Enough! Enough!

(MASHA *starts sobbing violently.*)

VERSHININ. Write to me . . . Don't forget me. Let me go now . . .
Time to go . . . Take her, Olga Sergeevna . . . I'm already . . . It's
time to . . . I'm late . . . (*Deeply moved, he kisses* OLGA's *hands, then embraces* MASHA *once more and exits quickly.*)
OLGA. There now, Masha! Don't cry, darling.
KULYGIN (*entering, embarrassed*). It's all right. Let her cry. It's all
right. Dear Masha, good Masha . . . You're my wife, and I'm
happy no matter what . . . I'm not complaining. I won't say a
word . . . Olga here is my witness. We'll go back to living the
way we did before, and I won't say a word or make the least
allusion . . .
MASHA (*stifling her sobs*).

> A green oak stands upon a firth,
> A chain of gold hangs round its trunk . . .

I'm going out of my mind . . .

> A green oak . . . stands upon a firth . . .

OLGA. Hush, Masha . . . Calm down . . . Give her some water.
MASHA. I'm not crying anymore.
KULYGIN. She's not crying anymore . . . Good girl . . .

(*The muted sound of a shot comes from the distance.*)

MASHA.

> A green oak stands upon a firth,
> A chain of gold hangs round its trunk . . .

Green cat . . . Green oak . . . I'm all mixed up . . . (*She drinks the water.*) My life is such a failure . . . I don't need anything else . . . I'll be all right in a minute . . . What difference does it make? What is a firth anyway? Why can't I get that word out of my head? I can't keep anything straight.

(*Enter* IRINA.)

OLGA. Hush, Masha. There's a good girl . . . Let's go inside.

MASHA (*angrily*). I'm not going in there. (*She starts sobbing again, but stops immediately.*) I'm never going into that house again, ever . . .

IRINA. Let's just sit here for a minute. No need to talk. Remember, I'm leaving tomorrow . . .

(*Pause.*)

KULYGIN. Yesterday I took this beard and mustache from a boy in my third-year class . . . (*He puts on the beard and mustache.*) I look like the German teacher . . . (*He laughs.*) Don't I? They're priceless, those boys.

MASHA. You really do look like that German.

OLGA (*laughing*). Yes.

(MASHA *starts crying.*)

IRINA. Now, Masha . . .

KULYGIN. Just like him . . .

NATASHA (*entering, to the maid*). What is it? Protopopov will keep an eye on baby Sophie. Tell your master to take Bobik for a stroll in the pram. Children are such a bother . . . (*To* IRINA.) So you're leaving tomorrow, Irina. What a shame. Do stay another week. (*She catches sight of* KULYGIN *and screams.* KULYGIN *laughs and takes off the beard and mustache.*) Goodness! What a fright you gave me! (*To* IRINA.) I'm so used to having you here. Don't think I'll find it easy to say good-bye. I'm moving Andrei and his violin into your room so he can saw away to his heart's content. That will leave his room free for baby Sophie. A heavenly child, a marvelous child. Isn't she something? Today she looked up at me with those big eyes of hers and you know what she said? "Mama."

KULYGIN. It's true. She *is* a lovely child.

NATASHA. So tomorrow I'll be all alone here. (*She sighs.*) The first thing I'll do is have the fir trees cut down ... Then that maple ... It looks so ugly at night ... (*To* IRINA.) Irina darling, that sash doesn't become you at all. It's in such poor taste ... What you need is something bright and gay ... And then I'll have all kinds of pretty little flowers put in everywhere. How nice it will smell ... (*Sternly.*) What is this fork doing on the bench? (*Going inside. To the maid.*) Will you tell me what this fork was doing on the bench? Well? (*She shouts.*) Silence!

KULYGIN. She's at it again.

(*A band starts playing a march offstage. They all listen.*)

OLGA. They're leaving.

(*Enter* CHEBUTYKIN.)

MASHA. Our friends are leaving. Well ... Let's hope they have a safe journey. (*To* KULYGIN.) We'd better be getting home ... Where's my hat and cape?

KULYGIN. I took them inside ... I'll go and fetch them. (*He goes into the house.*)

OLGA. Yes. Now we can all go home. About time too.

CHEBUTYKIN. Olga Sergeevna.

OLGA. What is it?

(*Pause.*)

What is it?

CHEBUTYKIN. Nothing ... I don't know how to tell you ... (*He whispers something in her ear.*)

OLGA (*stunned*). No! It can't be!

CHEBUTYKIN. Yes ... An awful mess ... I'm all worn out, exhausted ...

I don't want to say any more... (*Irritated.*) Though what difference does it make.

MASHA. What's happened?

OLGA (*embracing* IRINA). This has been a terrible day... I don't know how to tell you this, darling...

IRINA. What is it? Tell me quickly! What is it, for God's sake? (*She starts crying.*)

CHEBUTYKIN. The baron's been killed in a duel.

IRINA (*crying softly*). I knew it, I knew it...

CHEBUTYKIN (*sitting on a bench at the rear of the stage*). All worn out... (*He takes a newspaper out of his pocket.*) Let them have their cry... (*He sings softly.*)

> Ta-ra-ra boom-de-ay, ta-ra-ra boom-de-ay.
> Sat on a tomb all day, ta-ra-ra boom-de-ay.

What difference does it make.

(*The three sisters stand close together.*)

MASHA. Oh, listen to the music. They're leaving us. And one of them is gone forever. Forever and ever. While we stay on alone to start our lives anew. Life must go on. Life must go on...

IRINA (*laying her head on* OLGA*'s breast*). There will come a time when everyone knows what all this is for, all this suffering, when there will be no mysteries. But in the meantime life must go on... We must work, work and nothing else. I'll go off on my own tomorrow and teach, devote my life to anyone who needs it. It's autumn now. Soon winter will be here and cover everything with snow. And I'll be working, working...

OLGA (*embracing both sisters*). The music sounds so cheerful and lighthearted it makes me feel life's worth living. Dear God, the time will come when we too depart this earth forever and people forget us, forget our faces, our voices, even how many of us there were. But our sufferings will turn to joy: peace and happiness will reign on earth, and those who come after us will remember and bless those who live now. Our lives aren't over, dear sisters; we shall go on living. The music sounds so cheerful, so full of joy, it almost seems that any minute now we'll find out why we live, why we suffer . . . If only we knew. If only we knew.

(*The music grows fainter and fainter.* KULYGIN, *smiling cheerfully, enters with* MASHA'*s hat and cape.* ANDREI *enters, pushing the pram with Bobik in it.*)

CHEBUTYKIN (*singing softly*).

Ta-ra-ra boom-de-ay . . . Sat on a tomb all day . . .

(*He starts reading his newspaper.*) What difference does it make. What difference does it make.

OLGA. If only we knew. If only we knew.

CURTAIN

THE CHERRY ORCHARD

A COMEDY IN FOUR ACTS

CHARACTERS[1]

LYUBÓV ANDRÉEVNA RANÉVSKAYA (LYÚBA). A landowner.
ÁNYA. Her daughter, seventeen.
VÁRYA. Her foster daughter, twenty-four.
LEONÍD ANDRÉEVICH GÁEV (LYÓNYA). Her brother.
YERMOLÁI ALEXÉEVICH LOPÁKHIN. A merchant.
PYOTR SERGÉEVICH TROFÍMOV (PÉTYA). A student.
BORÍS BORÍSOVICH SIMEÓNOV-PÍSHCHIK. A landowner.
SHARLÓTTA IVÁNOVNA. A governess.
SEMYÓN PANTELÉEVICH YEPIKHÓDOV. A clerk.
DUNYÁSHA. A maid.
FIRS. A servant, eighty-seven.
YÁSHA. A young servant.
PASSERBY.
STATIONMASTER.
POSTMASTER.
GUESTS.
SERVANTS.

The action takes place on Madam RANEVSKAYA'*s estate.*

ACT ONE

A room still called the nursery. One of the doors leads to ANYA's *room. Day is breaking; the sun is about to rise. It is May and the cherry trees are in bloom, but it is still cold in the early morning. All the windows in the room are shut.*

Enter DUNYASHA, *carrying a candle, and* LOPAKHIN *with a book in his hand.*

LOPAKHIN. Thank God the train's in. What time is it?

DUNYASHA. Nearly two. (*She blows out the candle.*) It's light out.

LOPAKHIN. How late does that make the train? A couple of hours at least. (*He yawns and stretches.*) And you know what it makes me? A fool, that's what. I come all this way just to meet them at the station, and I sleep right through it . . . Dozed off sitting here, wouldn't you know it . . . Why didn't you wake me?

DUNYASHA. I thought you'd gone. (*She listens.*) I think I hear them coming.

LOPAKHIN (*listening*). No . . . They still have to get their bags and all . . .

(*Pause.*)

After the five years Lyubov Andreevna's been abroad I don't know what to expect . . . But she's a fine person. Easygoing, simple. I remember once when I was fifteen or so, my father—he was the village grocer—gave me a punch in the face that made my nose bleed . . . We were here at the house for some reason, and he'd been drinking. Well, Lyubov Andreevna—I can see her now, so young and slender—she took me over to this washstand, right here in the nursery. "Don't cry, little peasant," she said. "You'll be fine again in no time . . ."

(*Pause.*)

Little peasant . . . My father *was* a peasant, and look at me: white vest, tan shoes. A bull in a china shop . . . Oh, I'm rich, all right; I've got plenty of money. But it doesn't take much to see that deep down I'm still a peasant. (*He leafs through the book.*) Tried to read this book here; didn't understand a word, fell asleep over it.

(*Pause.*)

DUNYASHA. The dogs have been up all night. They can tell their masters are coming.

LOPAKHIN. What's wrong, Dunyasha?

DUNYASHA. My hands are shaking. I think I'm going to faint.

LOPAKHIN. Awfully sensitive lately, aren't you? Dressing like a lady. And that hairdo. It's not right. Know your place.

(*Enter* YEPIKHODOV *carrying a bunch of flowers. He is wearing a jacket and brightly polished boots that squeak loudly. On his way into the room he drops the flowers.*)

YEPIKHODOV (*picking up the flowers*). They're from the gardener. He said to put them in the dining room. (*He hands* DUNYASHA *the flowers.*)

LOPAKHIN. And bring me some kvass.[2]

DUNYASHA. Yes, sir. (*She exits.*)

YEPIKHODOV. It's several degrees below freezing out, and the cherry trees are all in bloom. I can't say I approve of our climate. (*He sighs.*) Not at all. It's not what you might call stimulative. And if I may appendix another observation: I bought these boots the day before yesterday, and—let me venture to assure you—they squeak so badly that there's no possibility whatsoever. What can I grease them with?

LOPAKHIN. Leave me alone. I'm sick of you.

YEPIKHODOV. Every day a new disaster. But you don't hear me complain. I'm used to it. I even smile. (*Enter* DUNYASHA. *She serves* LOPAKHIN *his kvass.*) Well, I'll be off. (*He bumps into a chair and knocks it over.*) There . . . (*Almost triumphantly.*) You see? The very circumstances, if you'll pardon the expression, I mean ... Simply remarkable, even! (*He exits.*)

DUNYASHA. You know what's happened? Yepikhodov has proposed to me!

LOPAKHIN. I see.

DUNYASHA. And I don't know what to say ... He's a nice quiet man, but there are times he starts talking and you can't make head or tail of it. Oh, it sounds all sweet and romantic; it just doesn't mean anything. I like him, kind of, and he's crazy about me. But he's so unlucky. Every day it's something different. You know what they call him for fun? Twenty-two disasters ...

LOPAKHIN (*listening*). I think they're coming.

DUNYASHA. They're coming! What's the matter with me? ... I'm all shivery.

LOPAKHIN. Yes, they're coming. Let's go and meet them. I wonder if she'll recognize me. It's five years now.

DUNYASHA (*excited*). I'm going to faint ... Oh dear, I'm going to faint!

(*Two carriages are heard pulling up to the house.* LOPAKHIN *and* DUNYASHA *exit quickly. The stage is empty. Noises start emerging from the adjoining rooms.* FIRS, *who has been to the station to meet* LYUBOV ANDREEVNA, *hurries across the stage, leaning on his cane. He is wearing old-fashioned livery and a top hat and mumbling to himself, though it is not clear what. The backstage noise grows louder and louder. A voice says, "Through here?" Enter* LYUBOV ANDREEVNA, ANYA, *and* SHARLOTTA. SHARLOTTA *has a little dog on a leash. They are all wearing traveling clothes. They are followed by* VARYA, *who is wearing a coat and kerchief,* GAEV, PISHCHIK, LOPAKHIN, DUNYASHA, *who is carrying a bundle and an umbrella, and other servants with luggage. They cross the room.*)

ANYA. Let's go through here. Remember what room this is, Mama?

LYUBOV ANDREEVNA (*joyfully, through tears*). The nursery!

VARYA. It's so cold my hands are numb. (*To* LYUBOV ANDREEVNA.) Your rooms are just the way you left them, Mama. The white room and the purple room.

LYUBOV ANDREEVNA. The nursery! My darling, precious nursery ...

This is where I slept as a child ... (*She cries.*) It's like being a child all over again ... (*She kisses* GAEV, *then* VARYA, *then* GAEV *again.*) Varya hasn't changed a bit either: still looks like a nun. I even recognize Dunyasha ... (*She kisses* DUNYASHA.)

GAEV. The train was two hours late. It's outrageous how they run things.

SHARLOTTA (*to* PISHCHIK). My dog eats nuts too.

PISHCHIK (*amazed*). Unbelievable!

(*All but* ANYA *and* DUNYASHA *exit.*)

DUNYASHA. It's been so long ... (*She takes off* ANYA*'s coat and hat.*)

ANYA. Four nights on the train. I didn't get any sleep ... Now I'm frozen solid.

DUNYASHA. It was snowing and cold when you left during Lent, and now look. Oh, Anya, sweet Anya! (*She laughs and kisses her.*) I've waited so long, Anya, precious ... Let me tell you now. I can't wait another minute ...

ANYA (*without enthusiasm*). What is it this time?

DUNYASHA. Yepikhodov, the clerk, he proposed to me just after Easter.

ANYA. That's all you ever talk about ... (*She tidies her hair.*) I've lost all my hairpins. (*She is so exhausted she can hardly stand.*)

DUNYASHA. I really don't know what to think. He loves me so much, so much ...

ANYA (*looking through the door into her own room, tenderly*). My room, my windows, as if I'd never been away. Home again! Tomorrow morning I'll get up and run straight to the orchard ... Oh, I hope I can fall asleep. I didn't sleep a wink the whole way. I was so worried.

DUNYASHA. The tutor has been here since the day before yesterday.

ANYA (*joyfully*). Petya!

DUNYASHA. He's in the bathhouse, sleeping. That's where he asked to stay. Said he didn't want to put anybody out. (*She glances at her pocket watch.*) I thought we should go and wake him, but your sister said, "No, you let him sleep."

(*Enter* VARYA, *a bunch of keys hanging from her belt.*)

VARYA. Quick, Dunyasha! Coffee ... Mama wants some coffee.

DUNYASHA. Won't take but a minute. (*She exits.*)

VARYA. Thank God you're home. Home again. (*Tenderly.*) My angel's back! My beauty's back!

ANYA. It was sheer torture.

VARYA. I can imagine.

ANYA. It was Easter week when I left, and cold. Sharlotta talked the whole way and did magic tricks. Whatever made you saddle me with her?

VARYA. You couldn't have traveled alone, angel. Not at seventeen.

ANYA. Anyway, we finally got to Paris. It was cold, snowing. My French was awful. Mama's place was on the fifth floor. I walked in. She had some French people there—some ladies and an old Jesuit with a prayer book. Smoke everywhere, no room to sit. Suddenly I felt sorry for her, so sorry I took her head in my arms and held it there, couldn't let go. And she kept hugging me and crying ...

VARYA (*through tears*). That's enough, that's enough ...

ANYA. She'd sold the villa near Menton by then, so there was nothing left, nothing. I had nothing either. We barely made it home. And Mama just can't understand! Whenever we ate at a station, she'd order the most expensive dish on the menu and give the waiter a ruble tip. Sharlotta too. Then Yasha would insist on a portion for himself. It was awful. You remember Mama's servant Yasha. We've brought him home.

VARYA. Yes, I've seen him, the swine.

ANYA. Well, how is everything? Have you kept up the mortgage payments?

VARYA. Don't be silly.

ANYA. O God, O God ...

VARYA. The estate is going up for sale in August ...

ANYA. O God ...

LOPAKHIN (*sticking his head through the door and mooing*). Moo-oo-oo ... (*He exits.*)

VARYA (*through tears*). I wish I could give him a taste of this ... (*She shakes her fist at him.*)

ANYA (*putting her arms around* VARYA, *softly*). Has he proposed, Varya?

(VARYA *shakes her head.*) But he does love you . . . Why don't the two of you talk it over? What are you waiting for?

VARYA. Nothing will ever come of it. He's too busy; he's got no time for me . . . Never even notices me. I'm through with him for good. It's hard for me even to look at him. Everyone talks about our wedding, congratulates me, and there's nothing to it. It's all a dream . . . (*In a different tone of voice.*) Your brooch—it's a bee, isn't it?

ANYA (*sadly*). Mama bought it. (*Walking in the direction of her room, talking cheerfully, like a child.*) Know what? In Paris I went up in a balloon!

VARYA. My angel's back! My beautiful angel! (DUNYASHA *has returned with a coffee urn and is making coffee.* VARYA *has moved to the door.*) All day long as I go about my chores I dream and dream. If only we could find you a rich husband, my mind would be at rest. I'd go to a hermitage, then on to Kiev, to Moscow, from one shrine to another . . . on and on. Oh, the glory of it . . .

ANYA. The birds are singing in the orchard. What time is it?

VARYA. Well past two. Time you were in bed, angel. (*Going into* ANYA*'s room.*) Bliss!

(*Enter* YASHA *with a traveling blanket and bag.*)

YASHA (*crossing the stage, genteelly*). Might I pass through?

DUNYASHA. I almost didn't recognize you, Yasha. You look so foreign.

YASHA. Hm . . . And who might you be?

DUNYASHA. I was no bigger than this when you left . . . (*She indicates her height with her hand.*) I'm Dunyasha, Fyodor Kozoedov's daughter. You wouldn't remember.

YASHA. Hm . . . A juicy little morsel. (*He looks this way and that, then puts his arms around her. She shrieks and drops a saucer. He exits quickly.*)

VARYA (*in the doorway, crossly*). What's going on in there?

DUNYASHA (*through tears*). I've broken a saucer . . .

VARYA. A good omen.

ANYA (*coming out of her room*). We'd better warn Mama that Petya's here.

VARYA. I gave orders not to wake him.

ANYA (*dreamily*). It's six years now. First Father dying, and a month later little Grisha drowning in the river. Only seven years old.

My beautiful baby brother. Mama couldn't bear it. She left, ran, and never looked back. (*She shudders.*) I understand her perfectly. If only she knew.

(*Pause.*)

And Petya—Grisha's tutor—he might bring back memories . . .

(*Enter* FIRS. *He is wearing a jacket and white vest.*)

FIRS (*going over to the coffee urn, solicitously*). Madam will have her coffee here . . . (*He puts on white gloves.*) Is it ready? (*To* DUNYASHA, *sternly.*) You there! Where's the cream?
DUNYASHA. Oh, goodness . . . (*She rushes off.*)
FIRS (*fussing about the urn*). A real numskull . . . (*He mumbles to himself.*) Back from Paris . . . The master used to go there too . . . His own horses . . . (*He laughs.*)
VARYA. What are you laughing at, Firs?
FIRS. Pardon, Miss? (*Joyfully.*) My mistress is back! Never thought I'd live to see it! Now I can die . . . (*He weeps for joy.*)

(*Enter* LYUBOV, GAEV, LOPAKHIN, *and* PISHCHIK. PISHCHIK *is wearing a long-waisted coat of fine cloth and a pair of full Russian trousers tucked into his boots.* GAEV *pantomimes a billiard player with his arms and body.*)

LYUBOV ANDREEVNA. How does it go again? Wait, I remember . . . Yellow into the corner pocket! Double into the middle!
GAEV. Cut into the corner. You and I used to sleep here in this room, Lyuba, and suddenly I'm fifty-one. Strange, isn't it.
LOPAKHIN. Yes, time flies.
GAEV. What?
LOPAKHIN. Time, I said. It flies.
GAEV. This place reeks of cheap cologne.
ANYA. I'm going to bed. Good night, Mama. (*She kisses* LYUBOV ANDREEVNA.)
LYUBOV ANDREEVNA. My beautiful baby. (*She kisses* ANYA's *hands.*) Glad to be home? I still can't believe it.
ANYA. Good night, Uncle Leonid.

GAEV (*kissing her face and hands*). God bless you. You're just like your mother! (*To* LYUBOV ANDREEVNA.) You looked just like her when you were her age, Lyuba.

(ANYA *shakes hands with* LOPAKHIN *and* PISHCHIK *and exits, closing the door behind her.*)

LYUBOV ANDREEVNA. She's so tired.

PISHCHIK. It's a long trip, after all.

VARYA (*to* LOPAKHIN *and* PISHCHIK). What do you say, gentlemen? It's nearly three. Time you were on your way.

LYUBOV ANDREEVNA (*laughing*). Same old Varya. (*She draws* VARYA *up to her and kisses her.*) Let me finish my coffee. Then we'll all go. (FIRS *places a cushion under her feet.*) Thank you, my dear. I drink coffee all the time now, day and night. Thank you, dear old Firs. (*She kisses* FIRS.)

VARYA. I'll go and make sure they've brought everything in . . . (*She exits.*)

LYUBOV ANDREEVNA. Is this really me sitting here? (*She laughs.*) I feel like jumping up and down and waving my arms. (*She covers her face with her hands.*) But what if I'm only dreaming? Dear God, how I love my country, how I cherish it! I couldn't see a thing from the train I was crying so hard. (*Through tears.*) But now I'd better drink my coffee. Thank you, Firs dear. Thank you, dear old Firs. I'm so glad you're still alive.

FIRS. The day before yesterday.

GAEV. He doesn't hear too well.

LOPAKHIN. Well, I'll be going now. I leave for Kharkov at about four. What a shame. Here I was hoping to have a good look at you, a chance to talk . . . You're as lovely as ever.

PISHCHIK (*having trouble breathing*). Even prettier . . . That Parisian outfit . . . A man could ruin himself over a woman like you.

LOPAKHIN. Your brother here calls me a profiteer and a boor, but I don't care. Let him. All I want is for you to trust me the way you used to and look at me with those wonderful gentle eyes. God! My father was your father's serf and your grandfather's before him, but you—you've done so much for me, you've made me forget the past. I love you like a member of my family . . . More.

LYUBOV ANDREEVNA. I can't sit still. I find it physically impossible . . . (*She jumps up and walks back and forth in great agitation.*) The joy is too much for me . . . Go ahead and laugh. I know I'm silly . . . Dear little bookcase . . . (*She kisses the bookcase.*) Sweet little table.

GAEV. Nanny died while you were away.

LYUBOV ANDREEVNA (*sitting and drinking coffee*). Yes, God rest her soul. They wrote and told me.

GAEV. Anastasy too. Oh, and cross-eyed Petrushka left us and moved to town. He's chief of police. (*He takes a box of fruit drops out of his pocket and pops one into his mouth.*)

PISHCHIK. My daughter Dasha . . . She sends her regards.

LOPAKHIN. I've got something to tell you, something nice and cheerful. (*He glances at his watch.*) No, I've got to go. There's no time . . . Well, I'll make it short. As you know, the cherry orchard is being sold to pay your debts. It goes up for auction on the twenty-second of August. But don't worry, dear lady. You can sleep in peace. There's a way out . . . Here's my plan. Listen carefully now. Your estate is only fifteen miles from town, and the railway line is nearby. Divide the cherry orchard and the land along the river into individual plots and lease them for summer cottages, and you'll have a yearly income of no less than twenty-five thousand rubles.

GAEV. Why, that's pure poppycock.

LYUBOV ANDREEVNA. I don't think I follow you.

LOPAKHIN. Each acre will bring in at least ten rubles a year. Advertise immediately, and I guarantee you won't have a scrap of land left by autumn. It'll all be grabbed up. In other words, congratulations! You're saved. The setting's magnificent, the river's deep. It needs a little work, of course, a little fixing up . . . You'll have to tear down all the old buildings, for instance, this house too—it's of no use to anyone anyway—then chop down the cherry orchard . . .

LYUBOV ANDREEVNA. Chop down the cherry orchard? My dear man, I'm sorry, but you don't know what you're saying. If there's anything interesting, anything noteworthy about this province, it's our cherry orchard.

LOPAKHIN. The one thing noteworthy about the orchard is its size. It only yields every other year, and even then you can't get rid of the crop: nobody buys the cherries.

GAEV. But it's in the encyclopedia.

LOPAKHIN (*glancing at his watch*). If we don't come up with something, some kind of plan, the cherry orchard, the whole estate, will be auctioned off on August twenty-second. Make up your minds! There's no other way, believe me. No other way.

FIRS. In the old days, forty or fifty years back, those cherries would be dried, pickled, marinated, made into jam. There was a time . . .

GAEV. Quiet, Firs.

FIRS. There was a time they sent them by the cartload to Moscow and Kharkov. The money they brought in! They were so soft and sweet and juicy, those dried cherries. They smelled so good . . . People knew the recipe then . . .

LYUBOV ANDREEVNA. And where's the recipe now?

FIRS. Gone and forgotten. Nobody remembers.

PISHCHIK (*to* LYUBOV ANDREEVNA). What's new in Paris? How was it? Eat any frogs?

LYUBOV ANDREEVNA. I ate crocodiles.

PISHCHIK. Unbelievable!

LOPAKHIN. Not so long ago if you lived in the country you were either master or man. Now the summer people are moving in. Every town, even the smallest, is surrounded by cottages, and within the next twenty years or so the number of summer people is bound to increase enormously. Now all they do is drink tea out on the balcony, but one day they may start growing things on their land, and then your cherry orchard will be happy, rich, productive . . .

GAEV (*indignant*). Pure poppycock!

(*Enter* VARYA *and* YASHA.)

VARYA. There are two telegrams waiting for you, Mama. (*She picks out the key to the old bookcase and unlocks it with a clatter.*) Here they are.

LYUBOV ANDREEVNA. From Paris. (*She tears up the telegrams without reading them.*) Paris is over and done with . . .

GAEV. You know how old that bookcase is, Lyuba? A week ago I pulled out the bottom drawer, and what did I find but some numbers burned into the wood. That bookcase was made exactly one hundred years ago. What do you think of that? We could celebrate its centenary. An inanimate object, true, but it does house books.

PISHCHIK (*amazed*). A hundred years old . . . Unbelievable!

GAEV. Yes . . . Quite a thing . . . (*He runs his hand over it.*) Most honorable bookcase! Allow me to salute you for more than a hundred years of service to the glorious principles of virtue and justice. Not once in an entire century has your silent summons to productive labor faltered. (*Through tears.*) From generation to generation you have maintained our family's courage and faith in a better future, you have nurtured in us the ideals of goodness and social consciousness.

(*Pause.*)

LOPAKHIN. Hm . . .

LYUBOV ANDREEVNA. Same old Lyonya.

GAEV (*slightly embarrassed*). Off the right into the corner! Cut into the middle!

LOPAKHIN (*glancing at his watch*). I'd better be going.

YASHA (*handing* LYUBOV ANDREEVNA *her medicine*). Care to take your pills now?

PISHCHIK. Never take medicine, my dear . . . Doesn't do a bit of good. Or harm either . . . Come, let me have them. (*He takes the pills, pours them all out into his palm, blows on them, puts them in his mouth, and washes them down with kvass.*) There!

LYUBOV ANDREEVNA (*alarmed*). You're out of your mind!

PISHCHIK. So much for the pills.

LOPAKHIN. Some gullet you've got there.

(EVERYONE *laughs.*)

FIRS. When the gentleman was here at Easter, he ate half a bucket of pickles . . . (*He goes on muttering.*)

LYUBOV ANDREEVNA. What's he saying?

VARYA. He's been muttering that way for three years. We're used to it.

YASHA. It's his advancing age.

(SHARLOTTA, *very thin and tightly laced, crosses the stage in a white dress with a lorgnette at her belt.*)

LOPAKHIN. Excuse me, Sharlotta Ivanovna. I haven't had a chance to say hello to you yet. (*He tries to kiss her hand.*)

SHARLOTTA (*pulling her hand away*). If I let you kiss my hand, you'll be wanting to kiss my elbow, then my shoulder ...

LOPAKHIN. This is my unlucky day.

(EVERYONE *laughs.*)

Show us a trick, Sharlotta Ivanovna.

LYUBOV ANDREEVNA. Yes, Sharlotta. Do!

SHARLOTTA. Not now. I'm going to bed. (*She exits.*)

LOPAKHIN. See you all in three weeks. (*He kisses* LYUBOV ANDREEVNA's *hand.*) Good-bye for now. Time to go. (*To* GAEV.) Farum-wellum. (*He exchanges kisses with* PISHCHIK.) Farum-wellum. (*He shakes hands with* VARYA *and then with* FIRS *and* YASHA.) I don't really feel like going. (*To* LYUBOV ANDREEVNA.) Let me know if you decide in favor of the cottages. I can find you a loan of fifty thousand or so. Think it over seriously.

VARYA (*angrily*). Well, go if you're going!

LOPAKHIN. I am, I am. (*He exits.*)

GAEV. The boor. Oh, I'm sorry ... Varya's going to marry him. He's Varya's intended.

VARYA. Oh, Uncle Leonid! How can you!

LYUBOV ANDREEVNA. Well, why not, Varya? It would make me very happy. He's a fine man.

PISHCHIK. There's no denying it ... The worthiest of the worthy ... My Dasha says ... She says ... She says all sorts of things ... (*He starts snoring, but wakes up immediately.*) By the way, my dear, could you ... lend me two hundred and forty rubles? ... The interest on my mortgage is due tomorrow.

VARYA (*alarmed*). No, no! We haven't got it!

LYUBOV ANDREEVNA. I haven't got a thing. Really.

PISHCHIK. Oh well. It'll turn up. (*He laughs.*) Never say die. Last time

I thought I was done for, ruined, when suddenly they put a railway line across my property, and . . . I was in the money again. Something's bound to turn up sooner or later . . . Maybe Dasha will win two hundred thousand . . . She's got a lottery ticket.

LYUBOV ANDREEVNA. That's the end of the coffee. Time for bed.

FIRS (*scolding* GAEV *while brushing his clothes*). The wrong trousers again! What am I going to do with you?

VARYA (*quietly*). Anya's asleep. (*She opens the window quietly.*) The sun is up. It's getting warm. Look how beautiful the trees are, Mama. And oh, that air! The starlings are singing!

GAEV (*opening another window*). The orchard is all white. You haven't forgotten, have you, Lyuba? The long path running on and on, straight as an arrow, shining on moonlit nights. You remember, don't you? You haven't forgotten.

LYUBOV ANDREEVNA (*gazing out of the window at the orchard*). Oh, my childhood! My pure, innocent childhood! Sleeping here in the nursery, looking out at the orchard, waking up happy every morning. It's just the same. Nothing has changed. (*She laughs with joy.*) White, all white! Oh, my orchard! After a dark and stormy autumn, a freezing winter, here you are, young again, full of joy. The heavenly hosts have not forsaken you . . . If only I could lift the millstone from my breast. If only I could forget the past.

GAEV. Yes, and now the orchard's being sold to pay our debts. Odd, isn't it? . . .

LYUBOV ANDREEVNA. Look! It's Mama walking through the orchard . . . in a white dress! (*She laughs joyfully.*) Look, there she goes!

GAEV. Where?

VARYA. Heavens, Mama!

LYUBOV ANDREEVNA. Oh, there's nobody there. I just imagined it. See that little white tree leaning over the path where it turns off to the gazebo? There on the right. It looks like a woman . . .

(*Enter* TROFIMOV *wearing a shabby student uniform and glasses.*)

An amazing orchard! Banks of white blossoms against a blue sky . . .

TROFIMOV. Lyubov Andreevna! (LYUBOV ANDREEVNA *turns and looks at him.*) I just wanted to welcome you back. Then I'll go. (*He kisses her hand with great emotion.*) They told me not to come till morning, but I couldn't wait. (LYUBOV ANDREEVNA *stares at him in bewilderment.*)

VARYA (*through tears*). It's Petya, Petya Trofimov . . .

TROFIMOV. Petya Trofimov, Grisha's tutor . . . Have I changed so much?

(LYUBOV ANDREEVNA *puts her arms around him and weeps softly.*)

GAEV (*embarrassed*). Now, now, Lyuba . . .

VARYA (*crying*). I told you to wait till tomorrow, Petya.

LYUBOV ANDREEVNA. Grisha . . . My baby . . . Grisha . . . My son . . .

VARYA. It had to be, Mama. It was God's will.

TROFIMOV (*gently, almost crying*). There now, there now . . .

LYUBOV ANDREEVNA (*weeping softly*). My little boy—lost, drowned . . . Oh why, Petya, why? (*Lowering her voice.*) Here I am, talking away, making noise, and Anya's asleep in there . . . But what's happened to you, Petya? Why do you look so awful? Why have you aged so?

TROFIMOV. A peasant woman in the train referred to me as "the seedy gentleman."

LYUBOV ANDREEVNA. You were just a boy then, a nice young student. And now you're losing your hair, wearing glasses . . . Don't tell me you're still a student. (*She moves in the direction of the door.*)

TROFIMOV. An eternal student, most likely.

LYUBOV ANDREEVNA (*kissing* GAEV *and then* VARYA). Well, time for bed, everybody . . . You look old too, Leonid.

PISHCHIK (*following her*). Time to go to bed . . . Oh, my gout. Think I'll stay the night. Then tomorrow morning . . . What do you say, dear lady? Two hundred and forty rubles . . .

GAEV. Persistent, isn't he?

PISHCHIK. Two hundred and forty rubles . . . The interest on my mortgage.

LYUBOV ANDREEVNA. But I have no money, my dear.

PISHCHIK. I'll pay it back, kind lady . . . It's such a piddling amount.

LYUBOV ANDREEVNA. Oh, all right. Leonid will let you have it . . . Take care of it, Leonid.

GAEV. I will not! What does he think I am?

LYUBOV ANDREEVNA. No, really. Go ahead. What can we do? ... He needs it ... He'll pay it back.

(*Exit* LYUBOV ANDREEVNA, TROFIMOV, PISHCHIK, *and* FIRS. *Only* GAEV, VARYA, *and* YASHA *remain*.)

GAEV. I see Lyuba hasn't stopped throwing money away. (*To* YASHA.) Step back a little, my good man. You smell like a chicken coop.

YASHA (*with a smirk*). Haven't changed a bit, have you.

GAEV. What was that? (*To* VARYA.) What did he say?

VARYA (*to* YASHA). Your mother's here from the village. She's been waiting since yesterday in the servants' quarters. She wants to see you.

YASHA. I wish she'd leave me be.

VARYA. You ought to be ashamed of yourself!

YASHA. Who needs her, anyway? Couldn't she have waited till tomorrow? (*He exits.*)

VARYA. Mama hasn't changed a bit, not a bit. She'd give everything away if we let her.

GAEV. Hm ...

(*Pause.*)

When many remedies are prescribed for a disease, it means the disease is incurable. I've given it a great deal of thought, serious thought. I've come up with any number of remedies, any number. Which basically means none at all. Wouldn't it be nice if someone left us a fortune. Wouldn't it be nice if we could find Anya a rich husband. Wouldn't it be nice if one of us went to Yaroslavl and tried his luck with our aunt the countess. She's very, very rich, you know.

VARYA (*crying*). God willing.

GAEV. Oh, stop blubbering! She's very rich, but she doesn't like us. In the first place, Lyuba married a lawyer, not a nobleman ... (ANYA *appears at the door.*) She married beneath her station. And her behavior—well, you can't exactly say she's been virtuous. Oh, she's sweet, kind, a wonderful person, and I love her dearly, but, mitigating circumstances or no, you must admit her morals are a bit loose. It shows in every move she makes.

VARYA (*in a whisper*). Anya's at the door.

GAEV. What?

(*Pause.*)

That's funny. I seem to have something in my right eye ... I can hardly see. Anyway, while I was at the District Court on Thursday ...

(*Enter* ANYA.)

VARYA. Why aren't you in bed, Anya?

ANYA. I can't seem to fall asleep.

GAEV. My little girl. (*He kisses* ANYA's *face and hands.*) My baby ... (*Through tears.*) You're not my niece; you're my angel. You're everything to me. Believe me, believe me ...

ANYA. I do believe you, Uncle Leonid. Everybody loves you, respects you ... There's only one thing: you must learn to keep your mouth shut. Keep your mouth shut. Those things you said just now about Mama, your sister—what made you say them?

GAEV. I know, I know ... (*He covers his face with her hand.*) You're right. It's awful. God help me, that speech I made today to the bookcase was ... stupid. And I didn't realize it until it was over.

VARYA. She's right, Uncle Leonid. You must learn to keep your mouth shut. Keep quiet—that's all.

ANYA. You'll feel a lot better for it.

GAEV. I won't say another word. (*He kisses* ANYA's *and* VARYA's *hands.*) Not another word. But this is important. While I was at the District Court on Thursday, a group of us got together and started talking about one thing and another, and it seems we can borrow enough to pay the bank its interest.

VARYA. God willing!

GAEV. I'm going in on Tuesday to have another chat with them. (*To* VARYA.) Stop blubbering. (*To* ANYA.) Your mother's going to talk to Lopakhin. He can't possibly refuse ... and as soon as you're good and rested, you can pay a visit to your great-aunt the countess in Yaroslavl. That way we'll be tackling the thing from three directions at once. We can't fail. We'll pay the interest. I know we will ... (*He puts a fruit drop into his mouth.*) I give you my word of honor. I swear by all I hold dear. The estate shall not be sold! (*Passionately.*) Here is my hand. You may call me a liar and a cheat if I let it come up for auction. I swear by my entire being!

ANYA (*calm again and happy*). You're so good, Uncle Leonid, so intelligent! (*She hugs him.*) Now I feel better. Calm and happy.

(*Enter* FIRS.)

FIRS (*reproachfully*). You ought to be ashamed of yourself, sir. It's long past your bedtime.

GAEV. Yes, yes. I'm on my way. You can go, Firs. It's all right. I'll undress myself. Well now, little ones, time for bed ... (*He kisses* ANYA *and* VARYA.) I am a man of the eighties ...³ And even if people don't think too much of the eighties, I've suffered for my convictions. Why do you think the peasants love me so? You have to get to know the peasants. You have to know the way they ...

ANYA. There you go again, Uncle Leonid.

VARYA. Not now, Uncle Leonid. Please keep quiet.

FIRS (*angrily*). Leonid Andreevich!

GAEV. Coming, coming ... You go to bed too. Double bank into the middle. Pot the white. (*He exits.* FIRS *hobbles out after him.*)

ANYA. I'm so relieved. I haven't the slightest desire to go to Yaroslavl—I don't like that great-aunt of ours—but still I'm relieved. Thanks to Uncle Leonid. (*She sits.*)

VARYA. We'd better get some sleep. I'm going. Oh, by the way, we had some trouble while you were gone. You know, don't you, that only the older servants are left in the old quarters: Yefimushka, Polya, Yevstignei, and of course Karp. Well, they started letting some tramps sleep there, and at first I closed my eyes to it. But one day I heard a rumor that I'd given orders to feed them nothing but dried peas. Because I'm so stingy, you see ... It was Yevstignei who started it ... "All right, then," I said to myself, "if that's the way you want it." So I told him to come and see me ... (*She yawns.*) Well, he came ... and I said to him, "How could you? How could you be such a fool?" (*She looks over at* ANYA.) Anya! ...

(*Pause.*)

Asleep!...(*She takes* ANYA *by the arm.*) Come to bed now...Come with me ... (*She leads her along.*) My angel's asleep. Come with me ... (*They proceed slowly.*)

(*The sound of a shepherd's pipe comes from the far side of the orchard.* TROFIMOV *starts across the stage, but stops when he sees* VARYA *and* ANYA.)

VARYA. Sh! She's asleep...Asleep...Come with me, precious.

ANYA (*softly, half asleep*). I'm so tired ... I keep hearing bells...Uncle... dear ... Mama and Uncle Leonid ...

VARYA. Come with me, precious. Come with me ... (*They exit into* ANYA's *room.*)

TROFIMOV (*deeply moved*). My sunshine! My spring!

CURTAIN

ACT TWO

A field. A tumbledown old chapel long since abandoned. It is flanked by a well, some large stone slabs that must once have been tombstones, and an old bench. A road leads to GAEV's estate. A dark strip of tall poplars off to the side marks the beginning of the cherry orchard. There is a row of telegraph poles in the distance, and even farther, on the horizon, the dim outline of a large town visible only on the clearest of days. The sun is about to set. SHARLOTTA, YASHA, and DUN-YASHA are sitting on the bench. YEPIKHODOV stands nearby playing the guitar. They are all lost in thought. SHARLOTTA, who is wearing an old peaked cap, has taken a shotgun off her shoulder and is adjusting the buckle on the strap.

SHARLOTTA (*pensively*). I have no real identity papers, no way of knowing how old I am, but I always think of myself as young. When I was a little girl, my mother and father toured the fairgrounds giving performances, good ones too. I did the *salto mortale*[4] and various other stunts. And when Mama and Papa died, a German lady took me in and saw to my education. So far so good. Then I grew up and took a post as a governess. But don't ask me where I'm from or who I am—I don't know . . . Don't ask me who my parents were or even if they were married—I don't know. (*She takes a small cucumber out of her pocket and bites into it.*) Don't know a thing.

(*Pause.*)

I want so much to talk to somebody. But who? . . . I'm all alone.
YEPIKHODOV (*playing the guitar and singing*).

> What care I for worldly pleasure.
> What care I for friend or foe . . .[5]

I do so enjoy playing the mandolin!

DUNYASHA. That's no mandolin; that's a guitar. (*She gazes at herself in a hand mirror and powders her face.*)

YEPIKHODOV. To a fool in love it's a mandolin . . . (*He sings softly.*)

> If my heart's most valued treasure
> Keeps the fire of love aglow . . .

(YASHA *joins in.*)

SHARLOTTA. What awful voices they have . . . Ugh! Like jackals.

DUNYASHA (*to* YASHA). You're so lucky, going abroad like that.

YASHA. I should say so. Couldn't agree with you more. (*He yawns, then lights a cigar.*)

YEPIKHODOV. It stands to reason. Everything abroad has long since reached a stage of complete complection.

YASHA. Indubitably.

YEPIKHODOV. I am a man of culture—I read the most sundry books—but I still can't quite decide what direction to take, what I really want to do—live on or shoot myself, so to speak. But to be on the safe side, I always carry a revolver with me. See? . . . (*He takes out a revolver.*)

SHARLOTTA. Well, that's that. I'm off. (*She slings the gun over her shoulder.*) You're so bright, Yepikhodov, so awe-inspiring, I bet all the ladies go crazy over you. Ugh! (*She starts off.*) All these bright lights are so dull I have no one to talk to . . . Alone, all alone with no one to talk to and . . . and no idea who I am or why I'm here . . . (*She exits slowly.*)

YEPIKHODOV. When all is said and done and keeping strictly to the point, I must state on my behalf that fate has dealt me a series of merciless blows. And if by any chance I am mistaken, then why did I wake up this morning to find a spider of enormous proportions sitting on my chest? . . . This big. (*He indicates its size with both hands.*) Or whenever I pick up a glass of kvass, why is there always something positively indecent floating in it? Like a cockroach.

(*Pause.*)

Has any of you read Buckle's *History of Civilization in England*? [6]

(*Pause.*)

May I trouble you for a few words, Dunya my dear?

DUNYASHA. What is it?

YEPIKHODOV. May I request that we should talk in private? . . .

DUNYASHA (*embarrassed*). All right . . . But first would you bring me my cape . . . I left it near the bookshelf . . . It's so damp out here . . .

YEPIKHODOV. Very well . . . I'll go . . . And now I know what to do with my revolver . . . (*He picks up his guitar and exits strumming.*)

YASHA. Twenty-two disasters! The man's a fool, if you ask me. (*He yawns.*)

DUNYASHA. I hope to God he doesn't shoot himself.

(*Pause.*)

I've been so worried lately, so on edge. I was only a girl when they brought me to the house to work, and now I've completely lost touch with the way ordinary people live. Look how white my hands are—white as a lady's. I'm so delicate, refined, so ladylike, afraid of everything . . . Scared. And if you ever deceive me, Yasha, I don't know what it will do to my nerves.

YASHA (*kissing her*). A real sugar plum. Of course a girl must keep herself in hand. If there's one thing I disapprove of in a woman, it's loose behavior.

DUNYASHA. I'm madly in love with you. You're so well educated. You can talk about anything.

(*Pause.*)

YASHA (*yawning*). Yes . . . Well, the way I see it, if a girl is in love, it means she's immoral.

(*Pause.*)

What could be more enjoyable than a cigar in the open air? . . . (*He listens.*) Somebody's coming . . . It's the masters . . .

(DUNYASHA *flings her arms around him impulsively.*)

Go back to the house and make believe you've been out swimming
in the river. And don't take the main road or they'll see you and
think we had a rendezvous. That would be unbearable.

DUNYASHA (*coughing, softly*). That cigar. It gives me a headache . . .
(*She exits.*)

(YASHA *takes a seat near the chapel. Enter* LYUBOV ANDREEVNA,
GAEV, *and* LOPAKHIN.)

LOPAKHIN. You've got to make up your minds once and for all.
Time's running out. It's a perfectly simple matter anyway: either
you're willing to lease the land for cottages or you're not. Just say
the word. Say the word.

LYUBOV ANDREEVNA. Who's been smoking those disgusting cigars
around here? . . . (*She sits.*)

GAEV. Now that they've finished the railway line, it's no trouble at
all. (*He sits.*) We took the train into town just for a bite to eat . . .
Yellow into the middle. Think I'll go inside for a game . . .

LYUBOV ANDREEVNA. What's your hurry?

LOPAKHIN. Just one word! (*Pleading with them.*) Tell me. Please!

GAEV (*yawning*). What's that?

LYUBOV ANDREEVNA (*looking into her purse*). Yesterday I had plenty of
money; today there's almost none left. Poor Varya's trying to econ-
omize by feeding us all milk soup, the old servants in the kitchen
get nothing but dried peas, and I throw my money away . . . (*She
drops her purse, scattering some gold coins.*) There it goes . . . (*She is
annoyed.*)

YASHA. Allow me, madam. (*He picks up the coins.*)

LYUBOV ANDREEVNA. Yes, Yasha. Please . . . What can have pos-
sessed me to go to town for lunch? . . . That pitiful restaurant of
yours—the orchestra, the tablecloths reeking of soap . . . Why
drink so much, Lyonya! And eat so much! And talk so much!
Rambling on in the restaurant today about the seventies and the
decadents. And to whom? Really now! Talking about decadents
to waiters!

LOPAKHIN. Hm.

GAEV (*dismissing her reproach with a wave of the hand*). I know, I know.

I'm hopeless ... (*Irritably, to* YASHA.) What are you doing, hanging around all the time?

YASHA (*laughing*). Your voice makes me laugh.

GAEV (*to* LYUBOV ANDREEVNA). Either he goes or I go ...

LYUBOV ANDREEVNA. You may leave now. Go on ...

YASHA (*handing* LYUBOV ANDREEVNA *her purse*). I'm on my way. (*He can hardly keep from laughing.*) On my way ... (*He exits.*)

LOPAKHIN. There's a rich man by the name of Deriganov who's thinking of buying your estate. They say he'll be at the auction in person.

LYUBOV ANDREEVNA. Where did you hear that?

LOPAKHIN. In town. People are talking.

GAEV. Our aunt in Yaroslavl has promised us some money, but when or how much isn't clear.

LOPAKHIN. Approximately, then. A hundred thousand? Two hundred?

LYUBOV ANDREEVNA. Well ... Ten. Fifteen maybe, if we're lucky.

LOPAKHIN. I'm sorry, but you and your brother—you're the most scatterbrained, the most strange and impractical people I've ever met. Here I tell you in no uncertain terms that your estate is up for sale, and you can't seem to get it into your heads.

LYUBOV ANDREEVNA. But what can we do about it? Tell us what to do.

LOPAKHIN. I *have* told you. I tell you every day. Lease both the cherry orchard and the land for summer cottages, and do it now, without delay! The auction will be here in no time. Try and understand. Once you decide in favor of the cottages, you can borrow as much as you like. You'll be saved.

LYUBOV ANDREEVNA. But all those cottages and people—I'm sorry, it's so vulgar.

GAEV. I quite agree.

LOPAKHIN. I think I'm going to break down and cry or scream or faint. I can't take it. You're too much for me. (*To* GAEV.) And you—you're an old maid!

GAEV. What was that?

LOPAKHIN. An old maid! (*He starts to go.*)

LYUBOV ANDREEVNA (*alarmed*). No, don't go! Please stay, please! Maybe we can come up with something.

LOPAKHIN. But I *have* come up with something.

LYUBOV ANDREEVNA. Don't go! Please! You do liven up the place . . .

(*Pause.*)

I keep expecting something terrible to happen—like the house caving in on us.

GAEV (*in deep thought*). Double into the corner . . . Cross shot into the middle . . .

LYUBOV ANDREEVNA. Oh, the sins we have on our conscience . . .

LOPAKHIN. Sins? You?

GAEV (*putting a fruit drop into his mouth*). People say I've eaten up my fortune in fruit drops . . . (*He laughs.*)

LYUBOV ANDREEVNA. Oh, my sins . . . I've always spent money like water. I'm like a madwoman. And to make matters worse, I married a man whose only talent was running up debts, who died of champagne, drank himself to death. I had the bad luck to fall in love with somebody else, and then, just after we'd become lovers—it was my first punishment, an awful blow—right here in the river . . . my little boy, he drowned. And I went abroad, went away for good. I never wanted to see that river again . . . I shut my eyes and ran, blindly. But *he* came after me . . . pitilessly, mercilessly. I bought a villa near Menton because *he* came down with something there, and for three years I nursed him day and night. He completely drained me—physically and emotionally. Then last year, when the place had to be sold for debts, I went to Paris, and there he robbed me, ran out on me, took up with another woman. I tried to poison myself . . . It was all so stupid and humiliating . . . And suddenly I felt I couldn't live without Russia, my country, my little girl . . . (*She wipes away her tears.*) O Lord, Lord, be merciful. Forgive me my sins! Don't punish me again. (*She takes a telegram out of her pocket.*) This came today from Paris. He begs me to forgive him, implores me to return . . . (*She tears up the telegram.*) Is that music I hear? (*She listens.*)

GAEV. Our famous Jewish orchestra. Remember? Four fiddles, flute, double bass.

LYUBOV ANDREEVNA. You mean it still exists? We should have them come and play sometime, give a party.

LOPAKHIN (*listening*). I don't hear anything . . . (*He sings softly.*)

> If you pay the Prussians,
> They'll Frenchify us Russians . . .[7]

(*He laughs.*) I saw a funny play at the theater last night. Very funny.

LYUBOV ANDREEVNA. How would you know it was funny? You people shouldn't go to plays. You should take a good look at yourselves—your gray lives, your empty talk . . .

LOPAKHIN. True. There's no getting away from it. We do live stupid lives.

(*Pause.*)

My father was a peasant, an empty-headed idiot whose only idea of education was to beat me when he was drunk—and with a stick. But when you think about it, I'm as much of a blockhead and idiot as he was. No schooling, and my penmanship's so bad I'm ashamed to let people see it—a pig could do better.

LYUBOV ANDREEVNA. What you need is a wife, my friend.

LOPAKHIN. Hm . . . True.

LYUBOV ANDREEVNA. Like our Varya. A nice girl.

LOPAKHIN. Hm.

LYUBOV ANDREEVNA. And from a nice, simple background. Works all day long. The main thing, though, is she loves you. And you've been fond of her all these years, haven't you?

LOPAKHIN. Well, it's all right with me . . . She's a nice girl.

(*Pause.*)

GAEV (*to* LYUBOV ANDREEVNA). Did you know I'd been offered a post at the bank? Six thousand a year . . .

LYUBOV ANDREEVNA. You? In a bank? Stay where you are . . .

(*Enter* FIRS *carrying an overcoat.*)

FIRS (*to* GAEV). Put this on now, sir. It's damp out.

GAEV (*putting on the coat*). I wish you'd stop pestering me.

FIRS. Now, now . . . You went off this morning without telling me.

(*He examines* GAEV *carefully.*)

LYUBOV ANDREEVNA. You look so much older, Firs.

FIRS. I beg your pardon, madam?

LOPAKHIN. She says you're looking old.

FIRS. I *am* old. They were ready to marry me off before your papa was born . . . (*He laughs.*) I was head footman by the time the serfs were freed. I didn't want my freedom. I stayed on with the master . . .

(*Pause.*)

I remember how happy they all were at the time—not that they knew why.

LOPAKHIN. Yes, those were the good old days . . . Plenty of floggings.

FIRS (*failing to catch* LOPAKHIN's *last words*). I should say so. Peasants had their masters; masters had their peasants. Now they're all scattered. You don't know where you stand.

GAEV. Quiet, Firs. I'm going into town tomorrow. I've been promised an appointment with a general who may let us have a loan.

LOPAKHIN. Don't count on it. Besides, you can't begin to pay the interest. Take my word for it.

LYUBOV ANDREEVNA. He's imagining things. There's no general.

(*Enter* TROFIMOV, ANYA, *and* VARYA.)

GAEV. Oh, here come the children.

ANYA. Look, there's Mama.

LYUBOV ANDREEVNA (*tenderly*). Over here . . . Over here, darlings . . . (*Embracing* ANYA *and* VARYA.) If you two knew how much I love you. Here, sit next to me. (EVERYONE *sits.*)

LOPAKHIN. Our eternal student here spends all his time with the ladies, I see.

TROFIMOV. Mind your own business.

LOPAKHIN. Pushing fifty and still a student.

TROFIMOV. I've had enough of your stupid jokes.

LOPAKHIN. I wonder what our crackpot here is so angry about.

TROFIMOV. Stop picking on me.

LOPAKHIN (*laughing*). Let me ask you something. What sort of man do you think I am?

TROFIMOV. You? Well, you're a rich man, a millionaire-to-be, and insofar as predators are necessary to maintain the cycle of nature by devouring everything in their path, you too are necessary.

(EVERYONE *laughs*.)

VARYA. Why don't you tell us some more about the planets, Petya.

LYUBOV ANDREEVNA. No, let's go back to where we left off yesterday.

TROFIMOV. What were we talking about?

GAEV. Pride.

TROFIMOV. Oh, yes. We did do a lot of talking yesterday. Didn't come to any conclusions, though. From your point of view, there's something mystical about the proud man, and you're right in a way. But look at the facts—the bare, simple facts. Why even talk about pride when man's physiological makeup is so shoddy, when the overwhelming majority of the species is coarse, ignorant, and profoundly unhappy. It's time we stopped admiring ourselves and started working.

GAEV. We're all going to die anyway.

TROFIMOV. Who knows? And who knows what dying means? Maybe man has a hundred senses and when he dies he loses only the five we're aware of. That leaves ninety-five to go on living.

LYUBOV ANDREEVNA. You're so clever, Petya! . . .

LOPAKHIN (*ironically*). Yes, terribly!

TROFIMOV. Mankind marches onward, ever perfecting its powers. Things that seem unattainable to us now will one day come within our reach, but only if we work, do all we can to help those seeking the truth. Here in Russia there are still very few of them. The overwhelming majority of the intellectuals I know aren't seeking anything or even doing anything; they're incapable of work. They call themselves the intelligentsia, but they talk down to their servants and treat the peasants like animals. They don't know how to study, don't take their reading seriously. They sit around doing nothing. Science for them is nothing but chitchat, art—a closed book. Oh, they're all very earnest and look very solemn, they discuss weighty issues, philosophize— and right under their noses poorly nourished workers sleep without bedding, thirty or forty to a room, plagued by bedbugs, dark, fetid air, and all manner of depravity ... It's obvious: the only reason for all our fine words is to pull the wool over people's eyes—our own included. Show me the public nurseries people shout about. Show me the public libraries. You find them in novels, not in life. Life is all filth, vulgarity, Asiatic barbarism ... I don't like those earnest faces. I'm afraid of them. I'm afraid of earnest words. We'd be better off keeping our mouths shut.

LOPAKHIN. Well, I'm up every day at four. I work from morning till night. I handle a lot of money—my own and other people's—and I see who's who and what's what. Try to get something done and you'll see how few honest, decent people there are. Sometimes, when I can't fall asleep, I think to myself, "Lord, you gave us vast forests, boundless plains, and sweeping horizons, and living in their midst we should be as giants ..."

LYUBOV ANDREEVNA. Why giants? ... They're all right in fairy tales, but otherwise they're scary.

(YEPIKHODOV *crosses the back of the stage strumming his guitar.*)

(*Pensively.*) There goes Yepikhodov.

ANYA (*pensively*). There goes Yepikhodov.

GAEV. The sun has set, ladies and gentlemen.

TROFIMOV. Hm.

GAEV (*in a subdued voice, as if reciting a poem*). O nature, glorious nature, glowing with eternal radiance, so beautiful, so indifferent! Thou, whom we call Mother, in whom the quick and the dead are joined together, who givest life and takest it away ...

VARYA (*beseechingly*). Uncle Leonid! ...

TROFIMOV. You'd do better with a double off the red into the middle.

GAEV. Not another word. Not a one.

(*They all sit deep in thought, their silence broken only by* FIRS'S *gentle mumbling. Suddenly they hear a distant sound that seems to come from the sky, the sound of a string that has snapped. It dies away mournfully.*)

LYUBOV ANDREEVNA. What was that?

LOPAKHIN. I don't know. A bucket must have snapped loose somewhere off in the mines. But a long way off.

GAEV. Maybe it's a bird of some kind . . . A heron . . .

TROFIMOV. Or an owl . . .

LYUBOV ANDREEVNA (*shuddering*). There was something disagreeable about it.

(*Pause.*)

FIRS. It was like that before the disaster: an owl hooting and the samovar humming and humming.

GAEV. What disaster?

FIRS. Freedom.

(*Pause.*)

LYUBOV ANDREEVNA. Come, let's go in, everybody. It's getting late. (*To* ANYA.) You've got tears in your eyes. What is it, child? (*She puts her arms around her.*)

ANYA. Nothing, Mama. I'm all right.

TROFIMOV. Somebody's coming.

(*A* PASSERBY *appears. He is wearing a battered white cap and an overcoat and is slightly drunk.*)

PASSERBY. Excuse me, but can you tell me if this is the way to the station?

GAEV. Yes. Just follow this road.

PASSERBY. Much obliged. (*Coughing.*) Nice weather we're having. (*He begins to recite a poem.*)

> Brother, long-suffering brother!
> Come down to the Volga, whose groan . . .[8]

(*To* VARYA.) You wouldn't have thirty kopecks for a starving Russian, would you, mam'selle? . . . (VARYA, *frightened, shrieks.*)

LOPAKHIN (*angrily*). Has indecency lost all bounds?

LYUBOV ANDREEVNA (*ruffled*). Here . . . This is for you . . . (*She rummages in her purse.*) No silver . . . Oh well . . . Here's a gold piece . . .

PASSERBY. Much obliged, ma'am! (*He exits.*)

(*Laughter.*)

VARYA (*still frightened*). I'm leaving . . . I'm going . . . Mama, how could you! The servants have nothing to eat, and you give him gold.

LYUBOV ANDREEVNA. Well, what can you do with a fool like me? I'll give you everything I've got when we're back at the house. You'll let me have another loan, won't you, Lopakhin?

LOPAKHIN. At your service.

LYUBOV ANDREEVNA. Let's go, everyone. Time to go. By the way, Varya, the matchmaking is over. Congratulations.

VARYA (*through tears*). Please, Mama. It's not a laughing matter.

LOPAKHIN. Get thee to a nunnery, Ovarya.[9]

GAEV. Look, my hands are shaking. What I need is a good game of billiards.

LOPAKHIN. Ovarya, nymph, in thine orisons be all my sins remembered.

LYUBOV ANDREEVNA. Come along, everybody. It's almost time for supper.

VARYA. He really frightened me! My heart's still pounding.

LOPAKHIN. May I remind you all that the cherry orchard's going up for auction on the twenty-second of August. Don't forget now . . . Don't forget . . .

(*All but* TROFIMOV *and* ANYA *exit.*)

ANYA (*laughing*). We ought to have thanked the stranger for scaring Varya like that. Now we're alone.

TROFIMOV. Varya's afraid we'll fall in love. She won't let us out of her sight. She's too limited to see we're above such things. The only purpose to our lives, the only meaning is to do away with all the petty, illusory concerns that keep us from being happy and free. Onward! On we go! Inexorable. Our goal—that bright star burning in the distance! Onward! Don't fall behind, my friends!

ANYA (*clasping her hands*). How beautifully you put things!

(*Pause.*)

Isn't it heavenly here today?

TROFIMOV. Yes, the weather is splendid.

ANYA. What have you done to me, Petya? Why don't I love the cherry orchard the way I used to? I used to love it so dearly. I thought it was the finest place on earth, our orchard.

TROFIMOV. All Russia is our orchard. The earth is vast and beautiful, filled with wonderful places.

(*Pause.*)

Think of it, Anya. Your grandfather, great-grandfather, all your ancestors were serf-owners: they owned live souls. Can't you see them? Human beings staring out at you from every tree in the orchard, from every leaf, every trunk. Can't you hear their voices? . . . Owning live souls—it's done something to you, your whole family, past and present. You, your mother, your uncle—you don't realize you're living on credit, at the expense of others, people you won't let past your front door . . . We're at least two hundred years behind the times, so destitute we have no real conception of the past. All we do is philosophize, complain about how depressing life is, and drink vodka. But it's perfectly clear that to live in the present we've got to expiate our past, make a clean break with it. And the only way we can do so is through suffering—suffering and relentless hard work. Can you see that, Anya?

ANYA. It's a long time since we could really call this house our own, and I'm going to leave. I swear I am.

TROFIMOV. If you have the keys, then fling them down the well and come away! Free as a bird!

ANYA (*in a state of rapture*). How beautifully you put it!

TROFIMOV. Take my word for it, Anya! Take my word! I'm not thirty yet; I'm young, still a student. But what I've been through! When winter comes, I'm hungry, ailing, plagued with anxiety, poor as a pauper. The places life has taken me—there's nowhere I haven't been. But through it all, every minute of it, every day and every night, I'm haunted by inexplicable premonitions of happiness. I can see it coming, Anya . . .

ANYA (*pensively*). The moon is rising.

(YEPIKHODOV *is heard strumming the same sad song as before. The moon rises. Over by the poplars* VARYA *is looking for* ANYA *and calling, "Anya! Where are you?"*)

TROFIMOV. Yes, the moon is rising.

(*Pause.*)

There it is—happiness. Here it comes, closer and closer. I can hear its footsteps. And if *we* never see it or know it, well, that's all right too. Others will. (VARYA*'s voice calls out, "Anya! Where are you?"*) Varya again! (*Angrily.*) She's impossible!

ANYA. Don't mind her. Let's go down to the river. It's so lovely there.

TROFIMOV. Yes, let's. (*They exit.*)

(VARYA*'s voice calls out, "Anya! Anya!"*)

CURTAIN

ACT THREE

The drawing room. An arch opens onto the ballroom. The chandelier is lit. The Jewish orchestra mentioned in Act Two is playing in the entrance hall. It is evening. The guests are dancing a grand rond *in the ballroom.*[10] PISHCHIK *calls out, "Promenade à une paire!"* PISHCHIK *and* SHARLOTTA *are the first couple to enter,* TROFIMOV *and* LYUBOV ANDREEVNA *the second,* ANYA *and the* POSTMASTER *the third,* VARYA *and the* STATIONMASTER *the fourth, and so on.* VARYA *is crying quietly and dries her eyes while dancing.* DUNYASHA *is in the last couple. They cross the drawing room as* PISHCHIK *calls out, "Grand rond! Balancez!" and "Les cavaliers à genoux et remerciez vos dames!"*

FIRS, *wearing a frock coat, carries in a tray of soda water.* PISHCHIK *and* TROFIMOV *reenter the drawing room.*

PISHCHIK. Dancing comes hard with my high blood pressure and my two strokes, but you know what they say: if you run with the pack, then at least wag your tail. I'm as strong as a horse, though. My dear departed father, who liked a joke, used to say that the ancient line of Simeonov-Pishchik descended from the horse that Caligula made a senator . . . (*He sits.*) My only problem is money. A hungry dog believes only in meat. (*He begins to snore, but wakes up immediately.*) It's the same with me . . . I've got money on the brain.

TROFIMOV. Come to think of it, there is something horsey about you.

PISHCHIK. Well . . . A horse is a fine animal . . . You can sell a horse . . .

(*The sounds of a game of billiards come from an adjoining room.* VARYA *appears in the ballroom.*)

TROFIMOV (*teasing her*). Madame Lopakhina! Madame Lopakhina! . . .

VARYA (*angrily*). Oh, the seedy gentleman!

TROFIMOV. Seedy and proud of it!

VARYA (*musing bitterly*). Hiring musicians! What are we going to pay them with? (*She exits.*)

TROFIMOV (*to* PISHCHIK). If the energy you've wasted in a lifetime of scrounging for interest payments had been put to better use, you'd have turned the world upside down.

PISHCHIK. Nietzsche . . . the philosopher . . . a great man, world-renowned, a man of the intellect . . . Nietzsche says it's all right to counterfeit money.

TROFIMOV. So you've read Nietzsche?

PISHCHIK. Well, no . . . My Dasha told me. And things have come to such a pass that I may well have to resort to counterfeiting . . . Three hundred and ten rubles due the day after tomorrow . . . I've scraped together a hundred and thirty . . . (*He feels his pockets in alarm.*) It's gone! The money! I've lost it! (*Through tears.*) Where's my money? (*Joyfully.*) Oh, here it is! In the lining . . . Look at me, sweating all over . . .

(*Enter* LYUBOV ANDREEVNA *and* SHARLOTTA.)

LYUBOV ANDREEVNA (*humming a lively Caucasian dance tune*). Why isn't Leonid back yet? What can he be doing in town? (*To* DUN-YASHA.) See if the musicians want some tea, Dunyasha . . .

TROFIMOV. The auction probably never took place.

LYUBOV ANDREEVNA. This wasn't the right time to have musicians. It wasn't the right time for a party . . . Oh well, never mind. (*She sits and hums quietly.*)

SHARLOTTA (*handing* PISHCHIK *a pack of cards*). Pick a card, any card.

PISHCHIK. All right. I've got one.

SHARLOTTA. Now shuffle the cards. Fine. And give them back to me, if you'll be so kind. *Eins, zwei, drei!*[11] Now have a look in your coat pocket. Is that your card?

PISHCHIK (*pulling a card out of his pocket*). The eight of spades. Absolutely right! (*Amazed.*) Unbelievable!

SHARLOTTA (*holding the pack out to* TROFIMOV *in the palm of her hand*). Quickly. Tell me what the top card is.

TROFIMOV. Well, say, the queen of spades.

SHARLOTTA. Right you are! (*To* PISHCHIK.) And what's the top card now?

PISHCHIK. The ace of hearts.

SHARLOTTA. Right again! (*She claps her hands and the cards disappear.*) Nice weather we've been having. (*A mysterious woman's voice that seems to come from underground answers, "Yes, madam. Marvelous weather."*) You're everything I'd always hoped for. (*The voice replies, "I'm quite taken with you too, madam."*)

STATIONMASTER (*clapping*). Three cheers for the ventriloquist!

PISHCHIK (*amazed*). Unbelievable! You're a real charmer, Sharlotta Ivanovna . . . I'm in love . . .

SHARLOTTA. In love? (*Shrugging her shoulders.*) You? In love. *Guter Mensch, aber schlechter Musikant.*[12]

TROFIMOV (*slapping* PISHCHIK *on the back*). There's a good horse . . .

SHARLOTTA. Attention, please! One more trick. (*She picks up a plaid traveling blanket from a chair.*) Now here's a fine specimen of plaid. Think I'll sell it . . . (*She shakes it out.*) Any customers?

PISHCHIK (*amazed*). Unbelievable!

SHARLOTTA. *Eins, zwei, drei!* (*She lifts the blanket with a flourish and out steps* ANYA, *who curtsies, runs over to* LYUBOV ANDREEVNA, *gives her a hug, and runs back to the ballroom amidst the oh's and ah's of the crowd.*)

LYUBOV ANDREEVNA (*clapping*). Bravo! Bravo!

SHARLOTTA. And for an encore: *eins, zwei, drei.* (*She lifts the blanket and out comes* VARYA *with a bow.*)

PISHCHIK (*amazed*). Unbelievable!

SHARLOTTA. That's it for today. (*She throws the blanket at* PISHCHIK, *curtsies, and runs off to the ballroom.*)

PISHCHIK (*rushing after her*). You little minx, you! . . . What a woman! What a woman! (*He exits.*)

LYUBOV ANDREEVNA. Still no sign of Leonid. What can he be doing there so long? I don't understand. It must be over by now. Either the estate is sold or the auction didn't take place. Why keep us in suspense?

VARYA (*trying to comfort her*). He's bought it. I'm sure he has.

TROFIMOV (*sarcastically*). Of course he has.

VARYA. Our great-aunt gave him power of attorney to buy it in her name and have the mortgage made over to her. She's doing it for Anya's sake. God will help us. I'm sure He will. Uncle Leonid's got to buy it.

LYUBOV ANDREEVNA. Your great-aunt gave him fifteen thousand to buy back the estate in her name—she doesn't trust us—and that won't even cover the interest. (*She puts her hands over her face.*) My future is in the balance today, my fate ...

TROFIMOV (*teasing* VARYA). Madame Lopakhina!

VARYA (*angrily*). Eternal student! Twice expelled!

LYUBOV ANDREEVNA. Don't get so upset, Varya. What if he does tease you. Marry Lopakhin if you want to. He's a nice man, an attractive man. And don't marry him if you don't. Nobody's forcing you, darling ...

VARYA. I've given it serious thought, Mama. Let me be frank. He's a nice man, and I'm attracted to him.

LYUBOV ANDREEVNA. Then marry him. What are you waiting for? I don't understand.

VARYA. I can't very well propose to him, can I? For two years now everyone's been talking about it. Everyone but him. He either dodges the subject or turns it into a joke. Oh, I know. He's busy getting rich; he has no time for me. Well, if I had any money— a hundred rubles—I'd drop everything and go away from here, the further the better. Enter a convent.

TROFIMOV. Oh, the glory of it!

VARYA (*to* TROFIMOV). The student has to show how clever he is. (*In a gentle, teary voice.*) You're so much uglier than you used to be, Petya. And older. (*To* LYUBOV ANDREEVNA, *no longer crying.*) I need to be busy all the time, Mama; I need something to do every minute.

(*Enter* YASHA.)

YASHA (*scarcely able to keep from laughing*). Yepikhodov's broken a billiard cue. (*He exits.*)

VARYA. What is Yepikhodov doing here? Who said he could play billiards? I don't understand these people ... (*She exits.*)

LYUBOV ANDREEVNA. Don't tease her, Petya. Can't you see she's miserable enough as it is?

TROFIMOV. I just wish she wouldn't pry so. She's such a busybody. She hasn't left Anya or me alone all summer. She's afraid we'll have an affair. Well, what business is it of hers? And anyway, I've never given her the least cause to think so. I'm beyond such trivialities. We're above that sort of thing.

LYUBOV ANDREEVNA. Which means, I suppose, that I'm beneath it. (*Greatly agitated.*) Why isn't he back? All I want to know is whether the estate's been sold. It's so inconceivable a disaster I don't know what to think. I'm at my wits' end . . . Help me, Petya, or I'll scream, make a fool of myself . . . Say something, anything . . .

TROFIMOV. Does it really matter whether the estate is sold today or not? It's all over and done with, dead and buried. You can't turn back the clock. Try and be calm, try and be honest with yourself. For once in your life look truth in the face.

LYUBOV ANDREEVNA. What truth? You see so clearly what's true and what's false. I must be going blind. I don't see a thing. You've got a bold solution for everything, but isn't that because you're young and haven't suffered the consequences of what you preach? You look ahead so boldly, but isn't that because you're sheltered and don't imagine or expect anything terrible to happen? You may be bolder, purer, and deeper than we are, but put yourself in my place. Show a little generosity. Give me the benefit of the doubt. I was born here; my mother and father, my grandfather all lived here. I love this house. Life means nothing to me without the cherry orchard, and if it has to be sold you might as well sell me along with it . . . (*She embraces* TROFIMOV *and kisses him on the forehead.*) My little boy drowned here . . . (*She weeps.*) Don't be too hard on me. You're so good, so kind.

TROFIMOV. You know you have my deepest sympathy.

LYUBOV ANDREEVNA. No, you've got it all wrong, all wrong . . . (*She takes out a handkerchief. A telegram falls to the floor.*) I'm so depressed today, you can't imagine. I can't stand the noise. I jump at every sound. I'm trembling all over. But I can't go to my room: I'm terrified of the silence and of being alone. Don't condemn me, Petya . . . I love you like my own child. I'd gladly let Anya marry you, believe me, only you really must go back and finish your studies. You don't do anything; you just drift from place to place.

Don't you see how odd that is? . . . Well, don't you? And you must do something about that beard, make it grow or something . . . (*She laughs.*) You look so funny . . .

TROFIMOV (*picking up the telegram*). I've no desire to be a dandy.

LYUBOV ANDREEVNA. A telegram from Paris. I get one every day. One yesterday, one today. That wild man is ailing again, in trouble again . . . He asks me to forgive him, begs me to come. I really should go back to him and take care of him for a while. I see you don't approve, Petya, but what else can I do, dear? What else can I do? He's ill, he's lonely and unhappy. Who'll look after him, keep him from making a fool of himself, give him his medicine on time? And anyway—why not come out and say it?—I love him. It's obvious. I love him, I love him . . . He's a millstone round my neck, he's dragging me down with him, but I love my millstone. I can't live without it. (*She presses* TROFIMOV'*s hand.*) Don't hold it against me, Petya. Don't say anything at all. Not a word . . .

TROFIMOV (*through tears*). Forgive me for being so blunt, but he's robbed you!

LYUBOV ANDREEVNA. No, no, no! You mustn't say that! . . . (*She puts her hands over her ears.*)

TROFIMOV. But the man's a scoundrel! You're the only one who doesn't see it. A petty scoundrel, a nobody . . .

LYUBOV ANDREEVNA (*angrily, but in control*). Here you are, twenty-six, twenty-seven, and still a schoolboy . . .

TROFIMOV. Well, what if I am!

LYUBOV ANDREEVNA. Why aren't you more of a man? At your age you should know what it means to be in love. You should be in love yourself . . . You should fall in love. (*Angrily.*) That's right! What's so pure about you? You're a prude, that's all. A crackpot, a freak . . .

TROFIMOV (*horrified*). What is she saying?

LYUBOV ANDREEVNA. So you're "beyond love." You're not beyond love; you're what our Firs would call a numskull. Not having a mistress at your age! . . .

TROFIMOV (*horrified*). This is awful! How can she be saying these things? (*He rushes off to the ballroom clutching his head.*) This is awful! . . . I can't stand it. I've got to get out of here . . . (*He exits, but comes back at once.*) I never want to see you again! (*He exits into the entrance hall.*)

LYUBOV ANDREEVNA (*shouting after him*). Wait, Petya, wait! Don't be silly. I was only joking. Petya!

(*There is a sound of rapid footsteps on the stairs in the entrance hall followed by a crash.* ANYA *and* VARYA *shriek, then burst out laughing.*)

What's going on out there?

ANYA (*running in, laughing*). Petya's fallen down the stairs! (*She runs out.*)

LYUBOV ANDREEVNA. Oh, that Petya . . .

STATIONMASTER (*going and standing in the middle of the ballroom*). "The Sinner Woman" by Alexei Tolstoy.[13]

> A swarming crowd: gay laughter's clang,
> The crash of gongs, the lutes' clear twang,
> Flowers and green'ry scattered round . . .

(*The guests listen for a while, but when the strains of a waltz reach them from the entrance hall, the recitation breaks off and they all start dancing.* TROFIMOV, ANYA, VARYA, *and* LYUBOV ANDREEVNA *enter from the hall.*)

LYUBOV ANDREEVNA. Now, now, Petya . . . Poor, pure Petya . . . I apologize . . . Come, let's dance . . . (*She dances with* TROFIMOV. ANYA *and* VARYA *dance.*)

(*Enter* FIRS. *He stands his cane near the side door.* YASHA *has entered from the drawing room and is watching the dancers.*)

YASHA. How's it going, old man?

FIRS. Not doing too well. Time was we had generals and barons and admirals at our parties, and now who do we get? The postmaster, the stationmaster. And even they have to be begged. Been feeling a mite weak lately. The old master, their grandfather, he used to treat all ailments with sealing wax. I've been taking sealing wax every day now for nigh on twenty years. No, more. Maybe that's what keeps me going.

YASHA. You know, I'm sick of you, old man. (*He yawns.*) Why don't you just curl up and die.

FIRS. Another numskull. (*He starts mumbling to himself.*)

(TROFIMOV *and* LYUBOV ANDREEVNA *dance first in the ballroom,
then in the drawing room.*)

LYUBOV ANDREEVNA. *Merci.* I think I'll sit for a while . . . (*She sits.*)
I'm tired.

ANYA (*entering, shaken*). Just now in the kitchen a man said the
cherry orchard had been sold today.

LYUBOV ANDREEVNA. Sold? Who bought it?

ANYA. He didn't say. He's gone now. (*She dances with* TROFIMOV. *Both
exit into the ballroom.*)

YASHA. Just some old man jabbering away. A stranger.

FIRS. The master's not back yet, not home yet. Wearing a light coat
too. No good for this weather. Catch cold he will. Oh, these
youngsters!

LYUBOV ANDREEVNA. This is killing me. Go and find out who
bought it, will you, Yasha?

YASHA. He's gone. The man's gone. (*He laughs.*)

LYUBOV ANDREEVNA (*mildly annoyed*). What are you laughing about?
Why are you in such a good mood?

YASHA. It's Yepikhodov. He's so funny, the ninny. Twenty-two
disasters.

LYUBOV ANDREEVNA. Firs, where will you go if the estate is sold?

FIRS. Wherever you say.

LYUBOV ANDREEVNA. What is that look on your face? Are you feeling all right? You ought to be in bed, you know.

FIRS. Hm . . . (*With the trace of a smile.*) If I went to bed, who'd do the
serving, look after things? There's nobody left but me.

YASHA (*to* LYUBOV ANDREEVNA). May I ask you a favor, madam?
Will you take me with you if you go back to Paris? I can't stay
here anymore. It's impossible. (*Looking around and lowering his
voice.*) I don't need to tell you. You can see for yourself. This
country is so uncivilized: people are immoral, life is dull, you
can't get a decent meal in the kitchen, and on top of it all Firs
here is always in the way, always mumbling some nonsense or
other. Take me with you, please.

PISHCHIK (*entering*). May I have the pleasure of this waltz, beautiful lady ... (LYUBOV ANDREEVNA *stands to go with him.*) I'll get that hundred and eighty rubles out of you yet, you charmer ... Just you wait ... (*He dances.*) A hundred and eighty rubles, that's all ... (*They waltz into the ballroom.*)

YASHA (*singing softly*). "If thou couldst grasp the torments of my heart ..."

(*In the ballroom a figure in a gray top hat and checked trousers is jumping up and down and waving her arms. There are cries of "Bravo, Sharlotta Ivanovna!"*)

DUNYASHA (*stopping to powder her nose*). The young mistress told me to dance—there are lots of gentlemen and not enough ladies to go round—but dancing makes my head spin and my heart pound. You should have heard what the postmaster said to me just now, Firs Nikolaevich. It fairly took my breath away.

(*The music stops.*)

FIRS. What did he say to you?

DUNYASHA. He said I was like a flower.

YASHA (*yawning*). The ignorance of these people. (*He exits.*)

DUNYASHA. Like a flower ... I'm so sensitive. I so love tender words ...

FIRS. They will be your undoing.

YEPIKHODOV (*entering*). You've been avoiding me, Dunyasha ... as if I were an insect. (*He sighs.*) Ah, life.

DUNYASHA. What is it you want?

YEPIKHODOV. You may undoubtedly be right, of course. (*He sighs.*) But on the other hand, if you look at things from a point of view, then—I hope you won't mind my putting it this way—you've reduced me—forgive me for being so blunt—you've reduced me to a state of mind. I know I'm doomed to a disaster a day, but I don't care; I face each day with a smile. You gave me your word, and even if I ...

DUNYASHA. I'm sorry, but couldn't we talk about it some other time? And would you please leave me alone for now. I'm dreaming. (*She plays with her fan.*)

YEPIKHODOV. A disaster a day and—if you don't mind my putting it like this—all I do is smile. I even laugh at times.

VARYA (*entering from the ballroom, to* YEPIKHODOV). What? You still here? How disrespectful can you be! Really! (*To* DUNYASHA.) You may go now, Dunyasha. (*To* YEPIKHODOV.) First you play billiards and break a cue, then you parade up and down the drawing room like a guest.

YEPIKHODOV. You have no right to lecture me—if you don't mind my putting it that way.

VARYA. I'm not lecturing you; I'm telling you. All you do is wander from one place to another; you never do a stroke of work. Sometimes I wonder why we ever hired a clerk.

YEPIKHODOV (*offended*). The only people qualified to judge my working or wandering or eating or billiards are older and wiser than you.

VARYA. How dare you talk to me like that! (*Furiously.*) How dare you! So I'm not "wise" enough for you. Well, then get out of here! Get out of here this instant!

YEPIKHODOV (*cowed*). Might I ask you to be a bit more refined in your choice of words?

VARYA (*beside herself*). Out! Out! This instant! (*He walks towards the door. She follows on his heels.*) Twenty-two disasters! Don't you ever set foot in here again! I never want to see you again! (*He exits, but calls back from behind the door, "I'm going to lodge a complaint against you!"*) Oh, so you're coming back in, are you? (*She picks up the cane* FIRS *left by the door.*) All right then. Come on, come on . . . Come on, I'll show you . . . Coming? Are you coming? Well, take that . . . (*She swings the stick.*)

LOPAKHIN (*entering as she swings*). Much obliged.

VARYA (*angrily and with sarcasm*). Quite sorry, I'm sure.

LOPAKHIN. That's all right. Many thanks for the warm welcome.

VARYA. Don't mention it. (*She walks away, then turns. Gently.*) I didn't hurt you, did I?

LOPAKHIN. Not at all. The bump's going to be enormous though.

(*Voices in the ballroom are saying, "Lopakhin is back!"*)

PISHCHIK. Well, well, well! His nibs in person!... (*He and* LOPAKHIN *exchange kisses.*) Had a few snorts of cognac, eh, my friend? Well, we've been living it up too.

LYUBOV ANDREEVNA (*entering*). Is that you, Lopakhin? Why did it take so long? Where's Leonid?

LOPAKHIN. He came back with me. He'll be along soon...

LYUBOV ANDREEVNA (*agitated*). Well, what happened? Did the auction take place? Say something!

LOPAKHIN (*embarrassed and afraid of showing his elation*). The auction was over by four... We missed our train and had to wait until half past nine. (*Sighing deeply.*) Oh dear, my head is spinning.

(*Enter* GAEV. *He is carrying some parcels in his right hand and wiping away tears with his left.*)

LYUBOV ANDREEVNA. Well, what happened, Leonid? Leonid! (*Impatiently, beginning to cry.*) Out with it, for heaven's sake!

GAEV (*making a helpless gesture instead of answering; to* FIRS, *crying*). Here, take these... Some anchovies and herring... I haven't had a thing to eat all day... Oh, what I've been through!

(*The door to the game room is open. From inside the room comes the click of billiard balls and* YASHA's *voice saying, "Seven and eighteen."* GAEV's *expression changes. He has stopped crying.*)

I'm terribly tired. Come and find something for me to change into, Firs. (*He exits through the ballroom.* FIRS *follows.*)

PISHCHIK. Well, what happened at the auction? Tell us.

LYUBOV ANDREEVNA. Has the cherry orchard been sold?

LOPAKHIN. It has.

LYUBOV ANDREEVNA. Who bought it?

LOPAKHIN. I did.

(*Pause.*)

(LYUBOV ANDREEVNA *is stunned. She would have fallen had she not been standing next to an armchair and table.* VARYA *undoes the ring of keys from her belt, flings it to the floor in the middle of the drawing room, and exits.*)

LOPAKHIN. I bought it. Wait a minute, everybody, please. I still can't think straight. I don't know what to say ... (*He laughs.*) Deriganov was there by the time we'd arrived. Leonid Andreevich had only fifteen thousand, and Deriganov started the bidding at thirty, over and above the arrears on the mortgage. I can see he means business, so I take the bull by the horns and bid forty. He goes to forty-five; I go to fifty-five. He jumps by fives, I by tens ... And suddenly it's over. I bid ninety thousand over and above the arrears, and I got it. The cherry orchard is mine! Mine! (*He gives a loud laugh.*) Good God in heaven, the cherry orchard is mine! Tell me I'm drunk, out of my mind. Tell me it's only a dream ... (*He stamps his feet.*) Don't laugh at me. If my father and grandfather could rise up from their graves and see me now. Little Yermolai, the boy everybody picked on; little Yermolai, the boy who barely learned to read and ran around barefoot in winter; little Yermolai—the owner of the cherry orchard, the most beautiful place on earth! I have bought the estate where my grandfather and father were slaves, where they weren't allowed in the kitchen ... I must be dreaming. I must be inventing it all. It can't be true ... No, it's a figment of your imagination, a dark delusion. (*He picks up the keys, smiling fondly.*) She's flung down the keys to show she's no longer in charge. (*He jangles the keys.*) Well, what's the difference.

(*The orchestra starts tuning up.*)

Hey, let's have some music out there! Everybody come and watch Yermolai Lopakhin take an ax to the cherry orchard. Watch those trees come down! Our grandchildren and great-grandchildren will live to see a new life here ... Hey, let's hear that music!

(*The orchestra plays.* LYUBOV ANDREEVNA *has collapsed into the armchair and is weeping bitterly.*)

(*Reproachfully.*) Why, oh why didn't you listen to me? It's too late now, dear friend, poor friend. (*Tearfully.*) I wish this was over and done with. I wish our miserable, muddled lives would change somehow.

PISHCHIK (*taking* LOPAKHIN *by the arm and speaking softly*). She's crying. Let's go out into the ballroom and leave her alone . . . Come on . . . (*He takes him by the arm and leads him into the ballroom.*)

LOPAKHIN. What's the matter in there? Loud and clear, orchestra! Loud and clear! I'm the one who gives the orders now! (*With irony.*) Here comes the new master, the new owner of the cherry orchard! (*He bumps into a small table, nearly knocking over some candlesticks.*) I can pay for it all! (*He exits with* PISHCHIK.)

(*No one is left in the ballroom or drawing room but* LYUBOV ANDREEVNA, *who huddles in her chair, weeping bitterly. The orchestra plays softly.* ANYA *and* TROFIMOV *run in.* ANYA *goes over to* LYUBOV ANDREEVNA *and kneels down in front of her.* TROFIMOV *remains standing at the entrance to the ballroom.*)

ANYA. Mother! . . . Mother, are you crying? Good, kind, sweet Mother, beautiful Mother. I love you . . . and bless you. Yes, the cherry orchard is sold, gone. True, true. But don't cry. You still have your life ahead of you; you still have your good, kind heart . . . Come with me, Mother. Come away with me, come! . . . We'll plant a new orchard, more splendorous than this. When you see it, you'll understand. And joy—deep, silent joy—will fill your heart, just as the setting sun fills the evening sky, and you will smile again, Mother. Come, Mother, come! . . .

CURTAIN

ACT FOUR

The same setting as in Act One. There are no curtains on the windows or pictures on the walls. What little furniture remains is stacked up in one corner as if for sale. There is a sense of emptiness. Upstage, near the main entrance, is a pile of suitcases, traveling bags, and the like. The voices of VARYA *and* ANYA *come through the open door on the left.*

    LOPAKHIN *is standing and waiting.* YASHA *is holding a tray with glasses of champagne.* YEPIKHODOV *is tying up a box in the entrance hall. A low hum of voices comes from offstage: the peasants are saying their good-byes.* GAEV *answers, "Thank you, my boys, thank you."*

YASHA. The peasants have come to say good-bye. I imagine they mean well, Yermolai Alexeevich. They're just so ignorant.

    (*The hum dies down.* LYUBOV ANDREEVNA *and* GAEV *enter through the hall. Although she is not crying, her face is pale and trembling. She can hardly speak.*)

GAEV. Giving them your purse like that, Lyuba. How could you? How could you?

LYUBOV ANDREEVNA. I couldn't help it. I couldn't help it. (*They both exit.*)

LOPAKHIN (*calling out at the door*). Have some champagne before you go. A farewell glass. I didn't think of ordering any from town, but I found a bottle at the station. Have some, please.

    (*Pause.*)

What's the matter? Don't want any? (*He walks away from the door.*) If I'd known, I wouldn't have bought it. Oh well. Then I won't have any either. (YASHA *carefully places the tray on a chair.*) You have some, Yasha. Nobody else wants any.

YASHA. To those who are leaving. (*He drinks.*) That's not the real thing, I can assure you.

LOPAKHIN. Eight rubles a bottle.

(*Pause.*)

Cold as the devil in here.

YASHA. No point in lighting the stoves. We're leaving. (*He laughs.*)

LOPAKHIN. What's so funny?

YASHA. Just happy, that's all.

LOPAKHIN. It's too sunny and calm for October. More like summer. Good building weather. (*He glances at his watch and the door.*) Don't forget, everybody. The train pulls out in forty-six minutes. That means leaving for the station in twenty. Better hurry.

TROFIMOV (*entering from outside in a coat*). Time to go, I think. The horses are waiting. Where are my galoshes, damn it? They've disappeared. (*Through the door.*) Anya! My galoshes are gone. I can't find them anywhere.

LOPAKHIN. I'm going to Kharkov. I'll be taking the same train as you. I'm spending the winter there. It's torture sitting around here with nothing to do. I can't live without work. I don't know what to do with my hands. They just hang there, like somebody else's.

TROFIMOV. As soon as we're gone, you can get back to work and be useful again.

LOPAKHIN. Come on. Have a glass.

TROFIMOV. Not for me.

LOPAKHIN. So you're going to Moscow.

TROFIMOV. Yes, I'm going into town with the others today, and tomorrow I leave for Moscow.

LOPAKHIN. I see . . . I suppose your professors are awaiting your arrival to start lecturing.

TROFIMOV. Oh, mind your own business.

LOPAKHIN. How many years have you been at the university?

TROFIMOV. Why not think up something original for a change. You can do better than that. (*Looking for his galoshes.*) You know, this may be the last time we see each other, and before we say good-bye let me give you a piece of advice. Don't wave your arms so much.

Try and stop waving your arms. And you know, building all those cottages and expecting the residents to till the soil—well, that's just so much arm-waving too . . . Still, I'm fond of you. You've got fine, sensitive fingers, the fingers of an artist. You're a fine, sensitive person . . .

LOPAKHIN (*hugging* TROFIMOV). Good-bye, my boy. Thanks for everything. Let me give you a little money for the road. Just in case.

TROFIMOV. No, what for? I don't need it.

LOPAKHIN. But you haven't got any.

TROFIMOV. Yes, I have. Thanks anyway. I've just received some for a translation. It's here in my pocket. (*Anxiously.*) Now where are those galoshes?

VARYA (*from the room next door*). Here are your filthy galoshes. (*She throws them onto the stage.*)

TROFIMOV. What are you so upset about, Varya? Hm . . . These aren't my galoshes.

LOPAKHIN. I planted nearly three thousand acres of poppies in the spring, netted forty thousand on them. It was a sight for sore eyes, my poppies in bloom! Anyway, I've just made forty thousand. I can afford a loan. Why turn your nose up at it? I'm a peasant . . . I mean what I say.

TROFIMOV. Your father was a peasant, mine a pharmacist. What does that prove?

(LOPAKHIN *takes out his wallet.*)

Stop, stop . . . You could offer me two hundred thousand and I wouldn't take it. I'm a free man, and the things all of you set such store by—rich and poor alike—have no hold on me whatever. They're like pieces of fluff wafting through the air. I can do without you, I can make my own way. I'm strong, I'm proud. Mankind is moving towards a higher truth, the greatest possible happiness on earth, and I am in the forefront.

LOPAKHIN. But will you get there?

TROFIMOV. I will.

(*Pause.*)

I'll either get there myself or show others the way.

(*The sound of an ax striking a tree comes from far off.*)

LOPAKHIN. Well, good-bye, my boy. Time to go. You talk big to me, I talk big to you, and life slips by. I can work for long stretches without getting tired. It calms my mind and gives me the feeling I know what I'm living for. Think of all the people in Russia with nothing to live for. Oh well, that's not the crux of the matter. Gaev has taken that post at the bank, I hear. Six thousand a year . . . He'll never stick it out: he's too lazy . . .

ANYA (*at the door*). Mama wondered if you wouldn't wait till she's gone. To start chopping down the orchard, I mean.

TROFIMOV. Not very tactful . . . (*He exits through the hall.*)

LOPAKHIN. I'll stop them immediately . . . The fools! (*He follows* TROFIMOV *out.*)

ANYA. Have they taken Firs to the hospital yet?

YASHA. I told them to this morning. They must have.

ANYA (*to* YEPIKHODOV, *who is passing through the ballroom*). Please see if Firs has been taken to the hospital.

YASHA (*offended*). I told Yegor this morning. How many times must you ask?

YEPIKHODOV. Immemorial Firs, in my utter opinion, is beyond repair. It is time he joined his ancestors. I can only envy him. (*He puts a suitcase down on a hatbox and squashes it.*) There, you see? Of course. I knew it. (*He exits.*)

YASHA (*sarcastically*). Twenty-two disasters.

VARYA (*from behind the door*). Have they taken Firs to the hospital?

ANYA. Yes, they have.

VARYA. Then why didn't they take the letter to the doctor?

ANYA. We'd better send somebody over with it now . . . (*She exits.*)

VARYA (*from the next room*). Where's Yasha? Tell him his mother's come to say good-bye.

YASHA (*with a gesture of annoyance*). Won't she ever stop pestering me!

(*All this time* DUNYASHA *has been busy with the luggage. Now that* YASHA *is alone, she goes up to him.*)

DUNYASHA. You might at least glance in my direction, Yasha. Going away like this... Deserting me... (*She flings herself on his neck in tears.*)

YASHA. No use crying. (*He takes a drink of champagne.*) Paris again in six days. Tomorrow we take the express, and we're off in a cloud of smoke. I can hardly believe it. *Vive la France!* ...[14] This is no place for me. I can't live here, that's all. I've seen enough ignorance to last me a lifetime. (*He takes a drink of champagne.*) It's no use crying. Behave yourself, and you won't cry.

DUNYASHA (*powdering her nose and looking into a pocket mirror*). Send me a letter from Paris. I loved you, Yasha, loved you so much! I'm so delicate, Yasha.

YASHA. They're coming. (*He pretends to be seeing to the suitcases and sings softly to himself.*)

(*Enter* LYUBOV ANDREEVNA, GAEV, ANYA, *and* SHARLOTTA.)

GAEV. We'd better be on our way. Not much time left. (*Glancing at* YASHA.) Who smells of herring here?

LYUBOV ANDREEVNA. Everybody seated in the carriages in ten minutes... (*She looks around the room.*) Good-bye, dear old house, dear old grandfather. Winter will pass, spring will come, and you'll be gone, demolished. The things these walls have seen! (*She kisses her daughter with great feeling.*) You're radiant, my treasure. Your eyes are like diamonds. Are you happy? Very happy?

ANYA. Very! This is the start of a new life, Mama!

GAEV (*cheerfully*). It's true. Everything's going to be just fine now. Before the cherry orchard was sold, we worried and suffered so; now that everything's settled, we're calmer, cheerful even... I'm a loyal bank employee, a financier... Yellow in the middle. You look better too, Lyuba. Really you do.

LYUBOV ANDREEVNA. Yes, my nerves are calmer, it's true.

(*They help her on with her hat and coat.*)

And I've been sleeping well. You can take my things out now, Yasha. It's time. (*To* ANYA.) My little girl. See you soon... I'll be living in Paris on the money your great-aunt sent to buy back the estate. Dear old auntie. It won't last long.

ANYA. You will come back soon, won't you, Mama? . . . Very soon. I'm going to study, take my exams, and then go to work to help you. We'll read all sorts of books together, won't we? . . . (*She kisses her hands.*) We'll read our way through the long autumn evenings, book after book, and a wonderful new world will open up before us . . . (*Dreamily.*) You will come back, Mama, won't you? . . .

LYUBOV ANDREEVNA. Yes, precious. I will. (*She embraces* ANYA.)

(*Enter* LOPAKHIN. SHARLOTTA *is singing to herself.*)

GAEV. Lucky Sharlotta. She's singing.

SHARLOTTA (*picking up a bundle that looks like a baby in swaddling clothes*). Hush-a-bye, baby . . . (*The sound of a baby crying comes from the bundle.*) Hush, mama's little darling. Hush, mama's little boy. (*The "crying" picks up again.*) You're breaking my heart. (*She flings the bundle down.*) Find me another position, please. I can't go on like this . . .

LOPAKHIN. We'll find you something, Sharlotta Ivanovna. Don't worry.

GAEV. Everyone's abandoning us. Varya's going off on her own . . . All at once nobody needs us.

SHARLOTTA. I've got nowhere to live in town. I have to go somewhere else . . . (*She hums to herself.*) Oh well, what difference does it make.

(*Enter* PISHCHIK.)

LOPAKHIN. Well, well! The freak of nature! . . .

PISHCHIK (*out of breath*). Phew! Let me catch my breath . . . I'm all in . . . Please, good people . . . Give me some water . . .

GAEV. After another loan, I bet. No thanks. I think I'll go while the going's good . . . (*He exits.*)

PISHCHIK. It's been so long . . . beautiful lady . . . (*To* LOPAKHIN.) You here too? Glad to see you . . . A man of the highest intelligence . . . Here . . . It's for you . . . (*He gives* LOPAKHIN *some banknotes.*) Four hundred rubles. Now all I owe you is eight hundred and forty.

LOPAKHIN (*shrugging his shoulders in bewilderment*). I must be dreaming . . . Where did you get it?

PISHCHIK. Just a second ... It's so hot in here ... A most extraordinary event ... Some Englishmen have discovered a sort of white clay on my land ... (*To* LYUBOV ANDREEVNA.) And four hundred for you ... you ravishing creature. (*He hands her the money.*) The rest will come later. (*He takes a drink of water.*) Just now in the train I heard a young fellow saying ... that a great philosopher has been advising people to jump off their roofs ... Jump. That's his whole message. (*Amazed.*) Unbelievable. More water!

LOPAKHIN. Who are those Englishmen?

PISHCHIK. I've leased them the land with the clay for twenty-four years ... But you must forgive me. I'm very busy ... Lots of stops to make ... First there's Znoikov ... then Kardamonov ... I owe everybody money ... (*He takes a drink of water.*) Best of health to one and all ... I'll be back on Thursday ...

LYUBOV ANDREEVNA. We're moving into town today, and tomorrow I'm going abroad.

PISHCHIK. What? To town. (*Alarmed.*) How come? What for? Oh, I see ... The furniture, the suitcases ... Oh well ... (*Through tears.*) Oh well ... Highly intelligent, those Englishmen ... Oh well ... I wish you all the best ... God be with you ... Oh well ... All good things must come to an end ... (*He kisses* LYUBOV ANDREEVNA'S *hand.*) And if you happen to hear my end has come, then think of ... you know ... that horse, and say "There once was a man ... What was his name? ... Simeonov-Pishchik ... May he rest in peace ..." Superb weather we've been having ... Hm ... (*He exits, overcome with embarrassment, but returns immediately and speaks from the doorway.*) Dasha sends her regards! (*He exits.*)

LYUBOV ANDREEVNA. Well, now we can go. I'm taking two worries with me. The first is poor Firs. (*Looking at her watch.*) We still have five minutes.

ANYA. Firs has been taken to the hospital, Mama. Yasha took him there this morning.

LYUBOV ANDREEVNA. The second is Varya. She's used to getting up early, getting to work. Now that there's nothing to do, she's like a fish out of water. The poor dear's so thin and pale, always crying ...

(*Pause.*)

You know very well, Lopakhin, I've dreamt of ... seeing the two of you married, and it did look as if you were going to propose. (*She whispers to* ANYA, ANYA *nods to* SHARLOTTA, *and they both exit.*) She loves you, you like her, and I can't see why you always seem to be avoiding each other. I don't understand it.

LOPAKHIN. Neither do I, to tell you the truth. The whole thing is so strange. I don't mind going through with it, though, if it's not too late ... Let's just get it over with. Once you're gone, I'll never ask her.

LYUBOV ANDREEVNA. Splendid. It only takes a minute, after all. I'll go and call her ...

LOPAKHIN. We even have some champagne. (*Glancing over at the glasses.*) Empty. Somebody's drunk it all.

(YASHA *coughs.*)

Or should I say guzzled it all ...

LYUBOV ANDREEVNA (*excited*). Perfect. We'll leave the room ... Yasha, *allez!*[15] I'll go and call her ... (*At the door.*) Varya! Drop everything and come here. Come at once! (*She exits with* YASHA.)

LOPAKHIN (*glancing at his watch*). Hm ...

(*Pause.*)

(*Stifled laughter and whispers come from behind the door. After some time* VARYA *enters.*)

VARYA (*looking through the luggage*). That's funny. I can't find it anywhere.

LOPAKHIN. What are you looking for?

VARYA. I packed it myself and can't remember where.

(*Pause.*)

LOPAKHIN. Where will you be going now?

VARYA. Me? To the Ragulins' ... I've arranged to look after their house ... act as a sort of housekeeper there.

LOPAKHIN. That's in Yashnevo, isn't it? About fifty miles from here.

(*Pause.*)

So life in this house has come to an end.

VARYA (*looking through the luggage*). Where can it be? ... Maybe I put it in the trunk . . . Yes, life in this house has come to an end . . . And never more shall be . . .

LOPAKHIN. Well, I'm on my way to Kharkov . . . On the next train. I'm very busy. I'm leaving Yepikhodov here . . . I've hired him . . .

VARYA. You have?

LOPAKHIN. Last year we had snow by this time, remember? And now it's calm and sunny. Cold, though . . . Three degrees below freezing.

VARYA. I hadn't looked.

(Pause.)

Actually, the thermometer's broken.

(A voice from the courtyard calls out, "Yermolai Alexeevich!")

LOPAKHIN *(as if long expecting the call)*. Coming! *(He exits in a hurry.)*

(VARYA sits on the floor with her head on a bundle of clothes and sobs softly. The door opens, and LYUBOV ANDREEVNA enters cautiously.)

LYUBOV ANDREEVNA. Well?

(Pause.)

We're leaving now.

VARYA *(no longer crying, wiping her eyes)*. Yes, Mama. Time to go. I can be at the Ragulins' today if we don't miss the train . . .

LYUBOV ANDREEVNA *(calling out through the door)*. Anya! Put your things on!

(Enter ANYA, then GAEV and SHARLOTTA. GAEV is wearing a heavy coat with a hood. The servants and coachmen come in. YEPIKHODOV fusses with the luggage.)

Now we can be on our way.

ANYA *(joyfully)*. On our way!

GAEV. Friends! Good friends, kind friends . . . As we leave this house forever, I feel compelled to speak out, to express the feelings welling up within me . . .

ANYA (*beseechingly*). Uncle Leonid!

VARYA. Please, Uncle Leonid!

GAEV (*despondently*). Double off the yellow into the middle . . . Not another word.

(*Enter* TROFIMOV *followed by* LOPAKHIN.)

TROFIMOV. Come on, everybody! Time to go!

LOPAKHIN. My coat, Yepikhodov!

LYUBOV ANDREEVNA. Let me sit just one minute more . . . It's as though I'd never seen what the walls in the house were like, or the ceiling, and now I can't take my eyes off them I love them so . . .

GAEV. I remember when I was six years old sitting on this window-sill on Trinity Sunday and watching Father go off to church.

LYUBOV ANDREEVNA. Is everything outside?

LOPAKHIN. I think so, yes. (*Putting on his coat, to* YEPIKHODOV.) Keep an eye on things, Yepikhodov.

YEPIKHODOV (*in a hoarse voice*). Don't worry.

LOPAKHIN. What's wrong with your voice?

YEPIKHODOV. I drank some water just now. Must have swallowed something.

YASHA. Oh, the ignorance!

LYUBOV ANDREEVNA. There won't be a soul left when we leave.

LOPAKHIN. Until spring.

VARYA (*pulling an umbrella out of a bundle in such a way that she seems about to strike* LOPAKHIN, *who feigns fright*). Don't be silly. It never entered my mind.

TROFIMOV. Everyone into the carriages now . . . It's time! The train will be in soon!

VARYA. There are your galoshes, Petya. Right by that suitcase. (*Tearfully.*) They're so old and dirty . . .

TROFIMOV (*putting on the galoshes*). Let's go, everybody . . .

GAEV (*overwrought, afraid of bursting into tears*). The train . . . The station . . . Cross shot into the middle, double off the white into the corner.

LYUBOV ANDREEVNA. Let's go.

LOPAKHIN. Everybody here? No one left behind? (*He locks the side door, left.*) I've got some things stored in there. Better lock up. Let's go.

ANYA. Good-bye, house! Good-bye, old life!

TROFIMOV. Hello, new life! . . . (*He exits with* ANYA.)

(VARYA *looks round the room and goes out slowly.* YASHA *and* SHARLOTTA, *with her dog, follow.*)

LOPAKHIN. See you in the spring. Everybody out now . . . Farum-wellum! . . . (*He exits.*)

(LYUBOV ANDREEVNA *and* GAEV *are left alone. As if waiting for this moment, they fall into each other's arms and sob softly, holding back, afraid to be heard.*)

GAEV (*in despair*). Oh, Lyuba, Lyuba . . .

LYUBOV ANDREEVNA. Oh, my dream, my sweet, my beautiful orchard! . . . My life, my youth, my happiness—good-bye! . . . Good-bye! . . .

(ANYA *calls out cheerfully but insistently,* "Mama!" TROFIMOV *calls out cheerfully and excitedly,* "Yoo-hoo! . . .")

One last look at the walls, the windows . . . Mother dear used to love walking about this room . . .

GAEV. Lyuba, Lyuba . . .

(ANYA *calls out,* "Mama! . . ." TROFIMOV *calls out,* "Yoo-hoo!")

LYUBOV ANDREEVNA. Coming! (*They exit.*)

(*The stage is empty. The noise of doors locking and carriages driving off is followed by silence. It is broken by the dull thud of an ax landing on a tree, a sad and lonely sound. There are footsteps.* FIRS *appears at the door, right. As usual he is wearing a jacket, white vest, and slippers. He looks ill.*)

FIRS (*going over to the door and trying the handle*). Locked. They're gone. (*He sits on the couch.*) Forgot about me . . . Oh well . . . I'll just sit here a while . . . I bet Leonid Andreevich didn't wear his fur coat, bet a while . . . I bet Leonid Andreevich didn't wear his fur coat, bet he put on that light one instead . . . (*He heaves a worried sigh.*) And I didn't even look to see . . . Oh, these youngsters! (*He mumbles something unintelligible.*) Life is over before you live it. (*He lies down.*) Think I'll lie down for a minute . . . No strength left, nothing left, nothing . . . A real . . . numskull! . . . (*He lies there motionless.*)

(*A distant sound is heard. It seems to come from the sky. It is the sound of a string that has snapped. It dies away mournfully. The silence that sets in is disturbed only by the thud of an ax striking a tree far away in the orchard.*)

CURTAIN

NOTES

1. Most of the surnames are "telling names," that is, their roots have a meaning: Arkadina, Irina Nikolaevna's stage name, evokes Arcadia, a rustic paradise; Treplev recalls the verb "ruffle, rumple"; Sorin implies "litter" and/or "weeds"; Zarechnaya includes the words "beyond the river," Trigorin—the words "three mountains"; Dorn means "thorn" in German; and Medvedenko combines the word "bear" with a suffix indicating Ukrainian origin.

   For the pronunciation of the names see "An Actor's Guide to Russian Names and Their Pronunciations" (p. xix). The following list indicates the proper stress for additional names of people and places occurring in characters' lines only.

   Arkadina: Petrúshka, Kíev, Khárkov

   Treplev: Nekrásov, Kíev, Yeléts

   Nina: Yeléts

   Shamraev: Pável Chádin, Rasplyúev, Sadóvsky, Súzdaltsev, Izmáilov, Yelízavetgrád. Latin vowels are pronounced like Russian vowels. The stress is as follows: De gústibus aut béne, aut níhil.

   Masha: Matryóna

   Trigorin: Popríshchin, Gógol, Tolstóy, Turgénev, Grokhólsky, Molchánovka.

2. Nikolai Nekrasov (1821–77). A major poet known for his wrenching depiction of peasant life. Eleonora Duse (1858–1924). A world-renowned

Italian actress whose trademark was a flamboyant emotionality. She toured Russia during the nineties.

3. Alexandre Dumas *fils*'s melodrama *Camille,* derived from his autobiographical novel of the same name, was a crowd-pleaser in the seventies and eighties. It also served as the basis for Verdi's *La Traviata. The Fumes of Life* is a forgotten play by the forgotten Russian playwright B. M. Markevich.

4. From "Zwei Grenadiere" by Schumann, based on a poem of the same name by Heine.

Moderato

To France were re-turn-ing two gre-na-diers

5. From "A Heavy Cross Has Fallen to Her Lot," based on a poem of the same name by Nekrasov. See note 2, above. No music is available.

6. From a text not uncommon in songbooks of the time. No music is available.

7. Poltava is a provincial Ukrainian city, and the fact that Arkadina performed at a fair only adds to the atmosphere of provinciality. Chadin appears to be Chekhov's invention, but Sadovsky was a respected actor known for creating the role of Rasplyuev in *Krechinsky's Wedding* (1855), a major work of nineteenth-century Russian drama by Alexander Sukhovo-Kobylin.

8. Shamraev is conflating two Latin proverbs: *De gustibus non est disputandum* (There is no accounting for tastes) and *De mortibus aut bene aut nihil* (Do not speak ill of the dead, or, literally, Of the dead either good or nothing). He has therefore said something that might be rendered in English as "Do not speak ill of tastes."

9. From Act III, Scene 4. Chekhov uses the 1837 prose translation by Nikolai Polevoy. A literal back translation of the Russian text reads as follows: "My son! Thou hast turned thine eyes into my soul, and I have seen it covered with such bloody, such deadly sores that it is beyond salvation." "And wherefore didst thou yield to vice, seeking love in the depths of transgression?"

10. Treplev is presumably following the French custom of sounding three knocks (*frapper les trois coups*) before the curtain rises.

11. Arkadina is referring to the late-nineteenth-century literary movement known as Decadence, which developed the aestheticist, antisocial, and to some extent morbid tendencies of Symbolism.

12. The opening of Siebel's aria in Act III, Scene 1 of Gounod's *Faust.*

13. The passage in question reads as follows: "Then, once she has him where she wants him, when she has moved him, won him over with her constant praise, she isolates him, gradually severing all bonds he has with the outside world and luring him into the habit of coming to see her, feeling at home with her . . ."

14. Maupassant describes the same phenomenon in *On the Water:* "There is no such thing as a simple feeling for the man of letters. Everything he sees, all his joys, his pleasures, his sufferings, his bouts of despair immediately become objects for observation. Hearts, faces, gestures, intonations—he cannot stop analyzing them in spite of everything, in spite of himself.[. . .] If he suffers, he takes note of it and files it away in his memory. Leaving the cemetery where he has buried the person who means the most to him in the world, he says to himself, 'A strange feeling I've just had. It's like being drunk with grief, etc.' "

15. Poprishchin is the title character in Gogol's "Diary of a Madman" (1842).

16. *Fathers and Sons* (1862) is Turgenev's signature novel.

17. From a serenade popular at the time. No music is available.

18. The miller in Pushkin's *The Water Nymph,* a dramatic fragment in verse (1832), goes mad after his daughter, seduced and abandoned, drowns herself. He tells her lover he has sprouted wings and caws on her grave.

19. The Man in the Iron Mask is the twin brother of Louis XIV in *The Vicomte de Bragelonne* (1848–50) by Alexandre Dumas *père,* the concluding volume of the swashbuckling *Three Musketeers* trilogy.

20. The passage comes from the conclusion to Turgenev's novel *Rudin* (1856).

NOTES TO *UNCLE VANYA*

1. All the surnames incorporate roots of recognizable words— Serebryakov "silver," Voinitsky "war," Astrov "astral," and Telegin "cart"—therefore qualifying as telling names. Two given names may also be construed as such: Yelena, the Russian equivalent of Helen, which possibly evokes Helen of Troy, and Sofya, the Greek for "wisdom." Vanya is the pet name for Ivan; Ivan is the Russian equivalent of

John. Vanya's mother calls him by the French equivalent, Jean, because her generation and class spoke French as a matter of course, but Vanya's use of the French *maman* to refer to his mother is tinged with irony. The same holds for his use of Hélène with Yelena and his reference to Sereb-ryakov as Herr Professor, an otherwise eminently respectful German form of address. Telegin's brother-in-law has the comical telling name of Lakademonov, which consists of an amalgam of "academic" and "demon" preceded by the French definite article (*l'*).

For the pronunciation of the characters' names see the "Actor's Guide to Russian Names" (p. xix). The following list indicates the proper stress for additional Russian names of people and places occurring in characters' lines only.

Serebryakov: Bátyushkov, Turgénev

Yelena: Yefím

Maria Vasilyevna: Pável Alexéevich, Khárkov

Astrov: Malítskoe, Khárkov, Túla, Turgénev, Petrúshka

Telegin: Grigóry Ilyích, Konstantín Trofímovich Lakademónov, Khárkov, Aivazóvsky, Marína Timoféevna

Watchman: Zhúchka, Málchik

2. Latin for "as much as necessary."

3. Alexander Ostrovsky (1823–86). A leading nineteenth-century play-wright. The play in question is *The Dowerless Bride* (1879).

4. Konstantin Batyushkov (1778–1855). A major poet who reached his apogee in the 1810s and 1820s, then sank into mental illness.

5. A Russian folk ditty. No music is available.

6. Italian for "enough."

7. Serebryakov is playing on the opening line of Gogol's comedy *The Inspector General* (1836).

8. The Latin proverb translates literally as "One night awaits us all."

9. Mikhail Aivazovsky (1800–71). A prolific painter known primarily for his dramatic seascapes. As usual, Telegin is wide of the mark.

10. An Italian expression meaning, literally, "The play is over," and, figuratively, "The game is up."

NOTES TO *THREE SISTERS*

1. Although the character names in *Three Sisters* are less "telling" than those in the earlier plays, the surname Prozorov could be construed as deriving from a verb meaning "to see clearly." Vershinin comes from "summit, peak," and Solyony evokes "salt." The name Tusenbach is

significant less for its etymology than for its unmistakable German origin, of which Tusenbach the character is clearly ashamed. (Russians have traditionally regarded Germans as hardworking to the point of ridicule, and the conflict between Tusenbach's ardent desire to work and total inability to do so reflects the German/Russian dichotomy in him.) The name of the offstage—but important—character Protopopov means, ironically, "archpriest."

For the pronunciation of the characters' names see the "Actor's Guide to Russian Names" (p. xix). The following list indicates the proper stress for additional Russian names of people and places occurring in characters' lines only.

Andrei: Protopópov, Bóbik, Téstov

Natasha: Bóbik, Protopópov, Sophie (the French form of the name and hence pronounced with the stress on the last syllable)

Olga: Kirsánov, Kolotílin

Masha: Protopópov, Gógol, Bóbik, Márfa. Note the stress pattern for the conjugation of "to love" in Latin: ámo, ámas, ámat; amámus, amátis, ámant.

Irina: Basmánnaya, Sarátov, Berdíchev, Bóbik, Protopópov

Kulygin: Kózyrev. The vowels in the Polish word *kochane,* "darling," are pronounced like the Russian vowels; the *ch* is pronounced like the English *h;* the stress falls on the *a.* Vowels in the Latin words are also pronounced like the Russian vowels; *c* (in *feci, faciant, corpore, fallacem, consecutivum*) is pronounced *k.* The stress is as follows:

> Féci quod pótui, fáciant mélior poténtes.
> mens sána in córpore sáno
> O fallácem hóminum spem
> in víno véritas
> ut consecutívum

Vershinin: Basmánnaya

Tusenbach: Aléko

Solyony: Aléko, Lérmontov, cheremshá

Chebutykin: Dobrolyúbov, Berdíchev, chekhartmá, Protopópov, Lérmontov, Skvortsóv

Fedotik: Pýzhikov

Anfisa: Mikhaíl, Protopópov

2. After the abolition of serfdom in 1861 local assemblies called District Councils were set up to administer education, public health, roads, and

agriculture and trade. They provided the first step towards self-government and democracy in Russia, their representatives being elected, and although the electoral system favored landowners over urban dwellers and peasants the Councils introduced a number of liberal reforms.

3. The day on which the saint whose name one has is commemorated. Orthodox Christians commonly celebrate name days in addition to birthdays.

4. Nikolai Dobrolyubov (1836–61). A major nineteenth-century literary critic, whose name any educated Russian at the time could have been expected to recognize.

5. The opening lines of Pushkin's playfully Orientalist narrative poem *Ruslan and Lyudmila* (1817–20).

6. From the fable "The Peasant and the Workman" by Ivan Krylov (1769–1844), Russia's foremost fabulist. Given Solyony's ominous role in the action, the line has a prophetic undertone to it.

7. From *The Werewolf,* a long-forgotten French comic opera by D.-G. A. Paris, popular in Russia during the early nineteenth century. No music is available.

8. A Latin adage meaning "I have done the best I could. May those who can do better."

9. The well-known Latin adage meaning "a sound mind in a sound body."

10. Russians are fond of flavoring vodka with herbs, which turn it various colors.

11. The concluding sentence in Gogol's "Tale About How Ivan Ivanovich Quarreled with Ivan Nikiforovich" (1835).

12. Balzac did in fact marry the Polish countess Ewelina Hanska in the Ukrainian backwater of Berdichev. The wedding took place in 1850 after a long liaison.

13. "Please excuse me, Maria, but you have somewhat crude manners." The French is correct, and Tusenbach's amused reaction may be due to Natasha's bad accent or simply to her desire to show off. However, her next French utterance, which is supposed to mean "It seems that my Bobik is no longer asleep," contains an error typical of Russian speakers and would sound to French ears like "It seems that my Bobik is already not asleep."

14. The first line comes from *Wit from Woe* (1824), a neoclassical comedy of manners in verse by Alexander Griboedov (1795–1829). The Aleko of the second line is the hero of Pushkin's Romantic narrative poem *The*

Gypsies (1824), but the line itself does not occur in the work. Nor, for that matter, does "Forget, forget thy dreams," the line he cites later.

15. Mikhail Lermontov (1814–41). Russia's major Romantic poet.

16. The Caucasus, a region of spectacular mountains between the Black and Caspian seas inhabited by numerous "primitive" tribes, provided the requisite exotic background for the Russian Romantics. Solyony's pose is compromised by Chebutykin's remark.

17. A well-known Russian folk song. (Stravinsky incorporated the melody into his ballet *Petrouchka* in 1911.)

18. A quotation from Cicero's *De Oratore* meaning "How deceitful is human hope!"

19. The well-known Latin adage "In wine is truth."

20. From an operetta so obscure that Chekhov, when asked, could not recall its title. No music is available.

21. From an aria sung by Prince Gremin in Tchaikovsky's opera *Eugene Onegin*.

22. From "The Geese," another Krylov fable.

23. The present tense conjugation of the Latin verb *amare* "to love."

24. The literal translation of the saying is, "Everything I own I carry with me." It implies that one's character counts more than one's worldly goods.

25. Another reference to Gogol's story "Diary of a Madman" (see *The Seagull,* note 15). The eponymous hero inserts the words "It doesn't matter, it doesn't matter. Silence" into his entries several times.

26. Polish for "darling." At the time Poland was a virtual province of Russia. The brigade was thus merely moving to a different part of the Russian Empire.

27. From a cancan melody popular at the time.

28. A Latin construction requiring the subjunctive after *ut,* "in order that."

29. Teachers belonged to the civil service, which followed a precise hierarchy and elaborate system of decorations. Needless to say, Kulygin's is anything but lofty.

30. The following is the introduction to "A Maiden's Prayer" by Thekla Badarzewska.

31. From Lermontov's poem "The Sail" (1832).
32. A mildly alcoholic drink made by letting rye or barley ferment in a mixture of malt and water.
33. "Don't make noise. Sophie is asleep. You are a bear." Natasha's French has gone downhill: she makes elementary mistakes in the first two sentences.

NOTES TO *THE CHERRY ORCHARD*

1. That none of the characters has a particularly "telling" surname (except perhaps the onomatopoeic "squeak" or "chirp" in Pishchik) represents the culmination of a trend away from the device in successive plays. If any meaning persists, it lies in the given rather than the family names: Lyubov means "love," though it is also perfectly common as a name, and the fact that Yermolai, Dunyasha (short for Yevdokia), and Firs all go back to Greek is less important than the fact that to a Russian they immediately betray their bearers' peasant origins. Sharlotta is the German—and, to Russian ears, very foreign—name Charlotte, and her Russian patronymic Ivanovna does not mean that her father's name was Ivan: Russians occasionally use that patronymic when the father's name is so foreign as to resist Russification or when the father's name is unknown. Sharlotta speaks standard Russian, but Chekhov is said to have indicated that she speaks it with a slight German accent.

   For the pronunciation of the characters' names see the "Actor's Guide to Russian Names" (p. xix). The following list indicates the proper stress for additional Russian names of people and places occurring in characters' lines only.

   Lyubov Andreevna: Grísha
   Anya: Grísha, Yaroslávl
   Varya: Yefímushka, Pólya, Yevstignéi, Ragúlin
   Gaev: Anastásy, Petrúshka, Yaroslávl
   Lopakhin: Derigánov, Khárkov, Yáshnevo
   Trofimov: Grísha, Lopákhina
   Pishchik: Dásha, Znóikov, Kardamónov
   Dunyasha: Fyódor Kozoédov, Nikoláevich
   Firs: Khárkov
   Yasha: Yegór
   Stationmaster: Alexéi Tolstóy
2. See note 32 to *Three Sisters*.

3. Russian intellectual history traditionally distinguishes two major groups of nineteenth-century thinkers: the "fathers" or generation of the forties, adherents of German idealism, and the "sons" or generation of the sixties, adherents of positivism and utilitarianism. Many of the latter went on to espouse populism and even terrorism, which culminated in the assassination of Tsar Alexander II in 1881. The eighties constituted a period of political reaction and intellectual stagnation.

4. The Italian term for an acrobatic maneuver in which a person turns head over heels in the air.

5. This song and the song sung by Yasha in Act Three belong to a genre known as the "cruel romance." It enjoyed great popularity at the time largely because it incorporated elements of Gypsy songs. No music is available.

6. Perhaps the fact that the English historian Henry Thomas Buckle (1821–62) gave pride of place to the "little man" in his depiction of events endears him to Yepikhodov. But this seemingly insignificant detail has further ramifications. It suggests there is more than meets the eye even in Yepikhodov (and thus, by extension, in everyone). It also signals Chekhov the protoabsurdist in the juxtaposition of cockroaches and English civilization.

7. Presumably a song from the play Lopakhin refers to in the next sentence. No music is available.

8. The first line comes from a poem by Semyon Nadson (1862–87), the second from a poem by Nikolai Nekrasov (1821–78). Both were known for their verse about the downtrodden.

9. Lopakhin's play on Hamlet's lines implies that he frequents more than the "funny plays" he brings up earlier in the act. In other words, there is more to Lopakhin, as there is to Yepikhodov (see note 6 above), than meets the eye. Moreover, here, as in *The Seagull,* Chekhov uses Shakespeare's relationships (Hamlet/Gertrude, Hamlet/Ophelia) to comment on the relationships between his own characters (Treplev/Arkadina, Lopakhin/Varya).

10. The *grand rond* is a reel-like circle dance. "Promenade à une paire!" indicates that the couples promenade one by one, "Balancez!" that they swing their arms, and "Les cavaliers à genoux et remerciez vos dames" that the men drop to their knees and thank their ladies.

11. German for "one, two, three."

12. A German adage that translates literally as "Good man, but bad musi-cian" and means that decent as he is he is not much good for anything.
13. Alexei Tolstoy (1817–78). A poet, distantly related to Lev Tolstoy, known largely for his historical verse dramas. The title figure in the moralistic poem the stationmaster recites is a wicked woman who sees the error of her ways when confronted by a Christlike figure.
14. French for "Long live France!"
15. French for "go."

MICHAEL HENRY HEIM is professor of Slavic languages and literatures and comparative literature at the University of California, Los Angeles, where he has taught for thirty years. He translates contemporary and classical fiction and drama from the Czech, French, German, Hungarian, Italian, Romanian, Russian, and Serbian/Croatian. His previous translations include *Anton Chekhov's Life and Thought: Selected Letters and Commentary* (with Simon Karlinsky); *The Unbearable Lightness of Being*, by Milan Kundera; *Too Loud a Solitude*, by Bohumil Hrabal; *My Century*, by Günter Grass; *Helping Verbs of the Heart*, by Péter Esterházy; and *The Encyclopedia of the Dead*, by Danilo Kiš. He has been a Fulbright Visiting Scholar, received fellowships from the National Endowment for the Humanities and the National Endowment for the Arts, and been awarded translation prizes by the Hungarian government, the Columbia University Translation Center, the American Literary Translators Association, and the PEN American Center West. He has also served as a juror for translation prizes awarded by the National Endowment for the Humanities, the National Endowment for the Arts, the PEN American Center, and the Goethe-Institut. He is a member of the American Academy of Arts & Sciences.

MODERN LIBRARY IS ONLINE AT
WWW.MODERNLIBRARY.COM

MODERN LIBRARY ONLINE IS YOUR GUIDE
TO CLASSIC LITERATURE ON THE WEB

THE MODERN LIBRARY E-NEWSLETTER

Our free e-mail newsletter is sent to subscribers, and features sample chapters, interviews with and essays by our authors, upcoming books, special promotions, announcements, and news.

To subscribe to the Modern Library e-newsletter, send a blank e-mail to: **sub_modernlibrary@info.randomhouse.com** or visit **www.modernlibrary.com**

THE MODERN LIBRARY WEBSITE

Check out the Modern Library website at
www.modernlibrary.com for:

- The Modern Library e-newsletter
- A list of our current and upcoming titles and series
- Reading Group Guides and exclusive author spotlights
- Special features with information on the classics and other paperback series
- Excerpts from new releases and other titles
- A list of our e-books and information on where to buy them
- The Modern Library Editorial Board's 100 Best Novels and 100 Best Nonfiction Books of the Twentieth Century written in the English language
- News and announcements

Questions? E-mail us at **modernlibrary@randomhouse.com**.
For questions about examination or desk copies, please visit
the Random House Academic Resources site at
www.randomhouse.com/academic